Undoubtedly Frederi PHI-
LOSOPHY is a mont[...]e of
the comments critics [...] the
series to date:

VOLUME 1
"There can be no doubt that this is the best text of the his-
tory of philosophy now available in English."
The Historical Bulletin

VOLUME 2
". . . unquestionably the finest account of mediaeval philosophy yet published in English."
The (London) Times Literary Supplement

VOLUME 3
". . . it constitutes a remarkable achievement, the most considerable work of scholarship produced by English Scholasti-
cism in our day, a work that has been received with respect
by philosophy scholars everywhere." *Book Reviews*

VOLUME 4
". . . offers a profound and well-organized introduction to
continental rationalism in the seventeenth century."
Cross Currents

VOLUME 5
"Obviously to be the standard history of philosophy for many
years to come." *Blackfriars*

VOLUME 6
"One thing at any rate is beyond doubt. No serious student
of western philosophy can dispense with Fr. Copleston's
History." *Duckett's Register*

VOLUME 7
"Each volume of Fr. Copleston's history provokes astonishment and wonder . . . The present volume is just as learned,
fair-minded, lucid and interesting as its predecessors."
The Month

Volumes of A HISTORY OF PHILOSOPHY now available in Image Books:

A HISTORY OF PHILOSOPHY: Volume 1
Parts I & II – Greece & Rome – D 134A & D 134B

A HISTORY OF PHILOSOPHY: Volume 2
Mediaeval Philosophy
Part I – Augustine to Bonaventure – D 135A
Part II – Albert the Great to Duns Scotus – D 135B

A HISTORY OF PHILOSOPHY: Volume 3
Late Mediaeval and Renaissance Philosophy
Part I – Ockham to the Speculative Mystics – D 136A
Part II – The Revival of Platonism to Suárez – D 136B

A HISTORY OF PHILOSOPHY: Volume 4
Modern Philosophy
Descartes to Leibniz – D 137

A HISTORY OF PHILOSOPHY: Volume 5
Modern Philosophy – The British Philosophers
Part I – Hobbes to Paley – D 138A
Part II – Berkeley to Hume – D 138B

A HISTORY OF PHILOSOPHY: Volume 6
Modern Philosophy
Part I – The French Enlightenment to Kant – D 139A
Part II – Kant – D 139B

A HISTORY OF PHILOSOPHY: Volume 7
Modern Philosophy
Part I – Fichte to Hegel – D 140A
Part II – Schopenhauer to Nietzsche – D 140B

A HISTORY OF PHILOSOPHY: Volume 8
Modern Philosophy – Bentham to Russell
Part I – British Empiricism and the Idealist Movement in
         Great Britain – D 141B
Part II – Idealism in America, The Pragmatist Movement
         The Revolt against Idealism – D 141B

A History of Philosophy

VOLUME VIII

Modern Philosophy

Bentham to Russell

PART I

British Empiricism and the Idealist Movement in Great Britain

by Frederick Copleston, S. J.

IMAGE BOOKS
A Division of Doubleday & Company, Inc.
Garden City, New York

Image Books Edition
by special arrangement with The Newman Press
Image Books Edition published September 1967

DI LICENTIA SUPERIORUM ORDINIS:
J. Corbishley, S.J.
Vice-Praep. Prov. Angliae Soc. Jesu

NIHIL OBSTAT:
T. Gornall, S.J.
Censor Deputatus

IMPRIMATUR:
✠ Joseph Cleary
Episcopus Cresimensis
Vic. Cap.

Birmingamiae die 25a Junii 1965

The *Nihil obstat* and *Imprimatur* are a declaration that a book or
pamphlet is considered to be free from doctrinal or moral error. It is
not implied that those who have granted the *Nihil obstat* and *Imprimatur* agree with the contents, opinions or statements expressed.

© Frederick Copleston, 1966
Printed in the United States of America

CONTENTS

PREFACE   9
ACKNOWLEDGMENTS   11

PART I

BRITISH EMPIRICISM

One: THE UTILITARIAN MOVEMENT (1)   17
Introductory remarks – The life and writings of
Bentham – The principles of Benthamism, followed by some critical comments – The life and
writings of James Mill – Altruism and the associationist psychology; Mill's polemic against
Mackintosh – James Mill on the mind – Remarks
on Benthamite economics.

Two: THE UTILITARIAN MOVEMENT (2)   42
Life and writings of J. S. Mill – Mill's develop-
ment of the utilitarian ethics – Mill on civil liberty and government – Psychological freedom.

Three: J. S. MILL: LOGIC AND EMPIRICISM   68
Introductory remarks – Names and propositions,
real and verbal – The nature of mathematics – Syllogistic reasoning – Induction and the principle of
the uniformity of Nature – The law of causation
– Experimental inquiry and deduction – Method
in the Moral Sciences – Matter as a permanent
possibility of sensations – The analysis of mind
and the spectre of solipsism – Mill on religion and
natural theology.

Four: EMPIRICISTS, AGNOSTICS, POSITIVISTS   113
Alexander Bain and the associationist psychology
– Bain on utilitarianism – Henry Sidgwick's com-

bination of utilitarianism and intuitionism –
Charles Darwin and the philosophy of evolution
– T. H. Huxley; evolution, ethics and agnosticism
– Scientific materialism and agnosticism; John
Tyndall and Leslie Stephen – G. J. Romanes and
religion – Positivism; the Comtist groups, G. H.
Lewes, W. K. Clifford, K. Pearson – B. Kidd; con-
cluding remarks.

Five: THE PHILOSOPHY OF HERBERT SPENCER   142
Life and writings – The nature of philosophy and
its basic concepts and principles – The general
law of evolution: the alternation of evolution and
dissolution – Sociology and politics – Relative and
absolute ethics – The Unknowable in religion and
science – Final comments.

PART II

THE IDEALIST MOVEMENT
IN GREAT BRITAIN

Six: THE BEGINNINGS OF THE MOVEMENT   171
Introductory historical remarks – Literary pio-
neers: Coleridge and Carlyle – Ferrier and the
subject-object relation – John Grote's attack on
phenomenalism and hedonism – The revival of interest in Greek philosophy and the rise of interest
in Hegel; B. Jowett and J. H. Stirling.

Seven: THE DEVELOPMENT OF IDEALISM   191
T. H. Green's attitude to British empiricism and
to German thought – Green's doctrine of the
eternal subject, with some critical comments –
The ethical and political theory of Green – E.
Caird and the unity underlying the distinction
between subject and object – J. Caird and the philosophy of religion – W. Wallace and D. G.
Ritchie.

Eight: ABSOLUTE IDEALISM: BRADLEY   214
Introductory remarks – *The Presuppositions of Critical History* – Morality and its self-transcending in religion – The relevance of logic to metaphysics – The basic presupposition of metaphysics – Appearance: the thing and its qualities, relations and their terms, space and time, the self – Reality: the nature of the Absolute – Degrees of truth and reality – Error and evil – The Absolute, God and religion – Some critical discussion of Bradley's metaphysics.

Nine: ABSOLUTE IDEALISM: BOSANQUET   248
Life and writings – Logic; judgment and reality – The metaphysics of individuality – Bosanquet's philosophy of the State – Hobhouse's criticism of Bosanquet – R. B. Haldane; Hegelianism and relativity – H. H. Joachim and the coherence theory of truth.

Ten: THE TURN TOWARDS PERSONAL IDEALISM   267
Pringle-Pattison and the value of the human person – The pluralistic idealism of McTaggart – The pluralistic spiritualism of J. Ward – General comments.

APPENDIX: A Short Bibliography   284

NOTES   300

PREFACE

In the preface to Volume VII of this *History of Philosophy* I said that I hoped to devote a further volume, the eighth, to some aspects of French and British thought in the nineteenth century. This hope has been only partially fulfilled. For the present volume contains no treatment of French philosophy but is devoted exclusively to some aspects of British and American thought. It covers rather familiar ground. But in a general history of Western philosophy this ground obviously ought to be covered.

As I have strayed over well into the twentieth century, some explanation may be needed of the fact that the philosophy of Bertrand Russell, who is happily still with us, has been accorded relatively extensive treatment, whereas the thought of Ludwig Wittgenstein, who died in 1951, has been relegated to the epilogue, apart from a few allusions in the chapter on Russell. After all, it may be pointed out, Russell was himself influenced to a certain extent by Wittgenstein, both in regard to the interpretation of the logical status of the propositions of logic and pure mathematics and in regard to logical atomism.

The explanation is simple enough. Russell's thought fits naturally into the context of the revolt against idealism; and though he has obviously exercised a powerful influence on the rise and development of the analytic movement in twentieth-century British thought, in some important respects he has maintained a traditional view of the function of philosophy. His lack of sympathy with Wittgenstein's later ideas and with certain aspects of recent 'Oxford philosophy' is notorious. Further, though he has emphasized the limitations of empiricism as a theory of knowledge, in some respects he can be regarded as prolonging the empiricist tradition into the twentieth century, even if he has enriched it with new techniques of logical analysis. Wittgenstein, however, frankly proposed a revolutionary concept of the nature, function and scope of philosophy. Certainly, there is a very considerable difference between the ideas of language expounded in the *Tractatus* and those expounded in *Philosophical Investiga-*

tions; but in both cases the concept of philosophy is far from being a traditional one. And as limitations of space excluded the possibility of according extensive treatment to the concentration on language which is associated with the name of Wittgenstein, I decided to confine my discussion of the subject to some brief remarks in an epilogue. This fact should not, however, be interpreted as implying a judgment of value in regard to the philosophy either of Russell or of Wittgenstein. I mean, the fact that I have devoted three chapters to Russell does not signify that in my opinion his thought is simply a hangover from the nineteenth century. Nor does the fact that I have relegated Wittgenstein to the epilogue, apart from some allusions in the chapters on Russell, mean that I fail to appreciate his originality and importance. Rather is it a matter of not being able to give equally extensive treatment to the ideas of both these philosophers.

A word of explanation may also be appropriate in regard to my treatment of Cardinal Newman. It will be obvious to any attentive reader that in distinguishing the currents of thought in the nineteenth century I have used traditional labels, 'empiricism', 'idealism' and so on, none of which can properly be applied to Newman. But to omit him altogether, because of the difficulty of classifying him, would have been absurd, especially when I have mentioned a considerable number of much less distinguished thinkers. I decided, therefore, to make a few remarks about some of his philosophical ideas in an appendix. I am well aware, of course, that this will not satisfy Newman enthusiasts; but a writer cannot undertake to satisfy everybody.

Volumes VII and VIII having been devoted respectively to German and British-American philosophy in the nineteenth century, the natural procedure would be to devote a further volume, the ninth, to aspects of French and other European philosophy during the same period. But I am inclined to postpone the writing of this volume and to turn my attention instead to the subject to which I referred in the preface to Volume VII, that is, to what may be called the philosophy of the history of philosophy or general reflection on the development of philosophical thought and on its implications. For I should like to undertake this task while there is a reasonable possibility of fulfilling it.

ACKNOWLEDGMENTS

The author has pleasure in expressing his gratitude to the Right Hon. the Earl Russell, O.M., for his generous permission to quote from his writings, and to the following publishers and holders of copyright for permission to quote from the works indicated below.

The Clarendon Press: *Collected Essays, Ethical Studies, Principles of Logic, Appearance and Reality, Essays on Truth and Reality,* by F. H. Bradley; *The Idea of God in the Light of Recent Philosophy* by A. S. Pringle-Pattison; *The Nature of Truth* by H. H. Joachim; *Statement and Inference* by J. Cook Wilson; and *Essays in Ancient and Modern Philosophy* by H. W. B. Joseph.

The Oxford University Press: *The Problems of Philosophy* and *Religion and Science* by Bertrand Russell; and *A Common Faith* by John Dewey.

Macmillan and Co., Ltd. (London): *Logic, Essentials of Logic, The Philosophical Theory of the State, The Principle of Individuality and Value, The Value and Destiny of the Individual* by Bernard Bosanquet; *Humanism, Formal Logic* and *Axioms as Postulates* (contained in *Personal Idealism,* edited by H. Sturt) by F. C. S. Schiller; and *Space, Time and Deity* by S. Alexander.

The Cambridge University Press: *The Nature of Existence* by J. M. E. McTaggart.

W. Blackwood and Sons, Ltd.: *Hegelianism and Personality* by A. S. Pringle-Pattison.

A. and C. Black, Ltd.: *Naturalism and Agnosticism* by James Ward.

Miss S. C. Campbell: *The Realm of Ends* by James Ward.

The Belknap Press of the Harvard University Press: *Collected Papers of Charles Sanders Peirce;* Vols. I and II, copyright 1931, 1932, 1959, 1960; Vols. III and IV, copyright 1933, 1961; Vols. V and VI, copyright 1934, 1935, 1962, 1963 by the President and Fellows of Harvard College.

G. Bell and Sons, Ltd.: *The Influence of Darwin on Philosophy* by John Dewey.

Constable and Co., Ltd.: *Experience and Nature* by John Dewey.

Yale University Press: *A Common Faith* by John Dewey; *The Meaning of God in Human Experience* and *Human Nature and Its Remaking* by W. E. Hocking. Acknowledgment is also due to Professor W. E. Hocking.

The University of Chicago Press: *Theory of Valuation* by John Dewey. (*International Encyclopaedia of Unified Science*, Vol. 2, no. 4, copyright 1939.)

The Philosophical Library Inc. (N.Y.): *Problems of Men* (copyright 1946) by John Dewey and *The Development of American Pragmatism* by John Dewey (contained in *Twentieth Century Philosophy*, edited by Dagobert D. Runes, copyright 1943).

Holt, Rinehart and Winston Inc. (N.Y.) and the John Dewey Foundation: *Human Nature and Conduct*, *Logic: The Theory of Inquiry* and *The Public and Its Problems* by John Dewey.

Putnam's and Coward-McCann (N.Y.): *Quest For Certainty* (copyright 1929, renewed 1957) by John Dewey.

The Macmillan Co. Inc. (N.Y.): *Democracy and Education* (copyright 1916) by John Dewey; *The New Realism: Cooperative Studies in Philosophy* (copyright 1912) by E. B. Holt and Others; *Process and Reality* (copyright 1929 and 1949) by A. N. Whitehead.

Professor G. Ryle, Editor of *Mind*: *The Nature of Judgment* (*Mind*, 1899) by G. E. Moore.

Mrs. G. E. Moore: *Principia Ethica* by G. E. Moore.

Routledge and Kegan Paul, Ltd.: *Philosophical Studies* by G. E. Moore; and *What I Believe* by Bertrand Russell.

George Allen and Unwin, Ltd.: *The Metaphysical Theory of the State* by L. T. Hobhouse; *Philosophical Papers and Some Main Problems of Philosophy* by G. E. Moore; *The Principles of Mathematics, Introduction to Mathematical Philosophy, Philosophical Essays, The Analysis of Mind, Our Knowledge of the External World, Principles of Social Reconstruction, Mysticism and Logic, An Outline of Philosophy, The Scientific Outlook, Power, An Inquiry into Meaning* and Truth, A History of Western Philosophy, Human Knowledge: Its Scope and Limits, Logic and Knowledge, My Philosophical Development, Unpopular Essays and Authority and the Individual by Bertrand Russell; Contemporary British Philosophy, First Series (1924) and Second Series (1925), edited by J. H. Muirhead.

W. W. Norton and Co., Inc. (N.Y.): The Principles of Mathematics by Bertrand Russell.

Simon and Schuster Inc. (N.Y.): A History of Western Philosophy (c. 1945), Human Knowledge: Its Scope and Limits (c. 1948), Authority and the Individual (c. 1949), Unpopular Essays (c. 1950) and My Philosophical Development (c. 1959), by Bertrand Russell.

Macdonald and Co., Ltd. (London) and Doubleday and Co. Inc. (N.Y.): Wisdom of the West by Bertrand Russell (copyright Rathbone Books Ltd., London 1959).

The Library of Living Philosophers Inc., formerly published by The Tudor Publishing Co., N.Y., and now published by The Open Court Publishing Co., La Salle, Illinois: The Philosophy of John Dewey (1939 and 1951) and The Philosophy of Bertrand Russell (1946), both edited by Paul Arthur Schilpp.

Part I

BRITISH EMPIRICISM

Chapter One

THE UTILITARIAN MOVEMENT (1)

Introductory remarks – The life and writings of Bentham – The principles of Benthamism, followed by some critical comments – The life and writings of James Mill – Altruism and the associationist psychology; Mill's polemic against Mackintosh – James Mill on the mind – Remarks on Benthamite economics.

1. The philosophy of David Hume, which represented the culmination of classical British empiricism, called forth a lively reaction on the part of Thomas Reid and his successors.[1] Indeed, as far as the Universities were concerned, in the first decades of the nineteenth century the so-called Scottish School was the one living and vigorous movement of thought. Moreover, though in the meantime it had received some serious blows and had lost its first vigour, its place in the Universities was eventually taken by idealism rather than by empiricism.

It would, however, be a great mistake to suppose that empiricism was reduced to a moribund condition by Reid's attack on Hume, and that it remained in this position until it was given a fresh lease of life by J. S. Mill. Philosophy is not confined to the Universities. Hume himself never occupied an academic chair, though, admittedly, this was not due to lack of effort on his part. And empiricism continued its life, despite attack by Reid and his followers, though its leading representatives were not university professors or lecturers.

The first phase of nineteenth-century empiricism, which is known as the utilitarian movement, may be said to have originated with Bentham. But though we naturally tend to think of him as a philosopher of the early part of the nineteenth century, inasmuch as it was then that his influence made itself felt, he was born in 1748, twenty-eight years be-

fore the death of Hume. And some of his works were published in the last three decades of the eighteenth century. It
is no matter of surprise, therefore, if we find that there is a
conspicuous element of continuity between the empiricism
of the eighteenth century and that of the nineteenth. For
example, the method of reductive analysis, the reduction,
that is to say, of the whole to its parts, of the complex to its
primitive or simple elements, which had been practised by
Hume, was continued by Bentham. This involved, as can be
seen in the philosophy of James Mill, a phenomenalistic
analysis of the self. And in the reconstruction of mental life
out of its supposed simple elements use was made of the
associationist psychology which had been developed in the
eighteenth century by, for instance, David Hartley,[2] not to
speak of Hume's employment of the principles of association
of ideas. Again, in the first chapter of his *Fragment on Government* Bentham gave explicit expression to his indebtedness to Hume for the light which had fallen on his mind
when he saw in the *Treatise of Human Nature* how Hume
had demolished the fiction of a social contract or compact
and had shown how all virtue is founded on utility. To be
sure, Bentham was also influenced by the thought of the
French Enlightenment, particularly by that of Helvétius.[3]
But this does not alter the fact that in regard to both method
and theory there was a notable element of continuity between the empiricist movements of the eighteenth and nineteenth centuries in Great Britain.

But once the element of continuity has been noted, attention must be drawn to the considerable difference in emphasis. As traditionally represented at any rate, classical British
empiricism had been predominantly concerned with the nature, scope and limits of human knowledge, whereas the
utilitarian movement was essentially practical in outlook,
orientated towards legal, penal and political reform. It is
true that emphasis on the role of the theory of knowledge in
classical empiricism can be overdone. Hume, for example,
was concerned with the development of a science of human
nature. And it can be argued, and has indeed been argued,
that he was primarily a moral philosopher.[4] But Hume's aim
was chiefly to understand the moral life and the moral judg-

ment, whereas Bentham was mainly concerned with providing the criterion for judging commonly received moral ideas and legal and political institutions with a view to their reformation. Perhaps we can apply Marx's famous assertion and say that Hume was primarily concerned with understanding the world, whereas Bentham was primarily concerned with changing it.

Of the two men Hume was, indeed, by far the greater philosopher. But Bentham had the gift of seizing on certain ideas which were not his own inventions, developing them and welding them into a weapon or instrument of social reform. Benthamism in a narrow sense, and utilitarianism in general, expressed the attitude of liberal and radical elements in the middle class to the weight of tradition and to the vested interests of what is now often called the Establishment. The excesses connected with the French Revolution produced in England a strong reaction which found notable expression in the reflections of Edmund Burke (1729–97), with their emphasis on social stability and tradition. But after the Napoleonic Wars at any rate the movement of radical reform was more easily able to make its influence felt. And in this movement utilitarianism possesses an undeniable historical importance. Considered as a moral philosophy, it is over-simplified and skates lightly over awkward and difficult questions. But its over-simplified character, together with an at least *prima facie* clarity, obviously facilitated its use as an instrument in the endeavour to secure practical reforms in the social and political fields.

During the nineteenth century social philosophy in Great Britain passed through several successive phases. First, there was the philosophical radicalism which is associated with the name of Bentham and which had been already expressed by him in the closing decades of the eighteenth century. Secondly, there was Benthamism as modified, added to and developed by J. S. Mill. And thirdly, there was the idealist political philosophy which arose in the last part of the nineteenth century. The term 'utilitarianism' covers the first two phases, but not, of course, the third. Utilitarianism was individualistic in outlook, even though it aimed at the welfare of society, whereas in idealist political theory the idea of the

State as an organic totality came to the fore under the influence of both Greek and German thought.

This and the following chapters will be devoted to an account of the development of utilitarianism from Bentham to J. S. Mill inclusively. The latter's theories in the fields of logic, epistemology and ontology will be discussed separately in a subsequent chapter.

2. Jeremy Bentham was born on February 15th, 1748. A precocious child, he was learning Latin grammar at the age of four. Educated at Westminster School and the University of Oxford, neither of which institutions captivated his heart, he was destined by his father for a career at the Bar. But he preferred the life of reflection to that of a practising lawyer. And in the law, the penal code and the political institutions of his time he found plenty to think about. To put the matter in simple terms, he asked questions on these lines. What is the purpose of this law or of this institution? Is this purpose desirable? If so, does the law or institution really conduce to its fulfilment? In fine, how is the law or institution to be judged from the point of view of utility?

In its application to legislation and to political institutions the measure of utility was for Bentham the degree of conduciveness to the greater happiness of the greatest possible number of human beings or members of society. Bentham himself remarks that the principle of utility, as so interpreted, occurred to him when he was reading the *Essay on Government* (1768) by Joseph Priestley (1733–1804) who stated roundly that the happiness of the majority of the members of any State was the standard by which all the affairs of the State should be judged. But Hutcheson, when treating of ethics, had previously asserted that that action is best which conduces to the greatest happiness of the greatest number.[5] Again, in the preface to his famous treatise on crimes and punishments (*Dei delitti e delle pene*, 1764), Cesare Beccaria (1738–94) had spoken of the greatest happiness divided among the greatest possible number. There were utilitarian elements in the philosophy of Hume, who declared, for example, that 'public utility is the sole origin of justice'.[6] And Helvétius, who, as already noted, strongly influenced Bentham, was a pioneer in utilitarian moral theory and in its application to the reform of society. In other words, Bentham did not invent the principle of utility: what he did was to expound and apply it explicitly and universally as the basic principle of both morals and legislation.

Bentham was at first principally interested in legal and penal reform. Radical changes in the British constitution did not enter into his original schemes. And at no time was he an enthusiast for democracy as such. That is to say, he had no more belief in the sacred right of the people to rule than he had in the theory of natural rights in general, which he considered to be nonsense. But whereas he seems to have thought at first that rulers and legislators were really seeking the common good, however muddled and mistaken they might be about the right means for attaining this end, in the course of time he became convinced that the ruling class was dominated by self-interest. Indifference and opposition to his plans for legal, penal and economic reform doubtless helped him to come to this conclusion. Hence he came to advocate political reform as a prerequisite for other changes. And eventually he proposed the abolition of the monarchy and the House of Lords, the disestablishment of the Church of England, and the introduction of universal suffrage and annual parliaments. His political radicalism was facilitated by the fact that he had no veneration for tradition as such. He was far from sharing Burke's view of the British constitution; and his attitude had much more affinity with that of the French *philosophes*,[7] with their impatience with tradition and their belief that everything would be for the best if only reason could reign. But his appeal throughout was to the principle of utility, not to any belief that democracy possesses some peculiarly sacred character of its own.

Nor was Bentham primarily moved by humanitarian considerations. In the movement of social reform in Great Britain throughout the nineteenth century, humanitarianism, sometimes based on Christian beliefs and sometimes without any explicit reference to Christianity, undoubtedly played a very important role. But though, for example, in his campaign against the outrageously severe penal code of his time and against the disgraceful state of the prisons, Bentham often demanded changes which humanitarian sentiment would in fact suggest, he was primarily roused to indignation by what he considered, doubtless rightly, to be the irrationality of the penal system, its incapacity to achieve its purposes and to serve the common good. To say this is not, of course, to say that he was what would normally be called inhumane. It is to say that he was not primarily moved by compassion for the victims of the penal system, but rather by the 'inutility' of the system. He was a man of the reason or understanding rather than of the heart or of feeling.

In 1776 Bentham published anonymously his *Fragment on Government* in which he attacked the famous lawyer Sir William Blackstone (1723–80) for his use of the fiction of a social compact or contract. The work had no immediate success, but in 1781 it brought Bentham the friendship of Lord Shelburne, afterwards Marquis of Lansdowne, who was Prime Minister from July 1782 to February 1783. And through Shelburne the philosopher met several other important people. He also formed a friendship with Étienne Dumont, tutor to Shelburne's son, who was to prove of invaluable help in publishing a number of his papers. Bentham not infrequently left manuscripts unfinished and went on to some other topic. And many of his writings were published through the agency of friends and disciples. Sometimes they first appeared in French. For example, a chapter of his *Manual of Political Economy*, written in 1793, appeared in the *Bibliothèque britannique* in 1798; and Dumont made use of the work in his *Théorie des peines et des récompenses* (1811). Bentham's work was published in English for the first time in John Bowring's edition of his *Works* (1838–43).

Bentham's *Defence of Usury* appeared in 1787 and his important *Introduction to the Principles of Morals and Legislation* in 1789.[8] The *Introduction* was intended as a preparation and scheme for a number of further treatises. Thus Bentham's *Essay on Political Tactics* corresponded to one section in this scheme. But though a part of this essay was sent to the Abbé Morellet in 1789, the work was first published by Dumont in 1816,[9] together with *Anarchical Fallacies* which had been written in about 1791.

In 1791 Bentham published his scheme for a model prison, the so-called *Panopticon*. And he approached the French National Assembly with a view to the establishment of such an institution under its auspices, offering his gratuitous services as supervisor. But though Bentham was one of the foreigners on whom the Assembly conferred the title of citizen in the following year, his offer was not taken up.[10] Similar efforts to induce the British government to implement the scheme for a model prison promised at first to be successful. But they eventually failed, partly, so Bentham at any rate liked to believe, through the machinations of King George III. However, in 1813 Parliament voted the philosopher a large sum of money in compensation for his expenditure on the Panopticon scheme.

In 1802 Dumont published a work entitled *Traités de législation de M. Jérémie Bentham*. This consisted partly of papers written by Bentham himself, some of which had been originally composed in French, and partly of a digest by Dumont of the philosopher's ideas. And the work contributed greatly to the rise of Bentham's fame. At first this was more evident abroad than in England. But in the course of time the philosopher's star began to rise even in his own country. From 1808 James Mill became his disciple and a propagator of his doctrines. And Bentham became what might be called the background leader or inspirer of a group of radicals devoted to the principles of Benthamism.

In 1812 James Mill published an *Introductory View of the Rationale of Evidence*, a version of some of Bentham's papers. A French version of the papers was published by Dumont in 1823 under the title *Traité des preuves judiciaires*; and an English translation of this work appeared in 1825. A five-volume edition of Bentham's papers on jurisprudence which was much fuller than James Mill's was published by J. S. Mill in 1827 under the title *Rationale of Judicial Evidence*.

Bentham also gave his attention both to questions of constitutional reform and to the subject of the codification of the law. Characteristically, he was impatient of what he regarded as the chaotic condition of English law. His *Catechism of Parliamentary Reform* appeared in 1817, though it had been written in 1809. The year 1817 also saw the publication of *Papers upon Codification and Public Instruction*. In 1819

Bentham published a paper entitled *Radical Reform Bill, with Explanations*, and in 1823 *Leading Principles of a Constitutional Code*. The first volume of his *Constitutional Code*, together with the first chapter of the second volume, appeared in 1830. The whole work, edited by R. Doane, was published posthumously in 1841.

It is not possible to list all Bentham's publications here. But we can mention two or three further titles. *Chrestomathia*, a series of papers on education, appeared in 1816, while in the following year James Mill published his edition of Bentham's *Table of the Springs of Action*[11] which is concerned with the analysis of pains and pleasures as springs of action. The philosopher's *Deontology or Science of Morality* was published posthumously by Bowring in 1834 in two volumes, the second volume being compiled from notes. Reference has already been made to Bowring's edition of Bentham's *Works*.[12] A complete and critical edition of the philosopher's writings is yet to come.

Bentham died on June 6th, 1832, leaving directions that his body should be dissected for the benefit of science. It is preserved at University College, London. This College was founded in 1828, largely as a result of pressure from a group of which Bentham himself was a member. It was designed to extend the benefits of higher education to those for whom the two existing universities did not cater. Further, there were to be no religious tests, as there still were at Oxford and Cambridge.

3. Benthamism rested on a basis of psychological hedonism, the theory that every human being seeks by nature to attain pleasure and avoid pain. This was not, of course, a novel doctrine. It had been propounded in the ancient world, notably by Epicurus, while in the eighteenth century it was defended by, for example, Helvétius in France and Hartley and Tucker in England.[13] But though Bentham was not the inventor of the theory, he gave a memorable statement of it. 'Nature has placed mankind under the governance of two sovereign masters, *pain* and *pleasure*. . . . They govern us in all we do, in all we say, in all we think: every effort we can make to throw off our subjection will serve but to demonstrate and confirm it. In words a man may pretend to abjure

their empire, but in reality he will remain subject to it all the while.'[14]

Further, Bentham is at pains to make clear what he means by pleasure and pain. He has no intention of restricting the range of meaning of these terms by arbitrary or 'metaphysical' definitions. He means by them what they mean in common estimation, in common language, no more and no less. 'In this matter we want no refinement, no metaphysics. It is not necessary to consult Plato, nor Aristotle. *Pain* and *pleasure* are what everybody feels to be such.'[15] The term 'pleasure' covers, for example, the pleasures of eating and drinking; but it also covers those of reading an interesting book, listening to music or performing a kind action.

But Bentham is not concerned simply with stating what he takes to be a psychological truth, namely that all men are moved to action by the attraction of pleasure and the repulsion of pain. He is concerned with establishing an objective criterion of morality, of the moral character of human actions. Thus after the sentence quoted above, in which Bentham says that Nature has placed mankind under the government of pain and pleasure, he adds that 'it is for them alone to point out what we ought to do, as well as to determine what we shall do. On the one hand the standard of right and wrong, on the other the chain of causes and effects, are fastened to their throne.'[16] If, therefore, we assume that pleasure, happiness and good are synonymous terms and that pain, unhappiness and evil are also synonymous, the question immediately arises whether it makes any sense to say that we ought to pursue what is good and avoid what is evil, if, as a matter of psychological fact, we always do pursue the one and endeavour to avoid the other.

To be able to answer this question affirmatively, we have to make two assumptions. First, when it is said that man seeks pleasure, it is meant that he seeks his greater pleasure or the greatest possible amount of it. Secondly, man does not necessarily perform those actions which will as a matter of fact conduce to this end.[17] If we make these assumptions and pass over the difficulties inherent in any hedonistic ethics, we can then say that right actions are those which tend to increase the sum total of pleasure while wrong actions are those which tend to diminish it, and that we ought to do what is right and not do what is wrong.[18]

We thus arrive at the principle of utility, also called the greatest happiness principle. This 'states the greatest happiness of all those whose interest is in question, as being the right and proper, and only right and proper and universally desirable, end of human action'.[19] The parties whose interest is in question may, of course, differ. If we are thinking of the individual agent as such, it is his greatest happiness which is referred to. If we are thinking of the community, it is the greater happiness of the greatest possible number of the members of the community which is being referred to. If we are thinking of all sentient beings, then we must also consider the greater pleasure of animals. Bentham is chiefly concerned with the greater happiness of the human community, with the common good or welfare in the sense of the common good of any given human political society. But in all cases the principle is the same, namely that the greatest happiness of the party in question is the only desirable end of human action.

If we mean by proof deduction from some more ultimate principle or principles, the principle of utility cannot be proved. For there is no more ultimate ethical principle. At the same time Bentham tries to show that any other theory of morals involves in the long run an at least tacit appeal to the principle of utility. Whatever may be the reasons for which people act or think that they act, if we once raise the question why we *ought* to perform a certain action, we shall ultimately have to answer in terms of the principle of utility. The alternative moral theories which Bentham has in mind are principally intuitionist theories or theories which appeal to a moral sense. In his opinion such theories, taken by themselves, are incapable of answering the question why we ought to perform this action and not that. If the upholders of such theories once try to answer the question, they will ultimately have to argue that the action which ought to be performed is one which conduces to the greater happiness or pleasure of whatever party it is whose interest is in question. In other words, it is utilitarianism alone which can provide an objective criterion of right and wrong.[20] And to show that this is the case, is to give the only proof of the principle of utility which is required.

In passing we can note that though hedonism represented only one element in Locke's ethical theory,[21] he explicitly stated that 'things then are good or evil only in reference to pleasure or pain. That we call good which is apt to cause or increase pleasure or diminish pain in us. . . . And on the contrary we name that evil which is apt to increase any pain or diminish any pleasure in us. . . .'[22] The property which is here called 'good' by Locke is described by Bentham as 'utility'. For 'utility is any property in any object, whereby it tends to produce benefit, advantage, pleasure, good or happiness, or . . . to prevent the happening of mischief, pain, evil or unhappiness to the party whose interest is considered.'[23]

Now, if actions are right in so far as they tend to increase the sum total of pleasure or diminish the sum total of pain of the party whose interest is in question, as Bentham puts it, the moral agent, when deciding whether a given action is right or wrong, will have to estimate the amount of pleasure and the amount of pain to which the action seems likely to give rise, and to weigh the one against the other. And Bentham provides a hedonistic or 'felicific' calculus for this purpose.[24] Let us suppose that I wish to estimate the value of a pleasure (or pain) for myself. I have to take into account four factors or dimensions of value: intensity, duration, certainty or uncertainty, propinquity or remoteness. For example, one pleasure might be very intense but of short duration, while another might be less intense but so much more lasting that it would be quantitatively greater than the first. Further, when considering actions which tend to produce pleasure or pain, I have to bear in mind two other factors, fecundity and purity. If of two types of action, each of which tends to produce pleasurable sensations, the one type tends to be followed by further pleasurable sensations while the other type does not or only in a lesser degree, the first is said to be more fecund or fruitful than the second. As for purity, this signifies freedom from being followed by sensations of the opposite kind. For instance, the cultivation of an appreciation of music opens up a range of enduring pleasure which does not yield those diminishing returns that result from the action of taking certain habit-forming drugs.

So far Bentham's calculus follows the same lines as that of Epicurus. But Bentham is chiefly concerned, in the application of his ethical theory, with the common good. And he adds that when a number of persons or community is the party whose interest is in question, we have to take into account a seventh factor in addition to the six just mentioned. This seventh factor is extent, that is, the number of persons who are affected by the pleasure or pain in question.

It has sometimes been said that Bentham's calculus is useless but that one could quite well discard it while retaining his general moral theory. But it seems to the present writer that some distinctions are required. If one chose to look on this theory as no more than an analysis of the meaning of certain ethical terms, it would doubtless be possible to maintain that the analysis is correct and at the same time to disregard the hedonistic calculus. But if one looks on Bentham's moral theory as he himself looked on it, that is, not simply as an analysis but also as a guide for action, the case is somewhat different. We could indeed maintain, and rightly, that no exact mathematical calculation of pains and pleasures can be made. It is fairly obvious, for example, that in many cases a man cannot make a precise mathematical calculation of the respective quantities of pleasure which would probably result from alternative courses of action. And if it is the community whose interest is in question, how are we going to calculate the probable sum total of pleasure when it is a notorious fact that in many cases what is pleasurable to one is not pleasurable to another? At the same time, if we admit, as Bentham admitted, only quantitative differences between pleasures, and if we regard hedonistic ethics as providing a practical rule for conduct, some sort of calculation will be required, even if it cannot be precise. And in point of fact people do make such rough calculations on occasion. Thus a man may very well ask himself whether it is really worth while pursuing a certain course of pleasurable action which will probably involve certain painful consequences. And if he does seriously consider this question, he is making use of one of the rules of Bentham's calculus. What relation this sort of reasoning bears to morality is another question. And it is irrelevant in the present context. For the hypothesis is that Bentham's general moral doctrine is accepted.

Now, the sphere of human action is obviously very much wider than legislation and acts of government. And in some cases it is the individual agent as such whose interest is in question. Hence I can have duties to myself. But if the sphere of morality is coterminous with the sphere of human action, legislation and acts of government fall within the moral sphere. Hence the principle of utility must apply to them. But here the party whose interest is in question is the community. Although, therefore, as Bentham says, there are many actions which are as a matter of fact useful to the community but the regulation of which by law would not be in the public interest, legislation ought to serve this interest. It ought to be directed to the common welfare or happiness. Hence an act of legislation or of government is said to conform with or be dictated by the principle of utility when 'the tendency which it has to augment the happiness of the community is greater than any which it has to diminish it'.[25]

The community, however, is 'a fictitious *body*, composed of the individual persons who are considered as constituting as it were its members'.[26] And the interest of the community is 'the sum of the interests of the several members who compose it'.[27] To say, therefore, that legislation and government should be directed to the common good is to say that they should be directed to the greater happiness of the greatest possible number of individuals who are members of the society in question.

Obviously, if we assume that the common interest is simply the sum total of the private interests of the individual members of the community, we might draw the conclusion that the common good is inevitably promoted if every individual seeks and increases his own personal happiness. But there is no guarantee that individuals will seek their own happiness in a rational or enlightened manner, and in such a way that they do not diminish the happiness of other individuals, thus diminishing the sum total of happiness in the community. And in point of fact it is clear that clashes of interest do occur. Hence a harmonization of interests is required with a view to the attainment of the common good. And this is the function of government and legislation.[28]

It is sometimes said that any such harmonization of interests presupposes the possibility of working altruistically for the common good, and that Bentham thus makes an abrupt and unwarranted transition from the egoistic or selfish pleasure-seeker to the public-spirited altruist. But some distinctions are required. In the first place Bentham does not assume that all men are by nature necessarily egoistic or selfish in the sense in which these terms would generally be understood. For he recognizes social affections as well as their contrary. Thus in his table of pleasures he includes among the so-called simple pleasures those of benevolence, which are described as 'the pleasures resulting from the view of any pleasures supposed to be possessed by the beings who may be the objects of benevolence; to wit the sensitive beings we are acquainted with'.[29] In the second place, though Benthamism doubtless assumes that the man who takes pleasure in witnessing the pleasure of another does so originally because it is pleasurable to himself, it invokes the principles of the associationist psychology to explain how a man can come to seek the good of others without any advertence to his own.[30]

At the same time there is obviously no guarantee that those whose task it is to harmonize private interests will be notably endowed with benevolence, or that they will in fact have learned to seek the common good in a disinterested spirit. Indeed, it did not take Bentham long to come to the conclusion that rulers are very far from constituting exceptions to the general run of men, who, left to themselves, pursue their own interests, even if many of them are perfectly capable of being pleased by the pleasure of others. And it was this conclusion which was largely responsible for his adoption of democratic ideas. A despot or absolute monarch generally seeks his own interest, and so does a ruling aristocracy. The only way, therefore, of securing that the greater happiness of the greatest possible number is taken as the criterion in government and legislation is to place government, so far as this is practicable, in the hands of all. Hence

Bentham's proposals for abolishing the monarchy[31] and the House of Lords and for introducing universal suffrage and annual parliaments. As the common interest is simply the sum total of private interests, everyone has a stake, so to speak, in the common good. And education can help the individual to understand that in acting for the common good he is also acting for his own good.

To avoid misunderstanding, it must be added that the harmonization of interests by law which Bentham demanded was primarily a removal of hindrances to the increase of the happiness of the greatest possible number of citizens rather than what would generally be thought of as positive interference with the freedom of the individual. This is one reason why he gave so much attention to the subject of penology, the infliction of penal sanctions for diminishing the general happiness or good by infringing laws which are or at any rate ought to be passed with a view to preventing actions which are incompatible with the happiness of the members of society in general. In Bentham's opinion the primary purpose of punishment is to deter, not to reform. Reformation of offenders is only a subsidiary purpose.

Bentham's remarks on concrete issues are often sensible enough. His general attitude to penal sanctions is a case in point. As already remarked, the primary purpose of punishment is to deter. But punishment involves the infliction of pain, of a diminution of pleasure in some way or other. And as all pain is evil, it follows that 'all punishment in itself is evil'.[32] And the conclusion to be drawn is that the legislator ought not to attach to the infringement of the law a penal sanction which exceeds what is strictly required to obtain the desired effect. True, it might be argued that if the primary aim of punishment is to deter, the most ferocious penalties will be the most efficacious. But if punishment is in itself an evil, even though in the concrete circumstances of human life in society a necessary evil, the relevant question is, what is the least amount of punishment which will have a deterrent effect? Besides, the legislator has to take into account public opinion, though this is indeed a variable factor. For the more people come to consider a given penal sanction to be grossly excessive or inappropriate, the more they tend to withhold their co-operation in the execution of the law.[33] And in this case the supposedly deterrent effect of the punishment is diminished. Again, it has a bad educative effect and is not for the public good if some heavy penalty, such as the death penalty, is inflicted for a variety of offences which differ very much in gravity, that is, in the amount of harm which they do to others or to the community at large. As for the subsidiary aim of punishment, namely to contribute to the reformation of offenders, how can this aim be fulfilled when the prisons are notoriously hotbeds of vice?

It is possible, of course, to hold a different view about the primary purpose of punishment. But it would require a considerable degree of eccentricity for a man of today to disagree with Bentham's conclusion that the penal system of his time stood in need of reform. And even if we do hold a somewhat different view about the function of punishment, we can none the less recognize that his arguments in favour of reform are, generally speaking, intelligible and persuasive.

But when we turn from such discussions about the need for reform to Bentham's general philosophy, the situation is somewhat different. For example, J. S. Mill objected that Bentham's idea of human nature betrayed a narrowness of vision. And inasmuch as Bentham tends to reduce man to a system of attractions and repulsions in response to pleasures and pains, together with an ability to make a quasi-mathematical computation of the pluses of pleasures and the minuses of pains, many would find themselves in full agreement with Mill on this point.

At the same time J. S. Mill awards high marks to Bentham for employing a scientific method in morals and politics. This consists above all in 'the method of detail; of treating wholes by separating them into their parts, abstractions by resolving them into things—classes and generalities by distinguishing them into the individuals of which they are made up; and breaking every question into pieces before attempting to solve it'.[34] In other words, Mill commends Bentham for his thoroughgoing use of reductive analysis and for this reason regards him as a reformer in philosophy.

In regard to the question of fact Mill is, of course, quite

right. We have seen, for example, how Bentham applied a kind of quantitative analysis in ethics. And he applied it because he thought that it was the only proper scientific method. It was the only method which would enable us to give clear meanings to terms such as 'right' and 'wrong'. Again, for Bentham terms such as 'community' and 'common interest' were abstractions which stood in need of analysis if they were to be given a cash-value. To imagine that they signified peculiar entities over and above the elements into which they could be analysed was to be misled by language into postulating fictitious entities.

But though there can obviously be no valid *a priori* objection to experimenting with the method of reductive analysis, it is also clear that Bentham skates lightly over difficulties and treats that which is complicated as though it were simple. For example, it is admittedly difficult to give a clear explanation of what the common good is, if it is not reducible to the private goods of the individual members of the community. But it is also difficult to suppose that a true statement about the common good is always reducible to true statements about the private goods of individuals. We cannot legitimately take it for granted that such a reduction or translation is possible. Its possibility ought to be established by providing actual examples. As the Scholastics say, *ab esse ad posse valet illatio*. But Bentham tends to take the possibility for granted and to conclude without more ado that those who think otherwise have fallen victims to what Wittgenstein was later to call the bewitchment of language. In other words, even if Bentham was right in his application of reductive analysis, he did not pay anything like sufficient attention to what can be said on the other side. Indeed, Mill draws attention to 'Bentham's contempt of all other schools of thinkers'.[35]

According to Mill, Bentham 'was not a great philosopher, but he was a great reformer in philosophy'.[36] And if we are devotees of reductive analysis, we shall probably agree with this statement. Otherwise we may be inclined to omit the last two words. Bentham's habit of over-simplifying and of skating over difficulties, together with that peculiar narrowness of moral vision to which Mill aptly alludes, disqualifies him from being called a great philosopher. But his place in the movement of social reform is assured. His premisses are often questionable but he is certainly skilled in drawing from them conclusions which are frequently sensible and enlightened. And, as has already been remarked, the over-simplified nature of his moral philosophy facilitated its use as a practical instrument or weapon.

4. James Mill, Bentham's leading disciple, was born on April 6th, 1773, in Forfarshire. His father was a village shoemaker. After schooling at the Montrose Academy Mill entered the University of Edinburgh in 1790, where he attended the lectures of Dugald Stewart.[37] In 1798 he was licensed to preach; but he never received a call from any Presbyterian parish, and in 1802 he went to London with the hope of earning a living by writing and editorship. In 1805 he married. At the end of the following year he began work on his history of British India which appeared in three volumes in 1817. In 1819 this brought him a post in the East India Company, and subsequent advancement, with increases in salary, set him free at last from financial worries.

In 1808 Mill met Bentham and became a fervent disciple. By this time the would-be Presbyterian minister had become an agnostic. For some years he wrote for the *Edinburgh Review*, but he was too much of a radical to win the real confidence of the editors. In 1816–23 he wrote for the *Supplement* to the *Encyclopaedia Britannica* series of political articles which set forth the views of the utilitarian circle.[38] In 1821 he published his *Elements of Political Economy* and in 1829 his *Analysis of the Phenomena of the Human Mind*. Between these two dates he contributed for a time to the *Westminster Review*, which was founded in 1824 as an organ of the radicals.

James Mill died on June 23rd, 1836, a champion of Benthamism to the last. He was not perhaps a particularly attractive figure. A man of vigorous though somewhat narrow intellect, he was extremely reserved and apparently devoid of any poetic sensibility, while for passionate emotions and for sentiment he had little use. His son remarks that though James Mill upheld an Epicurean ethical theory (Bentham's hedonism), he was personally a Stoic and combined Stoic qualities with a Cynic's disregard for pleasure. But he was certainly an extremely hard-working and conscientious man, devoted to propagating the views which he believed to be true.

With James Mill, as with Bentham, we find a combination of *laissez-faire* economics with a reiterated demand for political reform. As every man naturally seeks his own interest, it is not surprising that the executive does so. The executive, therefore, must be controlled by the legislature. But the House of Commons is itself the organ of the interests of a comparatively small number of families. And its interest cannot be made identical with that of the community in general unless the suffrage is extended and elections are frequent.[39] Like other Benthamites, Mill also had a somewhat simple faith in the power of education to make man see that their 'real' interests are bound up with the common interest. Hence political reform and extended education should go hand in hand.

5. James Mill undertook to show, with the aid of the associationist psychology, how altruistic conduct on the part of the pleasure-seeking individual is possible. He was indeed convinced that 'we never feel any pains or pleasures but our own. The fact, indeed, is, that our very idea of the pains or pleasures of another man is only the idea of our own pains, or our own pleasures, associated with the idea of another man.'[40] But these remarks contain also the key to understanding the possibility of altruistic conduct. For an inseparable association can be set up, say between the idea of my own pleasure and the idea of that of the other members of the community to which I belong, an association such that its result is analogous to a chemical product which is something more than the mere sum of its elements. And even if I originally sought the good of the community only as a means to my own, I can then seek the former without any advertence to the latter.

Given this point of view, it may seem strange that in his *Fragment on Mackintosh*, which was published in 1835 after having been held up for a time, Mill indulges in a vehement attack on Sir James Mackintosh (1765–1832), who in 1829 had written on ethics for the *Encyclopaedia Britannica*. For

Mackintosh not only accepted the principle of utility but also made use of the associationist psychology in explaining the development of the morality which takes the general happiness as its end. But the reason for the attack is clear enough. If Mackintosh had expounded an ethical theory quite different from that of the Benthamites, the Kantian ethics for example, Mill would presumably not have been so indignant. As it was, Mackintosh's crime in Mill's eyes was to have adulterated the pure milk of Benthamism by adding to it the moral sense theory, derived from Hutcheson and to a certain extent from the Scottish School, a theory which Bentham had decisively rejected.

Although Mackintosh accepted utility as the criterion for distinguishing between right and wrong actions, he also insisted on the peculiar character of the moral sentiments which are experienced in contemplating such actions and, in particular, the qualities of the agents as manifested in such actions. If we group together these sentiments as forming the moral sense, we can say that it is akin to the sense of beauty. True, a virtuous man's moral qualities are indeed useful in that they contribute to the common good or happiness. But one can perfectly well approve and admire them without any more reference to utility than when we appreciate a beautiful painting.[41]

In discussing Mackintosh's view James Mill urged that if there were a moral sense, it would be a peculiar kind of faculty, and that we ought logically to admit the possibility of its overriding the judgment of utility. True, Mackintosh believed that in point of fact the moral sentiments and the judgment of utility are always in harmony. But in this case the moral sense is a superfluous postulate. If, however, it is a distinct faculty which, in principle at least, is capable of overriding the judgment of utility, it should be described as an immoral rather than a moral sense. For the judgment of utility is the moral judgment.

Many people would probably feel that, apart from the question whether the term 'moral sense' is appropriate or inappropriate, we certainly can experience the kind of sentiments described by Mackintosh. So what is all the fuss about? A general answer is that both Bentham and Mill looked on the theory of the moral sense as a cloudy and in some respects dangerous doctrine which had been superseded by utilitarianism, so that any attempt to reintroduce it constituted a retrograde step. In particular, Mill doubtless believed that Mackintosh's theory implied that there is a superior point of view to that of utilitarianism, a point of view, that is to say, which rises above such a mundane consideration as that of utility. And any such claim was anathema to Mill.

The long and the short of it is that James Mill was determined to maintain a rigid Benthamism.[42] Any attempt, such as that made by Mackintosh, to reconcile utilitarianism with intuitionist ethics simply aroused his indignation. As will be seen later, however, his son had no such devotion to the letter of the Benthamite gospel.

6. Obviously, the use made by James Mill of the associationist psychology in explaining the possibility of altruistic conduct on the part of the individual who by nature seeks his own pleasure presupposes a general employment of the method of reductive analysis which was characteristic of classical empiricism, especially in the thought of Hume, and which was systematically practised by Bentham. Thus in his *Analysis of the Phenomena of the Human Mind* Mill tries to reduce man's mental life to its basic elements. In general he follows Hume in distinguishing between impressions and ideas, the latter being copies or images of the former. But Mill actually speaks of sensations, not of impressions. Hence we can also say that he follows Condillac[43] in depicting the development of mental phenomena as a process of the transformation of sensations. It must be added, however, that Mill groups together sensations and ideas under the term 'feelings'. 'We have two classes of feelings; one, that which exists when the object of sense is present; another, that which exists after the object of sense has ceased to be present. The one class of feelings I call sensations; the other class of feelings I call *ideas*.'[44]

After reducing the mind to its basic elements Mill is then faced with the task of reconstructing mental phenomena with the aid of the principles of the association of ideas. Hume, he remarks, recognized three principles of association, namely contiguity in time and place, causation and resemblance. But causation, in Mill's view, can be identified with contiguity in time, that is, with the order of regular succession. 'Causation is only a name for the order established between an antecedent and consequent; that is, the established or constant antecedence of the one, and consequence of the other.'[45]

Mill's work covers such topics as naming, classification, abstraction, memory, belief, ratiocination, pleasurable and painful sensations, the will and intentions. And at the end the author remarks that the work, which constitutes the theoretical part of the doctrine of the mind, should be followed by a practical part comprising logic, considered as practical rules for the mind in its search for truth, ethics and the study of education as directed to training the individual to contribute actively to the greatest possible good or happiness for himself and for his fellow men.

We cannot follow Mill in his reconstruction of mental phenomena. But it is worth while drawing attention to the way in which he deals with reflection, which was described by Locke as the notice which the mind takes of its own operations. The mind is identified with the stream of consciousness. And consciousness means having sensations and ideas. As, therefore, 'reflection is nothing but consciousness',[46] to reflect on an idea is the same thing as to have it. There is no room for any additional factor.

Commenting on his father's theory J. S. Mill remarks that 'to reflect on any of our feelings or mental acts is more properly identified with *attending* to the feeling than (as stated in the text) with merely having it'.[47] And this seems to be true. But James Mill is so obstinately determined to explain the whole mental life in terms of the association of primitive elements reached by reductive analysis that he has to explain away those factors in consciousness to which it is difficult to apply such treatment. In other words, empiricism can manifest its own form of dogmatism.

7. To turn briefly to Benthamite economics. As far as the economic market was concerned, Bentham believed that in a freely competitive market a harmony of interest is inevitably attained, at least in the long run. Such State action as he

demanded consisted in the removal of restrictions, such as the abolition of the tariffs which protected the English market in grain and which Bentham thought of as serving the sectional interest of the land-owners.

Behind this *laissez-faire* theory lay the influence of the French physiocrats, to whom allusion has already been made, though elements were also derived, of course, from English writers, particularly from Adam Smith.[48] But it was obviously not simply a question of deriving ideas from previous writers. For the *laissez-faire* economics can be said to have reflected the needs and aspirations of the expanding industrial and capitalist system of the time. In other words, it reflected the interests, real or supposed, of that middle class which James Mill considered to be the wisest element in the community.

The theory found its classical expression in the writings of David Ricardo (1772–1823), especially in his *Principles of Political Economy*, which was published in 1817. Bentham is reported to have said that James Mill was his spiritual child, and that Ricardo was the spiritual child of James Mill. But though it was largely as a result of Mill's encouragement that Ricardo published his *Principles* when he did, in economic theory Mill was more dependent on Ricardo than the other way round. In any case it was Ricardo's work which became the classical statement of Benthamite economics.

In the view of his disciple J. R. McCulloch (1789–1864) Ricardo's great service was to state the fundamental theorem of the science of value. This was to the effect that in a free market the value of commodities is determined by the amount of labour required for their production. In other words, value is crystallized labour.

Now, if this theory were true, it would appear to follow that the money obtained from the sale of commodities belongs rightfully to those whose labour produced the commodities in question. That is to say, the conclusion drawn by Marx[49] from the labour theory of value appears to be amply justified, unless perhaps we wish to argue that the capitalist is to be included among the labourers. But Ricardo and the other economists of the *laissez-faire* School were far from using the labour theory of value as a means of showing that capitalism by its very nature involves exploitation of the workers. For one thing they were conscious that the capitalist contributes to production by the investment of capital in machinery and so on. For another thing they were interested in arguing that in a competitive market, free from all restrictions, prices tend naturally to represent the real values of commodities.

This line of argument seems to involve the at least implicit assumption that a free market is governed by some sort of natural economic law which ultimately ensures a harmonization of interests and operates for the common good, provided that nobody attempts to interfere with its functioning. But this optimistic view represents only one aspect of Benthamite economics. According to T. R. Malthus (1766–1834), population always increases when living becomes easier, unless, of course, its rate of increase is restricted in some way. Thus population tends to outrun the means of subsistence. And it follows that wages tend to remain constant, at a subsistence level that is to say. Hence there is a law of wages which can hardly be said to operate in favour of the greater happiness of the greatest possible number.

If the Benthamites had made in the economic sphere a thoroughgoing application of the principle of utility, they would have had to demand in this sphere a harmonization of interests through legislation similar to the harmonization of interests through legislation which they demanded in the political sphere. Indeed, in his essay on government for the *Encyclopaedia Britannica* James Mill declared that the general happiness is promoted by assuring to every man the greatest possible amount of the fruit of his own labour, and that the government should prevent the powerful robbing the weak. But their belief in certain economic laws restricted the Benthamites' view both of the possibility and of the desirability of State action in the economic sphere.

And yet they themselves made breaches in the wall set up round the economic sphere by the belief in natural economic laws. For one thing Malthus argued that while wages tend to remain constant, rents tend to increase with the increasing fertility of the land. And these rents represent profit for the landlords though they contribute nothing to production. In other words, the landlords are parasites on society. And it was the conviction of the Benthamites that their power should be broken. For another thing, while those who were strongly influenced by Malthus's reflections on population may have thought that the only way of increasing profits and wages would be by restricting the growth of population, and that this would be impracticable, the very admission of the possibility in principle of interfering with the distribution of wealth in one way should have encouraged the exploration of other ways of attaining this end. And in point of fact J. S. Mill came to envisage legislative control, in a limited form at least, of the distribution of wealth.

In other words, if the Benthamite economists began by separating the economic sphere, in which a *laissez-faire* policy should reign, from the political sphere, in which a harmonization of interests through legislation was demanded, in J. S. Mill's development of utilitarianism the gap between the economic and political spheres tended to close. As will be seen presently, J. S. Mill introduced into the utilitarian philosophy elements which were incompatible with strict Benthamism. But it seems to the present writer at any rate that in proposing some State interference in the economic sphere with a view to the general happiness, Mill was simply applying the principle of utility in a way in which it might well have been applied from the start, had it not been for the belief in the autonomy of the economic sphere, governed by its own iron laws.

Chapter Two

THE UTILITARIAN MOVEMENT (2)

Life and writings of J. S. Mill – Mill's development of the utilitarian ethics – Mill on civil liberty and government – Psychological freedom.

1. John Stuart Mill was born in London on May 20th, 1806. A fascinating account of the extraordinary education to which he was subjected by his father is to be found in his *Autobiography*. Having apparently started to learn Greek at the age of three, by the time he was about twelve years old he was sufficiently acquainted with Greek and Latin literature, history and mathematics to enter on what he calls more advanced studies, including logic. In 1819 he was taken through a complete course of political economy, during which he read Adam Smith and Ricardo. As for religion, 'I was brought up from the first without any religious belief, in the ordinary acceptation of the term',[1] though his father encouraged him to learn what religious beliefs mankind had in point of fact held.

In 1820 J. S. Mill was invited to stay in the South of France with Sir Samuel Bentham, brother of the philosopher. And during his time abroad he not only studied the French language and literature but also followed courses at Montpellier on chemistry, zoology, logic and higher mathematics, besides making the acquaintance of some economists and liberal thinkers. Returning to England in 1821 Mill started to read Condillac, studied Roman law with John Austin (1790–1859), and gave further attention to the philosophy of Bentham. He also extended his philosophical reading to the writings of thinkers such as Helvétius, Locke, Hume, Reid and Dugald Stewart. Through personal contact with men such as John Austin and his younger brother Charles, Mill was initiated into the utilitarian circle. Indeed, in the winter of 1822–3 he founded a little Utilitarian Circle of his own, which lasted for about three and a half years.

In 1823 Mill obtained, through his father's influence, a clerkship in the East India Company. And after successive promotions he became head of the office in 1856 with a substantial salary. Neither father nor son ever held an academic chair.

Mill's first printed writings consisted of some letters published in 1822, in which he defended Ricardo and James Mill against attack. After the foundation of the *Westminster Review* in 1824 he became a frequent contributor. And in 1825 he undertook the editing of Bentham's *Rationale of Evidence* in five volumes, a labour which, so he tells us, occupied about all his leisure time for almost a year.

It is hardly surprising that prolonged overwork, culminating in the editing of Bentham's manuscripts, resulted in 1826 in what is popularly called a nervous breakdown. But this mental crisis had a considerable importance through its effect on Mill's outlook. In his period of dejection the utilitarian philosophy, in which he had been indoctrinated by his father, lost its charms for him. He did not indeed abandon it. But he came to two conclusions. First, happiness is not attained by seeking it directly. One finds it by striving after some goal or ideal other than one's own happiness or pleasure. Secondly, analytic thought needs to be complemented by a cultivation of the feelings, an aspect of human nature which Bentham had mistrusted. This meant in part that Mill began to find some meaning in poetry and art.[2] More important, he found himself able to appreciate Coleridge and his disciples, who were generally regarded as the antithesis to the Benthamites. In the course of time he even came to see some merit in Carlyle, a feat which his father was never able to achieve. True, the effect of Mill's crisis should not be exaggerated. He remained a utilitarian, and, though modifying Benthamism in important ways, he never went over to the opposite camp. As he himself puts it, he did not share in the sharp reaction of the nineteenth century against the eighteenth, a reaction represented in Great Britain by the names of Coleridge and Carlyle. At the same time he became conscious of the narrowness of Bentham's view of human nature, and he

formed the conviction that the emphasis laid by the French
philosophes and by Bentham on the analytic reason needed
to be supplemented, though not supplanted, by an understanding of the importance of other aspects of man and his
activity.

In 1829–30 Mill became acquainted with the doctrines of
the followers of Saint-Simon.[3] While he disagreed with them
on many issues, their criticism of the *laissez-faire* economics
appeared to him to express important truths. Further, 'their
aim seemed to me desirable and rational, however their
means might be inefficacious'.[4] In a real sense Mill always
remained an individualist at heart, a staunch upholder of
individual liberty. But he was quite prepared to modify in-
dividualism in the interest of the common welfare.

In 1830–1 Mill wrote five *Essays on Some Unsettled Ques-*
tions of Political Economy, though they were not published
until 1844.[5] In 1843 he published his famous *System of*
Logic, on which he had been working for some years. For
part of the work he found stimulus in W. Whewell's *History*
of the Inductive Sciences (1837) and in Sir John Herschel's
Discourse on the Study of Natural Philosophy (1830), while
in the final rewriting of the work he found further help in
Whewell's *Philosophy of the Inductive Sciences* (1840) and
the earlier volumes of Auguste Comte's *Cours de philosophie*
positive.[6] His correspondence with the celebrated French
positivist, whom he never actually met, began in 1841. But
in the course of time this epistolary friendship waned and
then ceased. Mill continued to respect Comte, but he found
himself entirely out of sympathy with the positivist's later
ideas for the spiritual organization of humanity.

In 1848 Mill published his *Principles of Political Econ-*
omy.[7] In 1851 he married Harriet Taylor, with whom he had
been on terms of intimate friendship from 1830 and whose
first husband died in 1849. In 1859, the year following that
of his wife's death, Mill published his essay *On Liberty*, in
1861 his *Considerations on Representative Government*, and
in 1863 *Utilitarianism*.[8] An *Examination of Sir William*
Hamilton's Philosophy and the small volume on *Auguste*
Comte and Positivism appeared in 1865.

From 1865 until 1868 Mill was a Member of Parliament

for Westminster. He spoke in favour of the Reform Bill of 1867, and he denounced the policy of the British government in Ireland. Of his pamphlet *England and Ireland* (1868) he remarks that it 'was not popular, except in Ireland, as I did not expect it to be.'[9] Mill also advocated proportional representation and the suffrage for women.

Mill died at Avignon on May 8th, 1873. His *Dissertations and Discussions* appeared in four volumes between 1859 and 1875, while his *Essays in Religion* were published in 1874. Further reference to the last-named work, in which Mill discusses sympathetically the hypothesis of a finite God, that is, God limited in power, will be made in the next chapter.

2. In *Utilitarianism* Mill gives an often-quoted definition or description of the basic principle of utilitarian ethics which is quite in accord with Benthamism. 'The creed which accepts as the foundation of morals, Utility, or the Greatest Happiness Principle, holds that actions are right in proportion as they tend to promote happiness, wrong as they tend to produce the reverse of happiness. By happiness is intended pleasure, and the absence of pain; by unhappiness, pain, and the privation of pleasure.'[10]

True, Mill is anxious to show that utilitarianism is not a philosophy either of egoism or of expediency. It is not a philosophy of egoism because happiness, in the moral context, 'is not the agent's own greatest happiness, but the greatest amount of happiness altogether'.[11] As for expediency, the expedient as opposed to the right generally means that which serves the interests of the individual as such, without regard to the common good, 'as when a minister sacrifices the interests of his country to keep himself in place'.[12] Such conduct is clearly incompatible with the greatest happiness principle. At the same time, though Mill is anxious to show that utilitarianism does not deserve the accusations to which Bentham's doctrine seemed to some people to lay it open, he provides plenty of evidence that his thought moves within a Benthamite framework. This can be seen easily enough if one considers his discussion of the sense in which the principle of utility is susceptible of proof.[13] Mill's first point is that happiness is universally recognized to be a good. 'Each person's happiness is a good to that person, and the general

happiness, therefore, a good to the aggregate of all persons.'[14]
This remark implies an acceptance of Bentham's analysis of
such terms as 'community' and 'common interest'. Mill then
goes on to argue that happiness is not merely *a* good but *the*
good: it is the one ultimate end which all desire and seek.
True, it can be objected that some people seek virtue or
money or fame for its own sake, and that such things cannot
properly be described as happiness. But the fact that such
things can be sought for their own sakes is explicable in terms
of the association of ideas. Take virtue, for example. 'There
was no original desire of it, or motive to it, save its conduciveness to pleasure; and especially to protection from pain.'[15]
But that which is originally sought as a means to pleasure
can, by association with the idea of pleasure, come to be
sought for its own sake. And it is then sought not as a means
to pleasure or happiness but as a constituent part of it. Evidently, this line of argument, with its appeal to the associationist psychology, is in line with Benthamism.

Nobody, of course, disputes the facts that Mill began with
the Benthamism in which he had been indoctrinated by his
father, and that he never formally rejected it, and that he
always retained elements of it. The significant aspect of Mill's
brand of utilitarianism, however, is not to be found in the
ideas which he took over from Bentham and James Mill. It
is to be found in the ideas which Mill himself added, and
which strained the original Benthamite framework to such
an extent that it ought to have been radically refashioned or
even abandoned.

Foremost among the ideas which Mill introduced was that
of intrinsic qualitative differences between pleasures. He does
indeed admit that 'utilitarian writers in general have placed
the superiority of mental over bodily pleasures chiefly in the
greater permanency, safety, uncostliness, etc., of the former
—that is, in their circumstantial advantages rather than in
their intrinsic nature'.[16] But he goes on to argue that the
utilitarians in question might have adopted another point of
view 'with entire consistency. It is quite compatible with the
principle of utility to recognize the fact, that some *kinds* of
pleasure are more desirable and more valuable than others.
It would be absurd that while, in estimating all other things,

quality is considered as well as quantity, the estimation of pleasures should be supposed to depend on quantity alone.'[17]

Mill may be quite right in claiming that it is absurd that in discriminating between pleasures no account should be taken of qualitative differences. But the suggestion that the recognition of intrinsic qualitative differences is compatible with Benthamism is quite unjustified. And the reason is clear. If we wish to discriminate between different pleasures without introducing any standard or criterion other than pleasure itself, the principle of discrimination can only be quantitative, whatever Mill may say to the contrary. In this sense Bentham adopted the only possible consistent attitude. If, however, we are determined to recognize intrinsic qualitative differences between pleasures, we have to find some standard other than pleasure itself. This may not be immediately evident. But if we reflect, we can see that when we say that one kind of pleasure is qualitatively superior to another, we really mean that one kind of pleasure-producing activity is qualitatively superior to or intrinsically more valuable than another. And if we try to explain what this means, we shall probably find ourselves referring to some ideal of man, to some idea of what the human being ought to be. For example, it makes little sense to say that the pleasure of constructive activity is qualitatively superior to that of destructive activity except with reference to the context of man in society. Or, to put the matter more simply, it makes little sense to say that the pleasure of listening to Beethoven is qualitatively superior to the pleasure of smoking opium, unless we take into account considerations other than that of pleasure itself. If we decline to do this, the only relevant question is, which is the greater pleasure, quantity being measured not simply by intensity but also according to the other criteria of the Benthamite calculus.

In point of fact Mill does introduce a standard other than pleasure itself. On occasion at least he appeals to the nature of man, even if he does not clearly understand the significance of what he is doing. 'It is better to be a human being dissatisfied than a pig satisfied; better to be Socrates dissatisfied than a fool satisfied.'[18] After all, when Mill is engaged in discussing explicitly Bentham's strong and weak points, one

of the main features of Bentham's thought to which he draws
attention is its inadequate conception of human nature. 'Man
is conceived by Bentham as a being susceptible of pleasures
and pains, and governed in all his conduct partly by the different modifications of self-interest, and the passions commonly classed as selfish, partly by sympathies, or occasionally
antipathies, towards other beings. And here Bentham's conception of human nature stops. . . . Man is never recognized
by him as a being capable of pursuing spiritual perfection as
an end; of desiring, for its own sake, the conformity of his
own character to his standard of excellence, without hope of
good or fear of evil from other source than his own inward
consciousness.'[19]

It is very far from being the intention of the present writer
to find fault with Mill for introducing the idea of human
nature as a standard for determining qualitative differences
between pleasure-producing activities. The point is rather
that he does not appear to understand the extent to which
he is subjecting the original Benthamite framework of his
thought to acute stresses and strains. There is no need to
consult Aristotle, said Bentham. But to come closer to Aristotle is precisely what Mill is doing. In his essay On Liberty
he remarks that 'I regard utility as the ultimate appeal on all
ethical questions; but it must be utility in the largest sense,
grounded on the permanent interests of man as a progressive
being.'[20] Mill does not hesitate to refer to man's 'higher
faculties',[21] to which higher or superior pleasures are correlative. And in the essay On Liberty he quotes with approval
the statement of Wilhelm von Humboldt that 'the end of
man is the highest and most harmonious development of his
powers to a complete and consistent whole.'[22] True, Mill
does not produce a clear and full account of what he means
by human nature. He lays stress, indeed, on the perfecting
and improving of human nature, and he emphasizes the
idea of individuality. Thus he says, for example, that 'individuality is the same thing with development', and that 'it
is only the cultivation of individuality which produces, or
can produce, well-developed human beings'.[23] But he makes
it clear that individual self-development does not mean for
him a surrender to any impulses which the individual is in-

clined to follow, but rather the individual fulfilment of the ideal of harmonious integration of all one's powers. It is not a question of sheer eccentricity, but of unity in diversity. Hence there must be a standard of excellence; and this is not fully worked out. The relevant point in the present context, however, is not Mill's failure to elaborate a theory of human nature. Rather is it the fact that he grafts on to Benthamism a moral theory which has little or nothing to do with the balancing of pleasures and pains according to the hedonistic calculus of Bentham, and that he does not see the necessity of subjecting his original starting-point to a thorough criticism and revision. As we have seen, he does indeed criticize Bentham's narrowness of moral vision. But at other times he tends to slur over the differences between them, especially, of course, when it is a question of uniting against what they would consider reactionary forces.

The reference to Aristotle in the last paragraph is not so far-fetched as may at first sight appear. As Bentham was primarily interested in questions of practical reform, he not unnaturally emphasized the consequences of actions. The moral character of actions is to be estimated according to the consequences which they tend to have. This view is, of course, essential to utilitarianism, in some form or other at least. And Mill often speaks in the same way. But he also sees, as Aristotle saw, that the exercise of human activities cannot properly be described as a means to an end, happiness, when the end is taken to be something purely external to these activities. For the exercise of the activities can itself constitute a part of happiness. The enjoyment of good health, for example, and the appreciative hearing of good music are, or can be, constituent elements in happiness, and not simply means to some abstract external end. 'Happiness is not an abstract idea, but a concrete whole.'[24] This is a thoroughly Aristotelian notion.

Now, in the first two paragraphs of this section we saw that according to Mill actions are right in proportion as they tend to promote happiness, wrong in so far as they tend to produce the reverse of happiness. We also noted Mill's explanation that in this ethical context happiness does not mean the individual agent's own greater happiness, but the greatest amount of happiness altogether. And if we ask why the general happiness is desirable, Mill answers that 'no reason can be given why the general happiness is desirable, except that each person, so far as he believes it to be attainable, desires his own happiness'.[25] It is therefore incumbent on him to make clear the relation between the agent's own happiness and the general happiness.

One line of argument employed by Mill represents orthodox Benthamism. 'Each person's happiness is a good to that person, and the general happiness, therefore, a good to the aggregate of all persons.'[26] If the general happiness is related to my happiness as a whole to a part, in desiring the general happiness I am desiring my own. And by the force of association of ideas I can come to desire the general happiness without adverting to my own. It can thus be explained not only how altruism is possible but also how egoism is possible. For it is no more necessary that all should attain to an altruistic point of view than it is necessary that all those who desire money as a means to an end should become misers, seeking money for its own sake.

This may sound reasonable. But reflection discloses a difficulty. If the general happiness is, as Bentham maintained, nothing but the sum total resulting from an addition of the happinesses of individuals, there is no reason why I should be unable to seek my own happiness without seeking the general happiness. And if I ask why I ought to seek the latter, it is no use replying that I seek the former. For this reply to have any relevance, it must be assumed that the general happiness is not simply the result of an addition sum, the aggregate which results from a juxtaposition of individual happinesses, but rather an organic whole of such a kind that he who promotes his own happiness necessarily promotes the general happiness. For he actualizes a constituent part of an organic whole. But it can hardly be shown that this is the case unless emphasis is placed on the social nature of man. For one can then argue that the individual does not attain his own real happiness except as a social being, a member of society, and that his happiness is a constituent element in an organic whole.

This seems indeed to be the sort of idea towards which

Mill is working. He remarks, for example, that the firm foundation of the utilitarian morality is to be found in 'the social feelings of mankind'.[27] These social feelings can be described as the 'desire to be in unity with our fellow creatures, which is already a powerful principle in human nature, and happily one of those which tend to become stronger, even without express inculcation, from the influences of advancing civilization. The social state is at once so natural, so necessary, and so habitual to man, that, except in some unusual circumstances, or by an effort of voluntary abstraction, he never conceives himself otherwise than as a member of a body.'[28] True, Mill emphasizes the fact that the social feelings grow through the influence of education and of advancing civilization, and that the more they grow the more does the common good or general happiness appear as desirable, as an object to be sought. At the same time he also emphasizes the fact that social feeling has its root in human nature itself, and that 'to those who have it, it possesses all the characters of a natural feeling. It does not present itself to their minds as a superstition of education, or a law despotically imposed by the power of society, but as an attitude which it would not be well for them to be without. This conviction is the ultimate sanction of the greatest happiness morality.'[29]

Once again, therefore, we receive the impression that Mill is working away from Benthamism to an ethics based on a more adequate view of the human person. At the same time the new theory is not developed in such a way as to make clear its relations to and differences from the framework of thought with which Mill started and which he never actually abandoned.

Though, however, the difficulty of passing from the man who seeks his own personal happiness to the man who seeks the common good is diminished in proportion as emphasis is laid on the nature of man as a social being, there remains an objection which can be brought against the utilitarian theory of obligation, whether utilitarianism is understood in its original Benthamite form or as developed by Mill.[30] For anyone at least who accepts Hume's famous assertion that an 'ought' cannot be derived from an 'is', an ought-statement from a purely factual or empirical statement, is likely to object that this is precisely what the utilitarians try to do. That is to say, they first assert that as a matter of empirical fact man seeks happiness, and they then conclude that he ought to perform those actions which are required to increase happiness and that he ought not to perform those actions which diminish happiness or increase pain or unhappiness.

One possible way of dealing with this objection is, of course, to challenge its validity. But if it is once admitted that an ought-statement cannot be derived from a purely factual statement, then, to defend utilitarianism, we have to deny the applicability of the objection in this case. Obviously, we cannot deny that the utilitarians start with a factual statement, namely that all men seek happiness. But it might be argued that this factual statement is not the only statement which functions as a premiss. For example, it might be maintained that a judgment of value about the end, namely happiness, is tacitly understood. That is to say, the utilitarians are not simply stating that as a matter of empirical fact all men pursue happiness as the ultimate end of action. They are also stating implicitly that happiness is the only end worthy of being an ultimate end. Or it might be maintained that together with the factual statement that all men seek for happiness as the ultimate end of action, the utilitarians tacitly include the premisses that to act in the way which effectively increases happiness is the only rational way of acting (given the fact that all seek this end), and that to act in a rational manner is worthy of commendation. Indeed, it is fairly clear that Bentham does assume that, as all seek pleasure, to act in the way which will effectively increase pleasure is to act rationally, and that to act rationally is commendable. And it is also clear that Mill assumes that to act in such a way as to develop a harmonious integration of the powers of human nature or of the human person is commendable.

It is not the purpose of these remarks to suggest that in the opinion of the present writer utilitarianism either in its original Benthamite form or in the somewhat incoherent shape that it assumes with J. S. Mill, is the correct moral philosophy. The point is that though in word the utilitarians derive ought-statements from a purely factual, empirical statement, it is perfectly reasonable to argue that they tacitly presuppose other premises which are not purely factual statements. Hence, even if it is admitted that an ought-statement cannot be derived from a purely factual statement, the admission is not by itself necessarily fatal to utilitarian moral theory.

As for the general merits and demerits of utilitarian moral theory, this is too broad a question for discussion here. But we can make two points. First, when we are asked why we think that one action is right and another action wrong, we frequently refer to consequences. And this suggests that a teleological ethics finds support in the way in which we ordinarily think and speak about moral questions. Secondly, the fact that a man of the calibre of J. S. Mill found himself driven to transcend the narrow hedonism of Bentham and to interpret happiness in the light of the idea of the development of the human personality suggests that we cannot understand man's moral life except in terms of a philosophical anthropology. Hedonism certainly tends to recur in the history of ethical theory. But reflection on it prompts the mind to seek for a more adequate theory of human nature than that which is immediately suggested by the statement that all men pursue pleasure. This fact is well illustrated by Mill's development of Benthamism.

3. Mill's idea of the self-development of the individual plays a central role in his reflections on civil or social liberty. As he follows Hume and Bentham in rejecting the theory of 'abstract right, as a thing independent of utility',[31] he cannot indeed appeal to a natural right on the part of the individual to develop himself freely. But he insists that the principle of utility demands that every man should be free to develop his powers according to his own will and judgment, provided that he does not do so in a way which interferes with the exercise of a similar freedom by others. It is not in the common interest that all should be moulded or expected to conform to the same pattern. On the contrary, society is enriched in proportion as individuals develop themselves freely. 'The free development of individuality is one of the principal ingredients of human happiness, and quite

the chief ingredient of individual and social progress.'[32] Hence the need for liberty.

When he is thinking of the value of free self-development on the part of the individual, Mill not unnaturally pushes the idea of liberty to the fullest extent which is consistent with the existence and maintenance of social harmony. 'The liberty of the individual must be thus far limited; he must not make himself a nuisance to other people.'[33] Provided that he refrains from interfering with other people's liberty and from actively inciting others to crime, the individual's freedom should be unrestricted. 'The only part of the conduct of anyone, for which he is amenable to society, is that which concerns others. In the part which merely concerns himself, his independence is, of right, absolute. Over himself, over his own body and mind, the individual is sovereign.'[34]

In the passage just cited the phrase 'of right' suggests, at first sight at least, that Mill has forgotten for the moment that the theory of natural rights does not form part of his intellectual baggage. It would not indeed be matter for astonishment if after inheriting the rejection of this theory from Bentham and his father Mill then tended to reintroduce the theory. But presumably he would comment that what he rejects is the theory of 'abstract' rights which are not based on the principle of utility and which are supposed to be valid irrespective of the historical and social context. 'Liberty, as a principle, has no application to any state of things anterior to the time when mankind have become capable of being improved by free and equal discussion.'[35] In a society of barbarians despotism would be legitimate, 'provided that the end be their improvement, and the means justified by actually effecting that end'.[36] But when civilization has developed up to a certain point, the principle of utility demands that the individual should enjoy full liberty, except the liberty to do harm to others. And if we presuppose a society of this sort, we can reasonably talk about a 'right' to liberty, a right grounded on the principle of utility.

Mill's general thesis is, therefore, that in a civilized community the only legitimate ground for the exercise of coercion in regard to the individual is 'to prevent harm to others.

His own good, either physical or moral, is not a sufficient warrant.'[37] But where does the boundary lie between what does harm to others and what does not, between purely self-regarding conduct and conduct which concerns others? We have noted that Mill quotes with approval Wilhelm von Humboldt's statement that the end of man is 'the highest and most harmonious development of his powers to a complete and consistent whole'.[38] And Mill is, of course, convinced that the common happiness is increased if individuals do develop themselves in this way. Might it not be argued, therefore, that harm is done to others, to the community, if the individual acts in such a way as to prevent the harmonious integration of his powers and becomes a warped personality?

This difficulty is, of course, seen and discussed by Mill himself. And he suggests various ways of dealing with it. In general, however, his answer is on these lines. The common good demands that as much liberty as possible should be conceded to the individual. Hence injury to others should be interpreted as narrowly as possible. The majority is by no means infallible in its judgments about what would be beneficial to an individual. Hence it should not attempt to impose its own ideas about what is good and bad on all. The community should not interfere with private liberty except when 'there is a definite damage, or a definite risk of damage, either to an individual or to the public'.[39]

Obviously, this does not constitute a complete answer to the objection from the purely theoretical point of view. For questions can still be asked about what constitutes 'definite damage' or 'a definite risk of damage'.[40] At the same time Mill's general principle is, by and large, that which tends to be followed in our Western democracies. And most of us would doubtless agree that restrictions on private liberty should be kept to the minimum demanded by respect for the rights of others and for the common interest. But it is idle to suppose that any philosopher can provide us with a formula which will settle all disputes about the limits of this minimum.

Mill's insistence on the value of private liberty and on the principle of individuality or originality, the principle, that is to say, of individual self-development, naturally affects his ideas on government and its functions. It affects his concept of the most desirable form of government, and it also leads him to see how democracy can be threatened by a danger to which Bentham and James Mill had not really paid attention. We can consider these two points successively.

Though Mill is well aware of the absurdity of supposing that the form of constitution which one considers to be, abstractly speaking, the best is necessarily the best in the practical sense of being suited to all people and to all stages of civilization, he none the less insists that 'to inquire into the best form of government in the abstract (as it is called) is not a chimerical, but a highly practical employment of scientific intellect'.[41] For political institutions do not simply grow while men sleep. They are what they are through the agency of the human will. And when a political institution has become obsolete and no longer corresponds to the needs and legitimate demands of a society, it is only through the agency of the human will that it can be changed or developed or supplanted by another institution. But this demands thought about what is desirable and practicable, about the ideally best form of government. For, 'the ideally best form of government, it is scarcely necessary to say, does not mean one which is practicable or eligible in all states of civilization, but the one which, in the circumstances in which it is practicable and eligible, is attended with the greatest amount of beneficial consequences, immediate and prospective.'[42]

If we presuppose that a stage of civilization has been reached in which democracy is practicable, the ideally best form of government is, for Mill, that in which sovereignty is vested in the community as a whole, in which each citizen has a voice in the exercise of sovereignty, and in which each citizen is sometimes called on to take an actual part in government, whether local or national, in some capacity or other. For one thing, the individual is more secure from being harmed by others in proportion as he is able to protect himself. And he can do this best in a democracy. For another thing, a democratic constitution encourages an active type of character, gifted with initiative and vigour. And it is more valuable to promote an active than a passive type of character. Obviously, this consideration weighs heavily with Mill. In his opinion a democratic constitution is the most likely to encourage that individual self-development on which he lays so much emphasis. Further, it promotes the growth in the individual of a public spirit, of concern with the common good, whereas under a benevolent despotism individuals are likely to concentrate simply on their private interests, leaving care for the common good to a government in which they have no voice or share.

It is clear that Mill is not primarily concerned with an external harmonization of interests among atomic human individuals, each of which is supposed to be seeking simply his own pleasure. For if this were the chief concern of government, one might conclude that benevolent despotism is the ideal form of government and that democracy is preferable only because despots are, in practice, generally as self-seeking as anyone else. It was partly this idea that drove Bentham to adopt a radically democratic point of view. Mill, however, while by no means blind to the need for harmonizing interests, is concerned above all with the superior educative effect of democracy. True, it presupposes a certain level of education. At the same time it encourages, more than any other form of government, private liberty and free self-development on the part of the individual.

Ideally, direct democracy would be the best form of government, at least in the sense of a democracy in which all citizens would have the opportunity of sharing in government in some capacity. 'But since all cannot, in a community exceeding a single small town, participate personally in any but some very minor portions of the public business, it follows that the ideal type of a perfect government must be representative.'[43]

Mill is not, however, so naïve as to suppose that a democratic constitution automatically ensures a due respect for individual liberty. When democracy means in effect the rule, by representation, of a numerical majority, there is no guarantee that the majority will not oppress the minority. For example, legislation might be made to serve the interest of a racial or religious majority or that of a particular economic class[44] rather than the interests of the whole community.

In fine, what Bentham called 'sinister interests' can operate in a democracy as elsewhere.

As a safeguard against this danger Mill insists that minorities must be effectively represented. And to secure this he advocates a system of proportional representation, referring to Thomas Hare's *Treatise on the Election of Representatives* (1859) and to Professor Henry Fawcett's pamphlet *Mr. Hare's Reform Bill Simplified and Explained* (1860). But constitutional devices such as universal suffrage and proportional representation will not be sufficient without a process of education which inculcates a genuine respect for individual liberty and for the rights of all citizens, whatever may be their race, religion or position in society.

Given Mill's insistence on the value of individual self-development and initiative, it is not surprising that he disapproves of any tendency on the part of the State to usurp the functions of voluntary institutions and to hand them over to the control of a State bureaucracy. 'The disease which afflicts bureaucratic governments, and which they usually die of, is routine. . . . A bureaucracy always tends to become a pedantocracy.'[45] The tendency for all the more able members of the community to be absorbed into the ranks of State functionaries 'is fatal, sooner or later, to the mental activity and progressiveness of the body itself.'[46]

This does not mean, however, that Mill condemns all legislation and State control other than that required to maintain peace and order in the community. It seems true to say that he is drawn in two directions. On the one hand the principle of individual liberty inclines him to disapprove of any legislation or State control of conduct which goes beyond what is required for preventing or deterring the individual from injuring others, whether assignable individuals or the community at large. On the other hand the principle of utility, the greatest happiness principle, might well be used to justify a very considerable amount of legislation and State control with a view to the common good or happiness. But, as we have seen, the principle of individuality is itself grounded on the principle of utility. And the idea of preventing the individual from injuring others can be interpreted in such a way as to justify a good deal of State 'interference' with the individual's conduct.

Education is a case in point. We have seen that according to Mill the community has no right to coerce the individual simply for his own good. But this applies, as Mill explains, only to adults, not to children. For the latter must be protected not only from being harmed by others but also from harming themselves. Hence Mill does not hesitate to say, 'is it not almost a self-evident axiom, that the State should require and compel the education, up to a certain standard, of every human being who is born its citizen?'[47] He is not suggesting that parents should be compelled to send their children to State schools. For 'a general State education is a mere contrivance for moulding people to be exactly like one another':[48] it might easily become an attempt to establish 'a despotism over the mind'.[49] But if parents do not provide in some way for the education of their children, they are failing in their duty and are harming both individuals, namely the children, and the community.[50] Hence the State should prevent them from injuring others in this way. And if the parents are genuinely unable to pay for their children's education, the State should come to their aid.

On occasion Mill's interpretation of the principle of preventing the individual from injuring others is astonishingly broad. Thus in the essay *On Liberty* he remarks that in a country in which the population is or threatens to become so great that wages are reduced through superabundant labour, with the consequence that parents are unable to support their children, a law to forbid marriages unless the parties could show that they had the means of supporting a family would not exceed the legitimate power of the State. True, the expediency of such a law is open to dispute. But the law would not constitute a violation of liberty. For its aim would be to prevent the parties concerned from injuring others, namely the prospective offspring. And if anyone objected to the law simply on the ground that it would violate the liberty of parties who wished to marry, he would give evidence of a misplaced notion of liberty.

In point of fact Mill came to modify his view that no man should be compelled to act or to refrain from acting in a certain way simply for his own good. Take the case of proposed legislation to reduce the hours of labour. Mill came to the conclusion that such legislation would be perfectly legitimate, and also desirable, if it were in the real interest of the workmen. To pretend that it violates the worker's freedom to work for as many hours as he likes is absurd. It is indeed obviously true that he would choose to work for an excessive length of time, if the alternative were to starve. But it by no means follows that he would not choose to work for shorter hours, provided that the reduction were universally enforced by law. And in enacting such a law the legislator would be acting for the good of the worker and in accordance with his real desire.

Given his belief in the value of voluntary associations and of initiative uncontrolled by the State, together with his rooted mistrust of bureaucracy, Mill would hardly take kindly to the idea of the so-called Welfare State. At the same time in his later years he came to envisage a degree of State-control of the distribution of wealth which he at any rate was prepared to describe as socialist in character. And the development of his thought on social legislation has often been depicted, though not necessarily with disapproval of course, as constituting an implicit desertion of his original principles. But though it is perfectly reasonable to see in his thought a shift of emphasis from the idea of private liberty to that of the demands of the common good, it seems to the present writer that the charge of inconsistency or of making a *volte-face* can easily be overdone. After all, Mill did not mean by liberty merely freedom from external control. He emphasized liberty as freedom to develop oneself as a human being in the full sense, a freedom which is demanded by the common good. Hence it is reasonable to conclude that it is the business of the community, that it makes for the common good or general happiness, to remove obstacles to such self-development on the part of the individual. But the removal of obstacles may very well entail a considerable amount of social legislation.

What is true, of course, is that Mill departs very far from Benthamism. And this departure from Benthamism can also be seen in the sphere of economics. For example, when Mill condemned laws against trade unions and associations formed to raise wage-levels, the condemnation may have been based primarily on his belief that free rein should be given to private enterprises in general and to voluntary economic experiments in particular. But it implied that, within the limits set by other factors, something can be done to raise wages by human effort. In other words, there is no iron law of wages which renders nugatory all attempts to raise them.

To conclude this section. Bentham, with what we may call his quantitative point of view, naturally emphasized the individual unit. Each is to count, so to speak, as one and not as more than one. And this idea naturally led him in the direction of democratic convictions. Mill shared these convictions; but he came to lay the emphasis on quality, on the development of the individual personality, a value which is best assured in a democratically constituted society. And this shift in emphasis, involving a change from the concept of the pleasure-seeking and pain-avoiding unit to the concept of the personality seeking the harmonious and integrated active development of all his powers, is perhaps the most salient characteristic of Mill's development of utilitarianism from the philosophical point of view. From the practical point of view, that of the reformer, the feature of Mill's thought which usually strikes the observer is the way in which he discerns the growing movement towards social legislation and approves it in so far as he feels that he can reconcile it with his profound belief in the value of individual liberty. But the two points of view go together, as has already been remarked. For Mill's qualified approval of social legislation is motivated very largely by his conviction that such legislation is required to create the conditions for, by the removal of hindrances to, the fuller self-development of the individual. To the extent that he envisages the removal by the State of obstacles or hindrances to the leading by all of a full human life, Mill approximates to the point of view expounded by the British idealists in the latter part of the nineteenth century. But veneration for the State as such, the kind of veneration which had been shown by Hegel, is entirely absent from his outlook. In a very real sense he remains an individualist to the last. What exists is the individual, though the individual character and personality cannot be fully developed apart from social relations.

4. The topics of civil liberty and government are obviously connected. Freedom of the will or liberty in a psychological sense is discussed by Mill in his *A System of Logic*, under the general heading of the logic of the mental sciences, and in his *An Examination of Sir William Hamilton's Philosophy*. But as interest in the problem of freedom of the will is generally prompted by its bearing on ethics and on questions, whether moral or legal, about responsibility, it seems permissible to take the problem out of the general logical setting in which Mill actually discusses it and to consider it here.

Mill assumes that according to libertarians, upholders, that is to say, of the doctrine of freedom of the will, 'our volitions are not, properly speaking, the effects of causes, or at least have no causes which they uniformly and implicitly obey'.[51] And as he himself believes that all volitions or acts of the will are caused, he embraces, to this extent at least, what he calls the doctrine of philosophical necessity. By causation he understands 'invariable, certain and unconditional sequence',[52] a uniformity of order or sequence which permits predictability. And it is this empiricist idea of causation which he applies to human volitions and actions.

The causes which are relevant in this context are motives and character. Hence the doctrine of philosophical necessity means that, 'given the motives which are present to an individual's mind, and given likewise the character and disposition of the individual, the manner in which he will act might be unerringly inferred'.[53] It is scarcely necessary to say that Mill is referring to predictability in principle. The less knowledge we have of a man's character and of the motives which present themselves to his mind with varying degrees of force, the less able are we to predict his actions in practice.

One obvious objection to this theory is that it presupposes either that a man's character is fixed from the start or that it is formed only by factors which lie outside his control. In point of fact, however, Mill is quite prepared to admit that 'our character is formed by us as well as for us'.[54] At the same time he adds, and indeed must add if he is to preserve consistency with his premiss about causality, that the will to shape our character is formed for us. For example, experience of painful consequences of the character which he already possesses, or some other strong feeling, such as admiration, which has been aroused in him, may cause a man to desire to change his character.

It is true that when we yield, for example, to a stray temptation, we tend to think of ourselves as capable of having acted differently. But, according to Mill, this does not mean that we are actually aware or conscious that we could have acted in a different manner, all other things being equal. We are not conscious of liberty of indifference in this sense. What we are conscious of is that we could have acted differently if we had preferred to do so, that is, if the desire not to act in the way in which we did act or to act in a different manner had been stronger than the desire which, as a matter of fact, operated in us and caused our choice.

We can say, therefore, if we like, that Mill embraces a theory of character-determinism. But though he speaks, as we have seen, about the doctrine of philosophical necessity, he does not relish the use of such terms as 'necessity' and 'determinism'. He argues instead that the predictability in principle of human actions is perfectly compatible with all that the upholders of freedom of the will can reasonably maintain. Some religious metaphysicians, for instance, have found no difficulty in claiming both that God foresees all human actions and that man acts freely. And if God's foreknowledge is compatible with human liberty, so is any other foreknowledge. Hence an admission of predictability in principle does not prevent us from saying that man acts freely. It is rather a question of analysing what is meant by freedom. If it is taken to mean that when I am faced with alternative courses of action, I could make a different choice from the one which I actually make, even though all factors, including character, desires and motives, are assumed to be the same, it cannot be allowed that man is free. For freedom in this sense would be incompatible with predictability in principle: it would follow that human actions are uncaused and random events. But if by saying that man is free we mean simply that he could act differently from the way in which he does act if his character and motives were otherwise than they are, and that he himself has a hand in shaping his character, it is then quite legitimate to say that man is free. Indeed, those who assert human freedom can mean no more than this unless they are prepared to say that human actions are chance, inexplicable events.

Mill is naturally convinced that his analysis of human freedom is not at odds with the utilitarian ethics. For he does not deny that character is malleable or that moral education is possible. All that follows from the causal activity of motives, in conjunction with character, is that moral education must be directed to the cultivation of the right desires and aversions, that is, to the cultivation of those desires and aversions which are demanded by the principle of utility. 'The object of moral education is to educate the will: but the will can only be educated through the desires and aversions.'[55] As for penal sanctions and punishment in general, the statement that all human actions are in principle predictable does not entail the conclusion that all punishment is unjust. Let us assume that punishment has two ends, 'the benefit of the offender himself and the protection of others'.[56] Appropriate punishment can serve to strengthen the offender's aversion to wrong-doing and his desire to obey the law. As for protection of others, punishment, provided that unnecessary suffering is not inflicted, needs no defence other than that provided by common sense. Whatever position we may adopt on the subject of free will, murderers can no more be allowed to commit their crimes with impunity than a mad dog can be allowed to roam the streets.

In maintaining that all human actions are predictable in principle, Mill can draw, of course, on some empirical evidence. For it is an undoubted fact that the better we know a man the more confident we feel that in a given set of circumstances he would act in one way rather than in another. And if he does not act as we expected, we may conclude either that his character was stronger than we suspected or that there was a hidden flaw in his character, as the case may be. Similarly, if we find that our friends are surprised that we have resisted, say, a temptation to use a given opportunity of making money by some shady means, we may very well comment that they ought to have known us better. But though plenty of examples can be found in ordinary speech which seem to imply that a perfect knowledge of a man's character would enable the possessor of the knowledge to predict the man's actions, examples can also be found which suggest a belief to the contrary. After all, there are occasions on which we resent the suggestion that all our utterances and actions can be predicted, as though we were automata, incapable of any originality. Ultimately, however, Mill asserts the predictability in principle of all human actions more as the alternative to admitting uncaused events than as an empirical generalization.

If we assume that Mill is right in saying that we have to choose between these two alternatives, and if we are not prepared to describe human volitions and actions as chance or random events which happen without being caused, the question then arises whether the admission that all human volitions and actions are predictable in principle is or is not compatible with describing some actions as free. In one sense at any rate it is certainly compatible. For some of our actions are performed deliberately, with a conscious purpose, while others are not, reflex acts for instance. And if we wish to use the word 'free' simply to describe actions of the first kind, as distinct from the second kind, the question of predictability is irrelevant. For even if actions of both types are predictable in principle, the difference between them remains. And the word 'free' is being used simply to mark this difference. If, however, we wish to maintain that to say that an action is performed freely necessarily implies that the agent could act otherwise without being a different sort of person, unerring predictability in virtue of a knowledge of the person's character is ruled out. And if we have already accepted the validity of Mill's thesis that we have to choose between asserting predictability in principle and asserting that free actions are random events, we shall find it difficult to claim at the same time that an agent is morally responsible for his free actions.

If, however, we wish to maintain that Mill is not justified in forcing us to choose between admitting that all human actions are predictable in principle in virtue of the agent's character and admitting that free actions are random or chance events, we have to find an acceptable alternative. And this is not easy to do. It is hardly sufficient to say that the action is indeed caused but that it is caused by the agent's will, and that no other cause is required save a final cause, namely a purpose or motive. For Mill would immediately ask, what is the cause of the volition? Or is it an uncaused event? As for the motive, what causes this motive rather than another to be the stronger, actually prevailing motive? Must it not be the agent's character, the fact that he is the sort of man that he is?

It may be said that Mill himself gets into difficulties. For example, he admits that the individual can play a part in shaping his own character. And it is indeed essential for him to admit this, if any sense is to be given to his idea of civil liberty as required for self-development. But on Mill's own premisses every effort that a man makes with a view to self-improvement must be caused. And in the long run what can be meant by the statement that a man plays an active part in shaping his own character except that the causes of his character are not simply external, educational and environmental, but also internal, physiological and psychological? But this hardly squares with what the ordinary person understands by the claim that man is free, and that he is not simply a product of his environment, but can freely play an active part in shaping his character. Hence Mill should either embrace and assert determinism, which he tries to avoid, or make it clear that he is using terms such as 'free' and 'freedom' in some peculiar sense of his own, in what Bentham would call a 'metaphysical' sense.

But the fact that difficulties can be raised in regard to Mill's position does not necessarily get other people out of their difficulties. And it might very well be argued that we cannot escape these difficulties if we once allow ourselves to share Mill's analytic approach, speaking about the agent, his character and his motives as though they were distinct entities which interact on one another. We ought instead to

find another way of talking, based on a conception of the
human person and his acting which cannot be expressed in
Mill's terms. Bergson made an attempt to develop, or at
least to indicate, such a language. And others have followed
suit. We cannot talk about God in the language of, say,
physics. For the concept of God is not a concept of physical
science. Nor can we talk about freedom in the language used
by Mill. If we try to do so, we shall find freedom being
translated into something else.

The aim of the foregoing remarks is not to solve the
problem of freedom, but simply to indicate some lines of
reflection which arise out of Mill's discussions of the matter.
For the matter of that, there is a great deal more that could
be said in connection with Mill's approach and line of
thought. But it would be inappropriate to devote more space
to the subject in a book which is not intended to be a treatise
on human liberty, whether in the civil or in the psychological
sense of the term.

Chapter Three

J. S. MILL: LOGIC AND EMPIRICISM

Introductory remarks – Names and propositions, real and verbal – The nature of mathematics – Syllogistic reasoning – Induction and the principle of the uniformity of Nature – The law of causation – Experimental inquiry and deduction – Method in the Moral Sciences – Matter as a permanent possibility of sensations – The analysis of mind and the spectre of solipsism – Mill on religion and natural theology.

1. In the eighteenth century the study of logic had been comparatively neglected. And in the introduction to his *System of Logic* Mill pays a tribute to Richard Whateley (1787–1863), Archbishop of Dublin, as 'a writer who has done more than any other person to restore this study to the rank from which it had fallen in the estimation of the cultivated class in our own country.'[1] But it does not follow, of course, that Mill is in full agreement with Whateley's idea of the nature and scope of logic. Logic was defined by Whateley as the science and art of reasoning.[2] But this definition, Mill contends, is in any case too narrow to cover all logical operations. More important, Whateley regarded syllogistic deduction as the standard and type of all scientific inference, and he refused to admit that the logic of induction could be given a scientific form analogous to the theory of the syllogism. He did not mean, he explained, that no rules for inductive investigation could be laid down. But in his opinion such rules must always remain comparatively vague and could not be synthesized in a properly scientific theory of inductive logic. Mill, however, sets out with the aim of showing that the opposite is true. He is careful to remark that he does not despise the syllogism. And in his *System of Logic* he deals with syllogistic inference. But he lays emphasis on the nature of logic as 'the science which treats of the operations

of the human mind in the pursuit of truth'.[3] That is to say, he lays emphasis on the function of logic in generalizing and synthesizing the rules for estimating evidence and advancing from known to unknown truths rather than on its function as providing rules for formal consistency in reasoning. Hence what is primarily required for the development of logic is precisely the fulfilment of the task which according to Whateley could not be fulfilled, or at least not with any degree of scientific exactitude, namely to generalize 'the modes of investigating truth and estimating evidence, by which so many important and recondite laws of nature have, in the various sciences, been aggregated to the stock of human knowledge'.[4]

But Mill is not interested simply in developing a systematic theory of inductive logic as employed in natural science. He is also concerned with working out a logic of what he calls the moral sciences, which include psychology and sociology. True, he actually considered this topic before he found himself able to complete a satisfactory account of inductive logic as given in the third book of the System of Logic. But this does not prevent Mill from presenting the sixth book, which deals with the logic of the moral sciences, as an application to them of the experimental method of the physical sciences. He thus makes his own the programme envisaged by David Hume, namely that of employing the experimental method in the development of a science of human nature.[5]

If it is asked whether Mill's point of view is that of an empiricist, the answer obviously depends to a great extent on the meaning which is given to this term. As Mill himself uses the term, he is not, or at any rate does not wish to be, an empiricist. Thus in the System of Logic he speaks of 'bad generalization a posteriori or empiricism properly so called',[6] as when causation is inferred from casual conjunction. Again, Mill refers to induction by simple enumeration as 'this rude and slovenly mode of generalization',[7] a mode of generalization which was demanded by Francis Bacon and which confuses merely empirical laws with causal laws. A simple example is offered by the way in which many people generalize from the people of their own country to the peoples of other countries, 'as if human beings felt, judged and

acted everywhere in the same manner'.[8] Again, in Mill's
work on Comte we are told that 'direct induction [is] usually no better than empiricism',[9] 'empiricism' being obviously employed in a depreciatory sense. And similar remarks
occur elsewhere.

But though Mill certainly rejects empiricism in the sense
in which he understands the term, in the sense, that is to
say, of bad and slovenly generalization, of a procedure which
bears little relation to scientific method or methods, he
equally certainly takes his stand with Locke in holding that
the material of all our knowledge is provided by experience.
And if this is what is meant by empiricism, Mill is indubitably an empiricist. True, he admits intuition as a source of
knowledge. Indeed, 'the truths known by intuition are the
original premises from which all others are inferred'.[10] But
by intuition Mill means consciousness, immediate awareness
of our sensations and feelings. If by intuition is meant 'the
direct knowledge we are supposed to have of things external to our minds',[11] he is not prepared to admit that
there is any such thing. Indeed, the *System of Logic* 'supplies
what was much wanted, a text-book of the opposite doctrine
—that which derives all knowledge from experience, and all
moral and intellectual qualities principally from the direction given to the associations'.[12]

Mill's rejection of what he calls the German or *a priori*
view of human knowledge, which is to be found in the philosophy of Coleridge and to a certain extent in that of
Whewell, is complicated by the fact that he regards it as
having undesirable consequences in moral and political
theory, or even as being invoked to support undesirable social
attitudes and convictions. 'The notion that truths external to
the mind may be known by intuition or consciousness, independently of observation and experience, is, I am persuaded, in these times the great intellectual support of false
doctrines and bad institutions. . . . There never was such
an instrument devised for consecrating all deep-seated prej-
udices.'[13] Hence when the *System of Logic* endeavours to
explain mathematical knowledge, the stronghold of the intuitionists, without recourse to the idea of intuitive or *a priori*

knowledge, it is performing a valuable social service as well as attempting to settle a purely theoretical problem.

It may be objected that these remarks are really quite inadequate for settling the question whether or not Mill is to be described as an empiricist. On the one hand, if empiricism is equated with bad and slovenly generalization, it is indeed obvious that neither Mill nor any other serious thinker would wish to be called an empiricist. For the term becomes one of abuse or at least of depreciation. On the other hand, a conviction that the material of our knowledge is furnished by experience is not by itself sufficient warrant for calling a philosopher an empiricist. Hence to observe that Mill attacks empiricism in a certain sense of the term while at the same time he maintains that all our knowledge is grounded in experience, does not do more than narrow down the question to a certain extent. It does not answer it. We are not told, for instance, whether Mill admits metaphysical principles which, though we come to know them as a basis of experience and not *a priori*, nevertheless go beyond any actual experience, in the sense that they apply to all possible experience.

This line of objection is perfectly reasonable. But it is difficult to give a simple answer to the question raised. On the one hand Mill certainly takes up an empiricist position when he explicitly asserts that we cannot attain absolute truth and that all generalizations are revisable in principle. On the other hand, when he is differentiating between properly scientific induction and slovenly generalization, he tends to speak in such a way as to imply that hitherto unknown truths can be inferred with certainty from known truths and, consequently, that Nature possesses a stable structure, as it were, which could be expressed in statements which would be true of all possible experience. In view of Mill's general position in the history of British philosophy and in view of the influence exercised by his thought it is perfectly natural that we should emphasize the first aspect of his thought and call him an empiricist. But it is as well to remember that he sometimes adopts positions which imply a different point of view. In any case the different strands in his thought can be seen only by considering what he says on particular topics.

2. Logic, Mill maintains, is concerned with inferences

from truths previously known, not, of course, in the sense that the logician increases our knowledge of the world by actually making substantial inferences, but in the sense that he provides the tests or criteria for determining the value of inference or proof, and consequently of belief in so far as it professes to be grounded on proof. But inference is 'an operation which usually takes place by means of words, and in complicated cases can take place in no other way'.[14] Hence it is proper to begin a systematic study of logic by a consideration of language.

We might perhaps expect that Mill would turn immediately to propositions. For it is propositions which are inferred. But as he regards the proposition as always affirming or denying a predicate of a subject, one name, as he puts it, of another name, he actually begins by discussing names and the process of naming.

It is unnecessary to mention here all the distinctions which Mill draws between different types of names. But the following points can be noted. According to Mill, whenever a name given to objects has in the proper sense a meaning, its meaning consists in what it connotes, not in what it denotes. All concrete general names are of this kind. For example, the word 'man' can denote or refer to an indefinite number of individual things which together are said to form a class; but its meaning resides in what it connotes, namely the attributes which are predicated when the word 'man' is applied to certain beings. It follows, therefore, that proper names, such as John, which can be applied to more than one individual but which have no connotation, possess, strictly speaking, no meaning. It does not follow, however, that the word 'God' has no meaning. For this term is not, according to Mill, a proper name. To be sure, as used by the monotheist the term is applicable to only one being. But this is because, as so used, it connotes a certain union of attributes which in fact limits its range of application. It is thus a connotative term, not a proper name like John or Mary.

Mill does indeed distinguish between words which name things or attributes and words which enter into the naming-process. For instance, in 'the wife of Socrates' the word 'of' is not itself a name.[15] But Mill has been criticized by later logicians for passing over words such as 'or' and 'if', which can certainly not be described as parts of names.

Turning to propositions, we find, as already indicated, that Mill's over-emphasis on names and naming leads him to regard all propositions as affirming or denying one name or another. The words which are commonly, though not necessarily, used to signify affirmative or negative predication are 'is' or 'is not', 'are' or 'are not'. Thus Mill takes the subject-copula-predicate form of proposition as the standard, though not invariable, form. And he warns his readers about the ambiguity of the term 'is'. For example, if we fail to distinguish between the existential use of the verb 'to be' and its use as a copula, we may be led into such absurdities as supposing that unicorns must possess some form of existence because we can say that the unicorn is an animal with one horn, or even because we can say that it is an imaginary beast.

In the course of his discussion of the import or meaning of propositions Mill distinguishes between real and verbal propositions. In a real proposition we affirm or deny of a subject an attribute which is not already connoted by its name, or a fact which is not already comprised in the signification of the name of the subject. In other words, a real proposition conveys new factual information, true or false as the case may be, information which is new in the sense that it cannot be obtained simply by analysis of the meaning of the subject term. As proper names are not connotative terms and, strictly speaking, possess no 'meaning', every proposition, such as 'John is married', which has as its subject a proper name, must necessarily belong to this class. Verbal propositions, however, are concerned simply with the meanings of names: the predicate can be obtained by analysis of the connotation or meaning of the subject term. For example, in 'man is a corporeal being' the predicate already forms part of the connotation or meaning of the term 'man'. For we would not call anything a man unless it were a corporeal being. Hence the proposition says something about the meaning of a name, about its usage: it does not convey factual information in the sense that 'John is married' or 'the

mean distance of the moon from the earth is 238,860 miles'
conveys factual information.

The most important class of verbal propositions are definitions, a definition being 'a proposition declaratory of the
meaning of a word: namely, either the meaning which it
bears in common acceptance or that which the speaker or
writer, for the particular purposes of his discourse, intends
to annex to it'.[16] Mill thus does not exclude the use of
words in new ways for specific purposes. But he insists on the
need for examining ordinary usage very carefully before we
undertake to reform language. For an examination of the
different shades of meaning which a word has in common
usage, or changes in its use, may bring to light distinctions and other relevant factors which it is important that the
would-be reformer of language should bear in mind.

Obviously, when Mill says that definitions are verbal propositions, he does not intend to imply that they are by nature purely arbitrary or that inquiries into matters of fact
are never relevant to the framing of definitions. It would be
absurd, for example, to define man with complete disregard for the attributes which those beings whom we call men
possess in common. Mill's point is that though the connotation of the term 'man' is grounded in experience of men,
and though inquiries into matters of fact can render this
connotation less vague and more distinct, what the definition
as such does is simply to make this connotation or meaning
explicit, either wholly or in part, that is, by means of selected
differentiating attributes. True, we may be inclined to suppose that the definition is not purely verbal. But the inclina-
tion can be easily explained if we bear in mind the ambiguity
of the copula. A general connotative term such as 'man' denotes an indefinite number of things and connotes certain
attributes which they have in common. When, therefore, it is
said that 'man is . . .', we may be inclined to suppose that
the definition asserts that there are men. In this case, however, we tacitly presuppose the presence of two propositions,
corresponding to two possible uses of the verb 'to be'; on the
one hand the definition, which simply makes explicit the
meaning of the term 'man', and on the other hand an existential proposition which asserts that there are beings which

possess the attributes mentioned in the definition. If we omit the existential proposition which we have surreptitiously introduced, we can see that the definition is purely verbal, concerned simply with the meaning of a name.

Let us return for a moment to real propositions and consider a general proposition such as 'All men are mortal.'[17] Looked at from one point of view, as a portion of speculative truth, as Mill puts it, this means that the attributes of man are always accompanied by the attribute of being mortal. And under analysis this means that certain phenomena are regularly associated with other phenomena. But we can also look at the proposition under the aspect of a memorandum for practical use. And it then means that 'the attributes of man are *evidence of*, are a *mark* of, mortality'.[18] In other words, it tells us what to expect. According to Mill these different meanings are ultimately equivalent. But in scientific inference it is the practical aspect of meaning, its predictive aspect, which is of special importance.

We have, therefore, a distinction between verbal propositions in which the predicate is either identical with or a part of the meaning of the subject term, and real propositions, in which the predicate is not contained in the connotation of the subject. And Mill remarks that 'this distinction corresponds to that which is drawn by Kant and other metaphysicians between what they term analytic and synthetic judgments; the former being those which can be evolved from the meaning of the terms used'.[19] We may add that Mill's distinction also corresponds more or less to Hume's distinction between propositions which state relations between ideas and propositions which state matters of fact.

If we mean by truth correspondence between a proposition and the extra-linguistic fact to which it refers,[20] it obviously follows that no purely verbal proposition can be properly described as true. A definition can be adequate or inadequate; it can correspond or not correspond with linguistic usage. But by itself it makes no statement about matters of extra-linguistic fact. The question arises, however, whether for Mill there are real propositions which are necessarily true. Does he agree with Hume that no real proposition can be necessarily true? Or, to use Kantian terminology, does he recognize the existence of synthetic *a priori* propositions?

It is a notorious fact that Mill tends to speak in different ways, his way of speaking being influenced by his reaction to the type of theory which he happens to be discussing. Hence it is difficult to say what *the* view of Mill is. However, he is undoubtedly opposed to the view that there is any *a priori* knowledge of reality. And this opposition naturally inclines him to reject synthetic *a priori* propositions. Mill is not indeed prepared to say that when the negation of a given proposition appears to us as unbelievable, the proposition must be merely verbal. For there are doubtless some real propositions which reflect a uniformity or regularity of experience such that the negations of these propositions seem to us unbelievable. And for all practical purposes we are justified in treating them as though they were necessarily true. Indeed, we can hardly do otherwise, because *ex hypothesi* we have had no experience which has led us to question their universal applicability. But a real proposition can be necessarily true in the psychological sense that we find its opposite unbelievable, without being necessarily true in the logical sense that it must be true of all possible experience, of all unobserved or unexperienced phenomena.

This seems to be more or less Mill's characteristic position. But to appreciate the complexity of the situation it is advisable to consider what he has to say about mathematical propositions, the great stronghold of intuitionists and upholders of *a priori* knowledge.

3. It is scarcely necessary to say that Mill recognizes that mathematics possesses some peculiar characteristics. He remarks, for example, that 'the propositions of geometry are independent of the succession of events'.[21] Again, the truths of mathematics 'have no connection with laws of causation. . . . That when two straight lines intersect each other the opposite angles are equal, is true of all such lines and angles, by whatever cause produced.'[22] Again, mathematical reasoning 'does not suffer us to let in, at any of the joints in the reasoning, an assumption which we have not faced in the shape of an axiom, postulate or definition. This is a merit which it has in common with formal Logic.'[23]

When, however, we start inquiring into Mill's general theory of mathematics, complications arise. Dugald Stewart maintained that mathematical propositions do not express matters of fact but only connections between suppositions or assumptions and certain consequences. He further maintained that the first principles of geometry are Euclid's definitions, not the postulates and axioms. And as he regarded the definitions as arbitrary, he made it difficult to explain how pure mathematics can be applied. That mathematics can fit reality, so to speak, and be successfully applied in physics becomes for him a matter of pure coincidence. Mill, however, was not satisfied with this position. He wished to say that mathematical propositions are true. Hence he could not admit that Euclid's theorems are deducible from definitions. For Mill held, as we have seen, that definitions are neither true nor false. He had to maintain, therefore, that Euclid's theorems are deduced from postulates, which can be true or false. And he argued that any Euclidean definition is only partly a definition. For it also involves a postulate. In other words, any Euclidean definition can be analysed into two propositions, of which one is a postulate or assumption in regard to a matter of fact while the other is a genuine definition. Thus the definition of a circle can be analysed into the following two propositions: 'a figure may exist, having all the points in the line which bounds it equally distant from a single point within it', (and) 'any figure possessing this property is called a circle'.[24] The first proposition is a postulate; and it is such postulates, not the pure definitions, which form the premisses for the deduction of Euclid's theorems. The gap which Stewart created between pure and applied mathematics is thus closed. For the propositions of geometry, for instance, are not derived from arbitrary definitions but from postulates or assumptions concerning matters of fact.

We can say, therefore, that in geometry 'our reasonings are grounded on the matters of fact postulated in definitions, and not on the definitions themselves'.[25] And 'this conclusion', Mills remarks, 'is one which I have in common with Dr. Whewell'.[26] But though Mill may find himself in agreement with Whewell when it is a question of attacking Stewart's idea that the theorems of Euclidean geometry are deduced from definitions, agreement immediately ceases when it is a question of our knowledge of the first principles of mathematics. According to Whewell these first principles are self-evident, underived from experience and known intuitively. They constitute examples of *a priori* knowledge. And this is a position which Mill is unwilling to accept. He maintains instead that in mathematics 'these original premisses, from which the remaining truths of the science are deduced, are, notwithstanding all appearances to the contrary, results of observations and experiences, founded, in short, on the evidence of the senses'.[27] We have never come across a case which would refute a mathematical axiom; and the operation of the laws of association is quite sufficient to explain our belief in the necessity of such axioms.

In the general class of 'original premisses' Mill makes a distinction between axioms and the postulates involved in definitions. Axioms are exactly true. 'That things which are equal to the same thing are equal to one another, is as true of the lines and figures in nature, as it would be of the imaginary ones assumed in the definitions.'[28] But the postulates or assumptions involved in the definitions of Euclidean geometry 'are so far from being necessary, that they are not even true; they purposely depart, more or less widely, from the truth'.[29] For example, it is not true that a line as defined by the geometer can exist. But it does not follow that the geometer intuits some peculiar mathematical entity. When he defines the line as having length but not breadth, he is deciding, for his own purposes, to ignore the element of breadth, to abstract from it, and to consider only length. Hence both axioms and postulates are derived from experience.

Obviously, when Mill describes the first principles of mathematics as generalizations from experience, he is not suggesting that our knowledge of all mathematical propositions is in fact the result of inductive generalization. What he is saying in effect is that the ultimate premisses of mathematical demonstration are empirical hypotheses. He therefore finds himself in agreement with Dugald Stewart as against Whewell. As we have seen, he disagrees with Stewart's derivation of Euclidean geometry from pure definitions; but this disagreement is played down when it is a question of noting their substantial agreement about the nature of mathematics. 'The opinion of Dugald Stewart respecting the foundations of geometry is, I conceive, substantially correct; that it is built on hypotheses.'[30] All that Whewell can show, when arguing against this opinion, is that the hypotheses are not arbitrary. But 'those who say that the premises of geometry are hypotheses, are not bound to maintain them to be hypotheses which have no relation whatever to fact'.[31]

Having said this, Mill then proceeds to get himself into an impossible position. An hypothesis, he remarks, is usually taken to be a postulate or assumption which is not known to be true but is surmised to be true, because, if it were true, it would account for certain facts. But the hypotheses of which he is speaking are not at all of this kind. For, as we have seen, the postulates involved in the definitions of Euclidean geometry are known *not* to be literally true. Further, as much as is true in the hypotheses under discussion 'is not hypothetical, but certain'.[32] The hypotheses, therefore, appear to fall into two parts, one part being known not to be literally true, the other part being certain. And it is thus rather difficult to see what justification there is for speaking of 'hypotheses' at all. Nor is the situation improved when Mill says that to call the conclusions of geometry necessary truths is really to say that they follow correctly from suppositions which 'are not even true'.[33] What he means, of course, is that the necessity of the conclusions consists in the fact that they follow necessarily from the premises. But if we were to take literally the suggestion that necessary truths are necessary because they follow from untrue assumptions, we should have to say that Mill was talking nonsense. However, it would be unfair to understand him in this way.

In his *Autobiography* Mill makes it clear that the interpretation of mathematics which he regards as his own is the explanation of so-called necessary truths in terms of 'experience and association'.[34] Hence it would be going too far if one suggested that after the publication of the *System of Logic* Mill later produced a new interpretation of mathematics. It may even be going too far if one suggests that he consciously entertained second thoughts about the interpretation, or interpretations, given in the *Logic*. But it can hardly be denied that he made remarks which implied a different conception of mathematics. For example, in his *Examination of Sir William Hamilton's Philosophy* Mill informs his readers that the laws of number underlie the laws of extension, that these two sets of laws underlie the laws of force, and that the laws of force 'underlie all the other laws of the material universe'.[35] Similarly, in the Address which he wrote in 1866 for the University of St. Andrews Mill implies that mathematics gives us the key to Nature, and that it is not so much that the first principles of mathematics are formed by inductive generalization from observation of phenomena which might be otherwise than they are as that phenomena are what they are because of certain mathematical laws. Obviously, this would not necessarily affect the thesis that we come to know mathematical truths on a basis of experience and not *a priori*. But it would certainly affect the thesis that the necessity of mathematics is purely hypothetical.

Perhaps the situation can be summed up in this way. According to Mill, for the development of the science of number or arithmetic no more is required than two fundamental axioms, namely 'things which are equal to the same thing are equal to one another' and 'equals added to equals make equal sums', 'together with the definitions of the various numbers'.[36] These axioms can hardly be described as empirical hypotheses, unless one resolutely confuses the psychological question of the way in which we come to recognize them with the question of their logical status. And though Mill speaks of them as inductive truths, he also speaks of their 'infallible truth'[37] being recognized 'from the dawn of speculation'.[38] It would thus be quite possible to regard such axioms as necessarily true by virtue of the meanings of the verbal symbols used, and to develop a formalist interpretation of mathematics. But Mill was not prepared to admit that the fundamental axioms of mathematics are verbal propositions. Hence, if he was determined, as he was, to undermine the stronghold of the intuitionists, he had to interpret them as inductive generalizations, as empirical hypotheses. And the necessity of mathematical propositions had to be interpreted simply as a necessity of logical connection between premisses and the conclusions derived from them. At the same time Mill was acutely conscious of the success of applied mathematics in increasing our knowledge of the world; and he came to make remarks which remind us of Galileo, not to mention Plato. He thought, no doubt, that talk about laws of number lying at the basis of the phenomenal world was quite consistent with his interpretation of the basic principles of mathematics. But though it was consistent with the psychological statement that our knowledge of mathematical truths actually presupposes experience of things, it was hardly consistent with the logical statement that mathematical axioms are empirical hypotheses. And we have seen how Mill got himself into a difficult position when he tried to explain in what sense they are hypotheses.

In fine, we can say one of two things. Either we can say that Mill held an empiricist view of mathematics, but that he made assertions which were inconsistent with this view. And this is the traditional way of depicting the situation. Or we can say with certain writers[39] that though Mill seems to have thought that he was expounding one unified interpretation of mathematics, in actual fact we can discern several alternative interpretations in his writings, interpretations between which he continued to hesitate, in practice if not in theory.

4. Most of the propositions which we believe, Mill remarks, are believed not because of any immediate evidence for their truth but because they are derived from other propositions, the truth of which we have already assumed, whether justifiably or not. In short, most of the propositions which we believe are inferred from other propositions. But inference can be of two main kinds. On the one hand we can infer propositions from others which are equally or more general. On the other hand we can infer propositions from others which are less general than the propositions inferred from them. In the first case we have what is commonly called deductive inference or ratiocination, while in the second case we have inductive inference.

Now, according to Mill there is 'real' inference only when

a new truth is inferred, that is, a truth which is not already contained in the premisses. And in this case only induction can be accounted real inference, inasmuch as 'the conclusion or induction embraces more than is contained in the premisses'.[40] When the conclusion is precontained in the premisses inference makes no real advance in knowledge. And this is true of syllogistic inference. For 'it is universally allowed that a syllogism is vicious if there be anything more in the conclusion than was assumed in the premisses. But this is, in fact, to say that nothing ever was, or can be, proved by syllogism, which was not known, or assumed to be known, before.'[41]

If this were all that Mill had to say on the matter, it would be natural to conclude that for him there are two distinct types of logic. On the one hand there is deductive inference, in which from more general propositions we infer less general propositions. And as the inference is invalid unless the conclusion is precontained in the premisses, no new truth can be discovered in this way. Syllogistic reasoning can ensure logical consistency in thought. For example, if someone speaks in such a way as to show that he is really asserting both that all X's are Y and that a particular X is not Y, we can employ the forms of syllogistic reasoning to make clear to him the logical inconsistency of his thought. But no new truth is, or can be, discovered in this way. For to say that all X's are Y is to say that every X is Y. On the other hand we have inductive inference, the inference employed in physical science, whereby the mind moves from what is known to a truth which is unknown before the process of inference establishes it. In short, on the one hand we have a logic of consistency, on the other hand a logic of discovery.

In reality, however, the situation is much more complicated than this preliminary account suggests. Consider one of the arguments mentioned by Mill: 'All men are mortal; the Duke of Wellington is a man: therefore the Duke of Wellington is mortal.' It is indeed obvious that to concede the major and minor premisses and deny the conclusion would involve one in logical inconsistency. But Mill sometimes speaks as though to assume the truth of the major premiss is to assume the truth of the conclusion in such a

way that to know the truth of the major is already to know
the truth of the conclusion. And this seems to be questionable on either of the interpretations of the major premiss
which he puts forward.

We have already seen that according to Mill the proposition 'all men are mortal', when it is considered as what he
calls a portion of speculative truth, means that 'the attributes of man are always accompanied by the attribute mortality'.[42] Mill here fixes his attention on the connotation of
the word 'man'. And if the proposition 'all men are mortal'
is interpreted in terms of the connotation of the word 'man',
it is natural to say that the proposition concerns universals,
not particulars. Further, if we were to interpret 'always' as
meaning 'necessarily', there would be no cogent ground for
saying that the man who asserts that the attributes which
make up the connotation of the word 'man' are always accompanied by the attribute of mortality, must already know
that the Duke of Wellington is mortal. True, the assertion
in question can be said to imply that if there is a being
which can properly be described as the Duke of Wellington
and which also possesses the attributes that make up the
connotation of the word 'man', this being also possesses the
attribute of mortality. But the fact remains that the assertion
does not necessarily presuppose any knowledge whatsoever of
the Duke of Wellington.

It may be objected that Mill does not interpret 'always' as
'necessarily'. If he did, this would make 'all men are mortal'
an essential or verbal proposition. For mortality would then
be one of the attributes which make up the connotation of
the word 'man'. In point of fact Mill regards 'all men are
mortal' as a real proposition. Hence 'always' does not mean
'necessarily' but 'so far as all observation goes'. Moreover,
though Mill may sometimes speak in a way which implies or
suggests a realistic theory of universals, it is a notorious fact
that in the course of his discussion of the syllogism he sup-
ports a nominalist theory. In other words, 'all men' must be
understood in terms of denotation. It means 'all particular
men'. And if we *know* that *all* particular men are mortal,
we know that any particular man is mortal.

The premisses of this argument are correct. That is to say,

Mill does regard 'all men are mortal' as a real and not as a verbal proposition, and he does take up a nominalist position in his discussion of the syllogism. But the conclusion of the argument does not follow from the premisses. For according to Mill's nominalist theory 'all men are mortal' is a record of experience of particular facts, that is, of facts such as that Socrates and Julius Caesar both died. And if the Duke of Wellington is a living man, his death is obviously not included among these particular facts. Hence it cannot be reasonably claimed that to know that all men are mortal presupposes or includes knowledge of the mortality of the Duke of Wellington. The conclusion that the Duke of Wellington is mortal is not precontained in the proposition 'all men are mortal'. And it seems to follow that inference from 'all men are mortal' to 'the Duke of Wellington is mortal' is invalid.

In order to make the inference valid we have to say that 'all men are mortal' is not simply a record of past experience of people dying but also an inductive inference which goes beyond the empirical evidence and serves as a prediction, telling us what to expect. Having observed in the past that the attributes which make up the connotation of the term 'man' have in fact been accompanied by mortality, we infer that the same is to be expected in the future. In other words, 'all men are mortal' becomes not so much a premiss from which the mortality of living and future men is deduced as a formula for making future inferences, that is, from the possession of certain other attributes to the attribute of mortality. And this is precisely what Mill says. 'General propositions are merely registers of such inferences already made, and short formulae for making more. The major premiss of a syllogism, consequently, is a formula of this description: and the conclusion is not an inference drawn *from* the formula, but an inference drawn *according* to the formula.'[43] And the rules of syllogistic inferences are rules for the correct interpretation of the formula. As such, they are useful. And Mill can enter 'a protest, as strong as that of Archbishop Whateley himself, against the doctrine that the syllogistic art is useless for the purposes of reasoning'.[44]

But if the major premiss is not a proposition *from* which the conclusion is derived but a formula *according to which* the conclusion is drawn, it follows that it is particular observed facts which constitute the real logical antecedent. In other words 'all inference is from particulars to particulars'.[45] A multitude of particular factual connections between being a man and being mortal have been observed in the past. As we cannot carry them all in our heads, we record them in a compendious memorandum. But the record is not simply an historical note. It runs beyond the empirical evidence observed in the past and predicts the future, serving as a guide to or formula for making inferences. And though we need not cast our reasoning according to the formula in syllogistic form, we can do so. The rules of syllogistic inference are a set of rules or precautions for ensuring correctness and consistency in our interpretation of the formula, correctness being measured by our purpose in establishing the formula, namely to simplify the making of future inferences in accordance with our past inferences. Syllogistic reasoning then becomes the latter half in the total process, as Mill puts it, of travelling from premisses to conclusions, that is, from particulars to particulars. In other words, the gap between deductive and inductive inference is diminished.

But there is more to come. Mill admits that there are cases in which syllogistic reasoning constitutes the whole process of reasoning from premisses to conclusion. These cases occur, for example, in theology and in law, when the major premiss is derived from the appropriate authority, and not by inductive inference from particular cases. Thus a lawyer may receive his major premiss, in the form of a general law, from the legislator and then argue that it applies or does not apply in some particular case or set of circumstances. But Mill adds that the lawyer's process of reasoning is then 'not a process of inference, but a process of interpretation'.[46]

We have already seen, however, that when syllogistic inference constitutes the second half of a total process of reasoning from premisses to conclusion, it is in effect a process of interpreting a formula, namely the major premiss. And in this case the sharp distinction between two kinds of logic collapses. Syllogistic reasoning is simply a process of interpretation. It can stand on its own, so to speak, as may happen when a theologian takes his major premiss from the authority

of the Scripture or the Church. Or it can form one phase
in a total process of inference from particulars to particulars.
But in neither case is it, taken in itself, an example of inference. And the rules of the syllogism are rules for the correct
interpretation of a general proposition, not rules of inference,
in the proper sense of the term at least.

5. In view of the fact that Mill represents syllogistic reasoning as a process of interpreting a general proposition
which is itself the result of induction, it is not surprising
that he defines inductive inference as 'the operation of dis-
covering and proving general propositions'.[47] At first sight the
definition may indeed appear somewhat strange. For, as we
have seen, all inference is said to be from particulars to particulars. However, 'generals are but collections of particulars
definite in kind but indefinite in number'.[48]

This amounts to saying that to prove a general proposition is to prove that something is true of a whole class of
particulars. Hence induction can be defined as 'that operation
of the mind by which we infer that what we know to be true
in a particular case or cases will be true in all cases which
resemble the former in certain assignable respects'.[49] Obviously, Mill is not thinking of so-called perfect induction,
in which the general proposition simply records what has
already been observed to be true in regard to every single
member of a class. For induction in this sense does not represent any advance in knowledge.[50] He is thinking of inference which goes beyond the actual data of experience and
argues, for example, from the known truth that some X's are
Y to the conclusion that anything at any time which possesses
the attributes in virtue of which X's are considered as members of a class will also be found to possess the attribute Y.

The basic presupposition implied by this process of going
beyond the actual empirical data to the enunciation of a
general proposition is, according to Mill, the principle of the
uniformity of Nature, that all phenomena take place according to general laws. 'The proposition that the course of Nature is uniform, is the fundamental principle, or general
axiom, of Induction.'[51] And he goes on to say that if inductive inference from particulars to particulars were to be put

in syllogistic form by supplying a major premiss, this same principle would constitute the ultimate major premiss.

Now, if the principle of the uniformity of Nature is described as a fundamental principle or axiom or postulate of induction, this may tend to suggest that the principle is explicitly conceived and postulated before any particular scientific inference is made. But this is not at all Mill's point of view. He means rather that the uniformity of Nature is the necessary condition for the validity of scientific inference, and that in embarking on any particular inference we tacitly presuppose it, even though we are not consciously aware of the fact. When, therefore, he says that if an inductive inference were to be cast into syllogistic form, the principle of the uniformity of Nature would be found to constitute the ultimate major premiss, he means that the principle is the 'suppressed' premiss of induction. And, following his general doctrine of syllogistic reasoning, he means that it is a tacit formula or axiom *in accordance with which* inferences are made, not a proposition *from* which the conclusion of the inference is deduced. True, mention of the syllogism is rather confusing. For, as we have seen, Mill regards syllogistic reasoning as the interpretation of a formula; and this suggests deliberate interpretation of a consciously conceived and enunciated formula. But though the principle of the uniformity of Nature would obviously have to be explicitly enunciated if we were actually to cast inference into syllogistic form by supplying the suppressed major premiss, it by no means follows that all scientific inference involves conscious awareness of the principle or axiom in accordance with which it operates.

Mill has no intention, therefore, of suggesting that the principle of the uniformity of Nature is a self-evident truth which is known antecedently to the discovery of particular regularities or uniformities. On the contrary, 'this great generalization is itself founded on prior generalizations.'[52] And so far from being the first induction to be made, it is one of the last. This may indeed appear at first sight to be incompatible with Mill's view that the uniformity of Nature is the basic presupposition of scientific inference. But his position seems to be more or less as follows. Scientific inference would not be valid unless there was uniformity in Nature. Hence when we turn to the investigation of Nature and embark on scientific inference, we tacitly presuppose that there is uniformity in Nature, even though we are unaware of the fact. The explicit idea of the uniformity of Nature arises through the discovery of particular uniformities. And the more we discover such uniformities, the more we tend to prove the validity of the idea, and thus of the implicit presupposition of all inference.

Now, if the principle of the uniformity of Nature is taken to mean that the course of Nature is always uniform in the sense that the future will always repeat or resemble the past, the principle, as a universal proposition, is patently untrue. As Mill observes, the weather does not follow a uniform course in this sense, nor does anyone expect it to do so. But what is called the uniformity of Nature 'is itself a complex fact, compounded of all the separate uniformities which exist in respect to single phenomena',[53] these separate uniformities being commonly called laws of Nature. Presumably, therefore, to say that scientific inference presupposes the uniformity of Nature is simply to say that the scientific investigation of Nature tacitly presupposes that there are uniformities in Nature. In other words, the condition of the validity of scientific inference is that there should be uniformities in the context or sphere with which the inference is concerned. And the progressive discovery of particular uniformities constitutes the progressive validation of scientific inference.

It is often said that Mill attempts to 'justify' scientific inference from the unknown to the known. And so he does in a sense. But in what sense? He tells us indeed that 'the real proof that what is true of John, Peter, etc. is true of all mankind, can only be, that a different supposition would be inconsistent with the uniformity which we know to exist in the course of Nature'.[54] But we do not know in advance that the course of Nature is uniform. We may assume it, and if the assumption is partly a rule for making inferences, consistency demands that we should follow it. But consistency alone can hardly constitute a proof of the assumption. If at any rate we concentrate our attention on the empiricist aspects of Mill's thought, on his denial of *a priori* knowledge and on his view that all inference is from particulars to particulars, generals being but collections of particulars, it seems that the only possible justification of inductive generalization is partial verification coupled with absence of falsification. We cannot observe all possible instances of a law or asserted uniformity. But if the law is verified in those cases where we do test it empirically and if we know of no case in which it is falsified, this appears to be the only sort of justification of the inductive leap from the known to the unknown, from the observed to the unobserved, from 'some' to 'all', which can be provided. And if the uniformity of Nature is simply the complex of particular uniformities, it follows that the uniformity of Nature in a general sense tends to be proved, in the only sense in which it can ever be proved, in proportion as particular inductive generalizations are found, through partial verification and absence of falsification, to be successful predictions of phenomena.

6. In common parlance, as Mill puts it, the various uniformities in Nature are called the laws of Nature. But in stricter scientific language the laws of Nature are the uniformities in Nature when reduced to their simplest expression. They are 'the fewest and simplest assumptions, which being granted, the whole existing order of Nature would result',[55] or 'the fewest general propositions from which all the uniformities which exist in the universe might be deductively inferred'.[56] The task of the scientific study of Nature is to ascertain what these laws are and what subordinate uniformities can be inferred from them, while the task of inductive logic is to determine the principles and rules governing the arguments by which such knowledge is established.

We can note in passing how Mill shifts his position under the influence of the actual nature of science. When speaking as an empiricist, he tells us that all inference is from particulars to particulars, and that general propositions, reached by inductive generalization, are formulas for making inferences but not propositions *from* which conclusions are deduced. Now he tells us that the scientific study of Nature involves deducing less general from more general laws. Obviously, it remains true that particulars as such cannot be deduced from any general proposition. The general proposition tells us what to expect, and we then have to examine empirically whether the prediction is confirmed or falsified. At the same time there seems to be a change of emphasis. When discussing the syllogism, Mill gives a nominalist account of the process of inference. When he turns to induction he tends to adopt a more realist position. He tends to assume that Nature possesses a stable structure which can be represented in the edifice of science.

Some laws or uniformities, such as the propositions of geometry, are unrelated to temporal succession. Others, such as the propositions of arithmetic, apply both to synchronous or coexisting and to successive phenomena. Others again are related only to temporal succession. And the most important of these is the law of causation. 'The truth that every fact which has a beginning has a cause, is coextensive with human experience.'[57] Indeed, recognition of the law of causation is 'the main pillar of inductive science'.[58] That is to say, inductive science establishes causal laws, and it presupposes that every event happens in accordance with such a law. Hence in developing a theory of induction it is essential to define the idea of causality as clearly as possible.

Mill disclaims any intention of concerning himself with ultimate causes in a metaphysical sense.[59] Moreover, as he intends to determine the idea of causality only in so far as it can be obtained from experience, he does not propose to introduce the notion of any mysterious necessary bond between cause and effect. Such a notion is not required for a theory of inductive science. There is no need to go beyond 'the familiar truth, that invariability of succession is found by observation to obtain between every fact in nature and some other fact which has preceded it'.[60]

At the same time it is misleading to assert that Mill reduces the causal relation to invariable sequence. For this might be taken to imply that in his view the cause of a given phenomenon can be identified with any other phenomenon which is found by experience always to precede it. Rather does he identify the cause of a given phenomenon with the totality of antecedents, positive and negative, which are required for the occurrence of the phenomenon and which are sufficient for its occurrence. 'Invariable sequence, therefore, is not synonymous with causation, unless the sequence, besides being invariable, is unconditional.'[61] And the cause of a phenomenon is, properly speaking, 'the antecedent, or the concurrence of antecedents, on which it is invariably and *unconditionally* consequent'.[62]

Now, Mill says of the law of causation that 'on the universality of this truth depends the possibility of reducing the inductive process to rules'.[63] And he certainly assumes in practice that every phenomenon has a cause in the sense explained above. All the phenomena of Nature are the 'unconditional' consequences of previous collocations of causes.[64] And any mind which knew all the causal agents existing at a given moment, together with their positions and the laws of their operations, 'could predict the whole subsequent history of the universe, at least unless some new volition of a power capable of controlling the universe should supervene'.[65]

But how do we know that the law of causation is a universal truth? Mill is certainly not prepared to say that it is a self-evident *a priori* proposition, nor that it is deducible from any such proposition. Hence he must hold that it is a product of inductive inference. But what sort of inductive inference? In ascertaining particular causal laws the method recommended by Mill is that of elimination, as will be seen in the next section. But the method, or rather methods, of experimental inquiry by the process of elimination presuppose the truth of the law of causation. Hence it can hardly be itself established by this process. And this means that we have to fall back on induction by simple enumeration. That is to say, we find in ordinary experience that every event has a cause. And when we come to the scientific study of Nature, we already believe in and expect to find causal connections.

It can hardly be denied, I think, that Mill is in rather a difficult position. On the one hand he wishes to say that the law of causation is a universal and certain truth which validates scientific inference. And he maintains that induction by simple enumeration becomes more and more certain in proportion as the sphere of observation is widened. Hence 'the most universal class of truths, the law of causation for instance, and the principles of number and of geometry, are duly and satisfactorily proved by that method alone, nor are they susceptible of any other proof'.[66] The law of causation 'stands at the head of all observed uniformities, in point of universality, and therefore (if the preceding observations are correct) in point of certainty'.[67] Again, 'the law of cause and effect, being thus certain, is capable of imparting its certainty to all other inductive propositions which can be deduced from it'.[68] On the other hand Mill maintains that induction by simple enumeration is fallible. True, the certainty of the law of causation is 'for all practical purposes complete'.[69] At the same time 'the uniformity in the succession of events, otherwise called the law of causation, must be received not as a law of the universe, but of that portion of it only which is within the range of our means of sure observation, with a reasonable degree of extension to adjust cases. To extend it further is to make a supposition without evidence, and to which, in the absence of any ground of experience for estimating its degree of probability, it would be idle to attempt to assign any.'[70]

The upshot seems to be more or less this. In ordinary experience we find that events have causes. And experience, together with the operation of the laws of the association of ideas, can explain our undoubting assurance in the universal validity of the law of causation. And the law can thus fulfil, in regard to scientific inference, the function which Mill assigns to the major premiss in a syllogism. That is to say, it is at once a record of past experience and a prediction of what we are to expect. It is a rule or formula for scientific induction. Moreover, scientific inference always confirms the law of causation and never falsifies it. If we in fact arrive at a wrong conclusion and assert that A is the cause of C when it is not, we eventually find that something else, say B, is the cause of C, not that C is uncaused. Hence for all practical purposes the law of causation is certain, and we can safely rely on it. But from the purely theoretical point of view we are not entitled to say that it infallibly holds good in regions of the universe which lie outside all human experience.

If it is objected that Mill clearly wishes to attribute to the law of causation an absolute certainty which enables it to constitute the absolutely sure foundation of scientific inference, the objection can be conceded. 'That every fact which begins to exist has a cause . . . may be taken for certain. The whole of the present facts are the infallible result of all past facts, and more immediately of all facts which existed at the moment previous. Here, then, is a great sequence, which we know to be uniform. If the whole prior state of the entire universe could again recur, it would again be followed by the present state.'[71] But though Mill may believe in the universality and infallibility of the law of causation, the point is that on his premises he has no adequate justification for his belief. And, as we have seen, he finds himself compelled to recognize this fact.

7. Mill is very far from thinking that empiricism, in the sense of mere observation, can do much to advance scientific knowledge. Nor does he think that experimentalism, in the sense of the making of controlled experiments, constitutes the whole of scientific method. He is conscious that the function of hypotheses is 'one which must be reckoned absolutely indispensable in science. . . . Without such assumptions, science could never have attained its present state; they are necessary steps in the progress to something more certain; and nearly everything which is now theory was once hypothesis.'[72] Nor, of course, does he pass over the role of deduction. 'To the Deductive Method, thus characterized in its three constituent parts, Induction, Ratiocination and Verification, the human mind is indebted for its most conspicuous triumphs in the investigation of Nature.'[73] As attention is generally concentrated on Mill's methods of experimental inquiry, of which a brief account will shortly be given, it is as well to recognize from the outset that the experimentalism which he contrasts with mere empiricism does not involve a total blindness to the actual nature of scientific method.

A distinction is made by Mill between purely descriptive and explanatory hypotheses. Take the bare assertion that the orbits of the planets are ellipses. This merely describes the movements of the planets without offering any causal explanation. And if the hypothesis is verified, this is the only proof of its truth which is required. 'In all these cases, verification is proof; if the supposition accords with the phenomena there needs no other evidence of it.'[74] But in the case of explanatory hypotheses the situation is different. Let us suppose that from hypothesis X we deduce that if the hypothesis is true, phenomena *a*, *b* and *c* should occur in certain given circumstances. And let us suppose that the prediction is verified. The verification does not prove the truth of X; for the same consequences might also be deducible from hypotheses Y and Z. We are then faced with three possible causes. And in order to discover the true one we have to eliminate two. When this has been done, what was originally an hypothesis becomes a law of Nature.

The implied view of physical science is clearly realistic. Mill speaks as though we already know that Nature is uniform, in the sense that 'the whole of the present facts are the infallible result of all past facts'.[75] But when we contemplate Nature, we are not immediately presented with particular uniformities. And no amount of mere observation will enable us to resolve general uniformity into particular uniformities. For 'the order of Nature, as perceived at a first glance, presents at every instant a chaos followed by another chaos'.[76] In other words, when we look for the cause of a given event, we are faced with a plurality of *prima facie* causes or of possible causes; and observation alone will not enable us to determine the true cause. Nor for the matter of that will purely mental analysis or reasoning. Reasoning is indeed indispensable. For in science we have to form hypotheses and deduce their consequences. But an hypothesis cannot be turned into a law of Nature unless alternative possibilities are eliminated. And this requires methods of experimental inquiry. Obviously, all this presupposes the existence of an objective uniformity of Nature, and so of real causal laws waiting to be discovered. Given the empiricist aspects of Mill's thought, we cannot indeed prove the general uniformity of Nature except *a posteriori* and progressively, in proportion as we discover factual causal connections. But this does not alter the fact that Mill is clearly convinced that there are such connections to be discovered. And this is doubtless why he tends to speak, as we have seen, as though the general uniformity of Nature can be known in advance of the scientific discovery of particular causal laws.

Mill gives four methods of experimental inquiry. The first two methods are respectively those of agreement and disagreement. The canon or regulating principle of the method of agreement states that 'if two or more instances of the phenomenon under investigation have only one circumstance in common, the circumstance in which alone all the instances agree is the cause (or effect) of the given phenomenon'.[77] The canon of the method of disagreement states that if we consider a case in which the phenomenon under investigation occurs and a case in which it does not occur, and if we find that the two cases have all circumstances in common save one, which is present only in the former case, this one circumstance is the effect or the cause, or an indispensable part of the cause, of the phenomenon in question. Both methods are obviously methods of elimination, the first resting on the axiom that whatever can be eliminated is not connected by any causal law with the occurrence of the phenomenon under investigation, the second on the axiom that whatever cannot be eliminated is so connected. And Mill combines the two methods in the joint method of agreement and disagreement.[78]

The canon of the third experimental method, the method of residues, is stated as follows. 'Subduct from any phenomenon such part as is known by previous inductions to be the effect of certain antecedents, and the residue of the phenomenon is the effect of the remaining antecedents.'[79] The fourth method, that of concomitant variations, is especially used in cases where artificial experiment is not practicable. Its canon declares that whatever phenomenon varies whenever another phenomenon varies in a given manner is either a cause of this phenomenon or its effect or connected with it through some causal fact. For example, if we find that variations in the moon's position are always followed by corresponding variations in the tides, we are entitled to conclude that the moon is the cause, total or partial, which determines the tides, even though we are obviously not able to remove the moon and see what happens in its absence.

Now, Mill does indeed speak as though his four methods of experimental inquiry, which he regards as 'the only possible modes of experimental inquiry',[80] were methods of discovery. And it has been sometimes objected that they are in reality only ways of checking the validity of scientific hypotheses which have been worked out by other means. But in justice to Mill it must be added that he insists more on the status of the methods as methods of proof than on their function as possible methods of discovery. 'If discoveries are ever made by observation and experiment without Deduction, the four methods are methods of discovery: but even if they were not methods of discovery, it would not be the less true that they are the sole methods of Proof; and in that character even the results of deduction are amenable to them.'[81]

Mill recognizes, of course, that experimentation has a limited field of application. In astronomy we cannot perform the experiments which we can perform in chemistry. And the same is more or less true of psychology and sociology. Hence the method of these sciences, 'in order to accomplish anything worthy of attainment, must be to a great extent, if not principally deductive'.[82] But his general principle is that 'observation without experiment (supposing no aid from deduction) can ascertain sequences and coexistences, but cannot prove causation'.[83] And the four methods mentioned above are the methods of proof, the methods of turning an hypothesis into an assured causal law. Mill is therefore not prepared to accept the view, which he attributes to Whewell, that in the absence of empirical falsification we should be content to let an hypothesis stand until a simpler hypothesis, equally consistent with the empirical facts, presents itself. In his opinion absence of falsification is by no means the only proof of physical laws which is required. And for this reason he insists on the use of the methods of experimental inquiry, whenever this is practicable.

Does Mill succeed in justifying inductive inference from the observed to the unobserved, from the known to the unknown? If we concentrate attention on his explicit assertion that all inference is from particulars to particulars, and if we take it that particulars are all entirely separate entities (that is, if we concentrate attention on the nominalist elements in Mill's thought), a negative answer must be given. Mill might, of course, have tried to work out a theory of probability. But in the absence of such a theory he would perhaps have done best to say that science is justified by its success and requires no further theoretical justification. At the same time we can say that he does provide such a justification. But he provides it only by assuming that throughout Nature there is a structure of real uniformities which are something more than purely factual sequences. In other words, he justifies scientific inference by assuming a realist position and forgetting the implications of nominalism.

8. Hume's programme of extending the reign of science from the study of the non-human material world to man himself, by creating a science of human nature, had found a partial fulfilment in Mill's empiricist predecessors. The associationist psychologists aimed at setting psychology, the study of man's mental life, on a scientific basis. And Bentham thought of himself as developing a science of man's moral life and of man in society. As we have seen, J. S. Mill considered that Bentham's idea of human nature was narrow and short-sighted. And he was well aware that the science of human nature had not made an advance comparable to that made by the physical sciences. Hence for the would-be creator of a logic of the 'moral sciences' it could not be simply a question of stating in abstract and explicit form a method or methods of proof which had already been employed to obtain impressive concrete results. His work must be necessarily in large measure tentative, a pointing out of a path to be followed in the future rather than a reflection on a road already traversed. But in any case it was natural that Mill should lay emphasis on the need for developing a logic of the moral sciences. I do not intend to imply that he was influenced exclusively by his British predecessors. For French social philosophy was also a stimulative factor. But, given the general movement of thought, it was natural that a man who wished to work out a logic of inductive inference and who was at the same time deeply interested in social thought and reform, should include man in society in the field of his reflections about scientific method.

The sixth book of the *System of Logic* is entitled 'On the Logic of the Moral Sciences'. By the moral sciences Mill means those branches of study which deal with man, provided that they are neither strictly normative in character nor classifiable as parts of physical science. The first condition excludes practical ethics or 'morality', that is, ethics in so far as it is expressed in the imperative mood. 'The imperative mood is the characteristic of art, as distinguished from science.'[84] The second condition excludes consideration of states of mind in so far as they are considered as caused immediately by bodily states. Study of the laws governing the relations between states of mind belongs to psychology as a moral science; but study of the laws governing sensations regarded as proximately dependent on physical conditions belongs to physiology, which is a natural science. Provided that we bear in mind these qualifications, we can say that the moral sciences include psychology, ethology or the science of the formation of character,[85] sociology and history, though the science of history is really part of general sociology, the science of man in society.

What is needed, in Mill's opinion, is to rescue the moral sciences from 'empiricism'. That is to say, purely empirical descriptive laws must be turned into explanatory or causal laws or deduced from such laws. We may, for example, have observed that in all known cases human beings behave in a certain way in certain circumstances. We then state in a generalized form that human beings behave in this way. But mere observation of a certain number of instances does not really provide us with any reliable assurance that the empirical law holds universally. Such assurance can be provided only by ascertaining the cause or causes which determine human behaviour under given conditions. And it is only by ascertaining such causal connections that a genuine science of human nature can be developed. It does not follow, of course, that we can always ascertain exact laws in practice. But this at least is the ideal. Thus once more, in the distinction between empiricism and science we see evidence of Mill's firm belief in the existence of objective causal connections waiting to be discovered.

The subject-matter of psychology as a moral science is 'the uniformities of succession, the laws, whether ultimate or derivative, according to which one mental state succeeds another; is caused by, or at least is caused to follow, another'.[86]

These laws are those of the association of ideas, which have been ascertained, and in Mill's opinion could only be ascertained, by the methods of experimental inquiry. Hence psychology is 'altogether, or principally, a science of observation and experiment'.[87]

When, however, in ethology we turn to the formation of character, especially national character, there is little room for experiment. But mere observation is not sufficient to establish ethology as a science. Hence its method must be 'altogether deductive'.[88] That is to say, it must presuppose psychology, and its principles must be deduced from the general laws of psychology, while the already accepted empirical laws relating to the formation of character, individual or national, must be shown to be derivable from, and hence to function as verifications of, these principles. Moreover, once the principles of ethology have been firmly established, the way will lie open for the development of a corresponding art, namely that of practical education, which will be able to make use of the principles with a view to producing desirable effects or preventing undesirable effects.

Social science, the science of man in society, studies 'the actions of collective masses of mankind, and the various phenomena which constitute social life'.[89] It includes, of course, the study of politics. In social science or sociology, as in ethology, the making of artificial experiments is impracticable, while mere observation is not sufficient to create a science. At the same time the deductive method as practised in geometry does not provide an appropriate model. Bentham, indeed, endeavoured to deduce a social-political theory from one principle, namely that men always seek their own interests. But in point of fact it is not always true that men are always governed in their actions by selfish interests. Nor, for that matter, is it universally true that they are governed by altruistic motives. In general, social phenomena are too complex and are the results of too many diverse factors for it to be possible to deduce them from one principle. If he is seeking a model of method, the sociologist should look not to geometry but to physical science. For the physical scientist allows for a variety of causes contributing to the production of an effect, and so for a variety of laws.

Mill emphasizes the utility in social science of what he calls the inverse deductive or historical method. In employing this method the sociologist does not deduce conclusions *a priori* from laws and then verify them by observation. He first obtains the conclusions, as approximate empirical generalizations, from experience and then connects them 'with the principles of human nature by *a priori* reasonings, which reasonings are thus a real Verification'.[90] This idea was borrowed, as Mill frankly acknowledges, from Auguste Comte. 'This was an idea entirely new to me when I found it in Comte: and but for him I might not soon (if ever) have arrived at it.'[91]

But while he emphasizes the utility of the inverse deductive method Mill is not prepared to allow that it is the only method suitable for employment in sociology. For we can also make use of the direct deductive method, provided that we recognize its limitations. For example, if we know that X is a law of human nature, we can deduce that human beings will tend to act in a certain manner. But we cannot know and positively predict that they will act in this way in concrete fact. For we cannot know in advance, or at any rate only rarely, all the other causal agents at work, which may counteract the operation of the cause which we have in mind or combine with it to produce an effect rather different from that which would be produced if there were no other causal agents. However, the direct deductive method undoubtedly has its own use in predicting tendencies to action. And this is of value for practical politics. Further, it is especially fitted for use in a science such as political economy which 'considers mankind as occupied solely in acquiring and consuming wealth'.[92] Obviously, this is not all that mankind does. But the point is that the more simplified a view of man we take, the more scope can we attribute to the direct deductive method. Conversely, the more complex the situation considered, the more we have to turn to the inverse deductive method.

In sociology Mill follows Comte in making a distinction between social statics and dynamics. The former is concerned with ascertaining and verifying uniformities of coexistence in society. That is to say, it investigates the mutual actions and reactions of contemporaneous social phenomena, abstracting, as far as possible, from the continuous process of change which is always, if gradually, modifying the whole complex of phenomena. Social dynamics, however, studies society considered as being in a constant state of movement or change, and it tries to explain the historical sequences of social conditions. But though we can ascertain some general laws of historical change or progress, we cannot predict the rate of progress. For one thing, we cannot predict the appearance of those exceptional individuals who exercise a marked influence on the course of history.

In this connection Mill refers to Macaulay's essay on Dryden and criticizes the view, there expressed, of the comparative inoperativeness of great historical individuals. We cannot legitimately assume, for example, that without Socrates, Plato and Aristotle European philosophy would have developed as it did, or even that it would have developed at all. Nor can we justifiably assume that if Newton had not lived his natural philosophy would have been worked out practically just as soon by someone else. It is a complete mistake to suppose that the truth that all human volitions and actions are caused, entails the conclusion that outstandingly gifted individuals cannot exercise an exceptional influence.

Obviously, Mill's conception of social science as involving the explanation of human behaviour in terms of causal laws presupposes the predictability in principle of all human volitions and actions. This subject has already been touched on in connection with Mill's ethical theory. But he insists that this predictability is not to be confused with 'fatalism', when fatalism is understood as meaning that the human will is of no account in determining the cause of events. For the human will is itself a cause, and a powerful one.[93] Further, in sociology we have to steer a middle course between thinking that no definite causal laws can be ascertained and imagining that it is possible to predict the course of history. Social laws are hypothetical, and statistically-based generalizations by their very nature admit of exceptions.

Mill does indeed express his belief that with the progress of civilization collective agencies tend to predominate more and more, and that in proportion as this happens prediction becomes easier. But he is thinking, for example, of the difference between a society in which much depends on the caprices of an individual, the absolute monarch, and a society in which the people at large expresses its will through universal suffrage. In other words, empirical generalizations have a greater predictive power when we are dealing with men in the mass than when we are dealing with the individual agent.[94] True, one of the main aims of social science is to connect these empirical generalizations with the laws of human nature. But the situation is too complex for it to be possible to predict infallibly the course of history, even if, in Mill's opinions, changes in human society have made it easier to approximate to a science of history or of social dynamics.

9. Mill's whole conception of the sciences, whether physical or moral, obviously presupposes the existence of the external world. And we can now turn to his discussion of the grounds of our belief in such a world, a discussion which is carried on for the most part within the framework of his criticism of Sir William Hamilton's philosophy.

Hamilton maintained that in perception we have an immediate knowledge of the ego and the non-ego, of the self and of something existing which is external to the self. Mill, however, while readily admitting that we have, as Hume claimed, a natural belief in the existence of an external world, endeavours to show how this belief can be psychologically explained without its being necessary to suppose that it expresses an original datum of consciousness. He makes two postulates. The first is that the mind is capable of expectation, while the second is the validity of the associationist psychology. On the basis of these two postulates he argues that there are associations 'which, supposing no intuition of an external world to have existed in consciousness, would inevitably generate the belief in a permanent external world, and would cause it to be regarded as an intuition'.[95]

Let us suppose that I have certain visual and tactual sensations which produce in my mind an association of ideas. For example, when sitting at the table in my study, I have those visual sensations which I call seeing the table and the tactual sensations which I call touching or feeling the table. And an association is set up such that when I have a visual sensation of this kind, a tactual sensation is present as a possibility. Conversely, when I have only a tactual sensation, as when the room is completely dark, a visual sensation is there as a possibility. Further, when I leave the room and later re-enter it, I have similar sensations. Hence an association is formed in my mind of such a kind that when I am out of the room, I am firmly persuaded that, if I were at any moment to re-enter it, I should or could have similar sensations. Further, as these possible sensations form a group, and as moreover the group is found to enter into various causal relations, I inevitably think of the permanent possibilities of sensations as an abiding physical object. Actual sensations are transient and fugitive. But the possibilities of sensation, associated as a group, remain. Hence we come to distinguish between sensations and physical objects. But the ground of our belief in these external objects is the existence of different mutually associated clusters or groups of possible sensations, these groups being permanent in comparison with actual sensations.[96]

A further point. We find that the permanent possibilities of sensation which we think of as physical objects 'belong as much to other human or sentient beings as to ourselves',[97] though they certainly do not experience the same actual sensations as we do. And this puts the final seal to our belief in a common external world.

Now, Mill's theory, as so far outlined, might possibly be taken as being simply a psychological account of the genesis of a belief. That is to say, it might be understood as being free from any ontological commitment, as not involving any statement about the ontological nature of physical objects. In point of fact, however, Mill proceeds to define matter as 'a Permanent Possibility of Sensation',[98] bodies being groups of simultaneous possibilities of sensation. To be sure, he remarks that it is a question of defining matter rather than of denying its existence. But he makes it clear that he, like 'all Berkeleians',[99] believes in matter only in the sense of this definition, a definition which, he claims, includes the whole meaning which ordinary people attach to the term, whatever some philosophers and theologians may have done.

Hence Mill clearly commits himself to an ontological statement.

The definition of matter as a permanent possibility of sensation is, however, ambiguous. For it easily suggests the idea
of a permanent ground of possible sensations, a ground
which is itself unknowable. And if this were what Mill intended to imply, a rift would inevitably be introduced between the world of science and the underlying physical reality. Scientific truths would relate to phenomena, not to
things-in-themselves. But though he remarks elsewhere that
'all matter apart from the feelings of sentient beings has but
an hypothetical and unsubstantial existence: it is a mere assumption to account for our sensations',[100] he makes it clear
that he does not intend to assert the validity of this hypothesis.

Of course, if we interpret Mill on the lines on which Berkeley is often interpreted, namely as saying simply that material things are simply what we perceive and can perceive
them to be, and that there is no unknowable substratum as
postulated by Locke, the nature of science, as depicted by
Mill, does not appear to be affected. But though it is doubtless part of what Mill means, as is shown by his conviction
that in defining matter as he does he is on the side of the
common man, the fact remains that he speaks of material
things as 'sensations'. Thus he says, for example, that 'the
brain, just as much as the mental functions, is, like matter
itself, merely a set of human sensations either actual or inferred as possible—namely, those which the anatomist has
when he opens the skull. . . .'[101] And from this it appears
to follow that physical science inquires into the relations between sensations, principally, of course, possible sensations,
but still sensations. Indeed, Mill himself speaks of causal
relations or constant sequences as being found to exist between sets of possible sensations.

It is understandable that later empiricists have endeavoured to avoid this conclusion by forbearing from saying that
material things *are* sensations or sense-data. Instead they have
contented themselves with claiming that a sentence in which
a physical or material object is mentioned can in principle
be translated into other sentences in which only sense-data

are mentioned, the relation between the original sentence and the translation being such that if the former is true (or false), the latter is true (or false), and conversely. The question whether this claim has been made good need not detain us here.[102] The point is that, as far as Mill himself is concerned, he speaks in such a way that the subject-matter of physical science is human sensations.

This, however, is a very difficult position to maintain. Let us suppose that sensations are to be understood as subjective states. This would make great difficulties in regard to Mill's account of the genesis of our belief in an external world, as outlined above. For instance, Mill says that we 'find' that there are possibilities of sensation which are common to other people as well as to ourselves. But other people will be for me simply permanent possibilities of sensation. And if the word 'sensation' is understood in terms of a subjective state, it seems to follow that other people, and indeed everything else, are reduced to my subjective states. As for science, this would become a study of the relations between my sensations. But is it credible that if an anatomist looks at a human brain, the object of his examination is simply a set of his own subjective states, actual and possible? In short, the logical result of defining physical objects in terms of sensations, when sensation is understood as a subjective state, is solipsism. And nobody really believes that solipsism is true.

It may be objected that Mill never intended to say that science is simply concerned with subjective states in any ordinary sense of the term. And the objection is obviously valid. It is perfectly clear that Mill had no intention of maintaining that the whole physical world consisted of his, Mill's, sensations in a subjective sense. But then we must either reify sensations, turning them into public physical objects, or we must assume that to say that a physical object is a permanent possibility of sensations is to say that a physical object is that which is capable of causing sensations in a sentient subject. The first alternative would be a very peculiar thesis, while the second would tend to reintroduce the concept of things-in-themselves and the rift between the world of science and physical reality to which allusion has already been made.

The fact of the matter is that after showing, to his own satisfaction at least, how our belief in the external world can be explained genetically in terms of the association of ideas, Mill slides into ontological assertions without really considering their implications in regard to the nature of physical science. And it seems clear to the present writer at any rate that Mill's empiricist analysis of the physical object is not really compatible with the realist conception of science which underlies his doctrine about causal laws.

10. Mill was obviously predisposed by the empiricist tradition to give an analogous analysis of the concept of the mind. 'We have no conception of Mind itself, as distinguished from its conscious manifestations. We neither know nor can imagine it, except as represented by the succession of manifold feelings which metaphysicians call by the name of States or Modifications of Mind.'[103] It is quite true, of course, that we tend to speak of the mind as something permanent in comparison with changing mental states. But if there were no special factor in the situation to be considered, we could perfectly well define the mind as a permanent possibility of mental states.

In point of fact, however, the phenomenalistic analysis of the mind presents special difficulties. For 'if we speak of the Mind as a series of feelings, we are obliged to complete the statement by calling it a series of feelings which is aware of itself as past and future'.[104] And how can the series be aware of itself as a series? We have no reason to suppose that the material thing enjoys self-consciousness. But the mind certainly does.

But though he draws attention to this difficulty and admits that language suggests the irreducibility of the mind to the series of mental phenomena, Mill is unwilling to sacrifice phenomenalism. Hence he is compelled to hold that the series of feelings, as he puts it, can be aware of itself as a series, even though he is admittedly unable to explain how this is possible. 'I think, by far the wisest thing we can do, is to accept the inexplicable fact, without any theory of how it takes place; and when we are obliged to speak of it in terms which assume a theory, to use them with a reservation as to their meaning.'[105]

In connection with the analysis of the concept of mind Mill raises the question of solipsism. According to Reid, he remarks, I have no evidence at all of the existence of other selves if I am but a series of feelings or a thread of consciousness. My so-called awareness of other selves is simply an awareness of my own private feelings. But this line of argument, Mill contends, is 'one of Reid's most palpable mistakes'.[106] For one thing, even if I believe that my own mind is a series of feelings, there is nothing to prevent my conceiving other minds as similar series of feelings. For another thing, I have inferential evidence of the existence of minds other than my own, as the following line of reflection shows.

Modifications in the permanent possibility of sensations which I call my body evoke in me actual sensations and mental states which form part of the series which I call my mind. But I am aware of the existence of other permanent possibilities of sensations which are not related to my mental life in this way. And at the same time I am aware of actions and other external signs in these permanent possibilities of sensation or bodies, which I am warranted in interpreting as signs or expressions of inner mental states analogous to my own.

The view that we know the existence of other minds by inference from overt bodily behaviour is common enough. The trouble is, however, that Mill has already analysed bodies in terms of sensations. Obviously, he never intended to say or to imply that another person's body is simply and solely a group of *my* sensations, actual and possible. But he has at any rate to meet the objection that I am aware of another person's body only through my sensations, and that if the body is defined in terms of sensations, he must admit either that these sensations are mine or that sensations can exist on their own or that a body is a ground of possible sensations. In the first case solipsism is the logical conclusion. In the second case we are presented with a very peculiar thesis. In the third case, as has already been noted, the phenomenalistic analysis of the material thing collapses. And as, on Mill's own explicit admission, there is a special difficulty in the phenomenalistic analysis of mind, this is *a fortiori* subject to doubt.

Solipsism has proved the haunting spectre of phenomenalism. It is not that phenomenalists have actually embraced solipsism. For they have done nothing of the kind. The difficulty has been rather that of stating phenomenalism in such a way that it leads neither to a solipsistic conclusion on the one hand nor to an implicit abandonment of phenomenalism on the other. Perhaps the most successful attempt to state the phenomenalist position has been the modern linguistic version, to which reference was made in the previous section. But this can easily appear as an evasion of critical problems. At the same time, if we once start looking for hidden substrates, we shall find ourselves in other difficulties. And one can sympathize with the down-to-earth common-sense approach of some recent devotees of the cult of ordinary language. The trouble is, however, that once we have brought things back to ordinary language, the familiar philosophical problems tend to start up all over again.

11. Mill, as was mentioned in the sketch of his life, was brought up by his father without any religious beliefs. But he did not share James Mill's marked hostility to religion as inherently detrimental to morality. Hence he was more open to considering evidence for the existence of God. Of the ontological argument in its Cartesian form he remarks that it 'is not likely to satisfy anyone in the present day'.[107] And as he regarded the causal relation as being essentially a relation between phenomena, it is not surprising that he argues with Hume and Kant that 'the First Cause argument is in itself of no value for the establishment of Theism'.[108] But he is prepared to give serious consideration to the argument from design in Nature, as this is 'an argument of a really scientific character, which does not shrink from scientific tests, but claims to be judged by the established canons of Induction. The design argument is wholly grounded on experience.'[109] Whether any argument to a metaphenomenal reality can properly be called a 'scientific' argument is open to question. But Mill's main point is that even if the argument from design in Nature concludes with affirming the existence of a divine being which in itself transcends the reach of scientific inquiry, it bases itself on empirical facts in a manner which is easily understood and makes an infer-

ence, the validity of which is open to reasonable discussion.

Paley's form of the argument will not do. It is true that if we found a watch on a desert island, we should indeed infer that it had been left there by a human being. But we should do so simply because we already know by experience that watches are made and carried by human beings. We do not, however, have previous experience of natural objects being made by God. We argue by analogy. That is to say, we argue from resemblances between phenomena which we already know to be products of human design and other phenomena which we then attribute to the productive work of a supramundane intelligence.

It must be added, however, that the argument from design in Nature rests on a special resemblance, namely the working together of various factors to one common end. For instance, the argument infers the operation of a supramundane intelligence from the arrangement and structure of the various parts of the visual apparatus which together produce sight. We cannot indeed exclude all other explanations of such phenomena. Hence the argument cannot lead to a conclusion which possesses more than some degree of probability. But the argument is none the less a reasonable inductive inference.[110] 'I think it must be allowed that, in the present state of our knowledge, the adaptations in Nature afford a large balance of probability in favour of creation by intelligence.'[111]

In Mill's opinion, however, we cannot accept the existence of God as a probable truth and at the same time affirm the divine omnipotence. For design implies the adaptation of means to an end, and the need to employ means reveals a limitation of power. 'Every indication of Design in the Kosmos is so much evidence against the omnipotence of the designer.'[112]

This does not seem to me a very telling argument. For though the argument from design, taken by itself, concludes simply with assertion of the existence of a designer, not a creator, this does not show that the designer is not the creator. And it is difficult to see how the mere fact of using means to an end is any argument against omnipotence. But Mill's chief interest lies elsewhere, namely in arguing that there is an evident incompatibility between asserting at the same time that God is omnipotent and infinitely good. And this is a much more impressive line of argument.

Mill's point is that if God is omnipotent, he can prevent evil, and that if he does not do so, he cannot be infinitely good. It is no use saying with Dean Mansel that the term 'good' is predicated of God analogically and not in the same sense in which it is used of human beings. For this is really equivalent to saying that God is not good in any sense which we can give to the term. In fine, if we wish to maintain that God is good, we must also say that his power is limited or finite.

Mill is prepared to admit the reasonableness of believing that God desires the happiness of man. For this is suggested by the fact that pleasure seems to result from the normal functioning of the human organism and pain from some interference with this functioning. At the same time we can hardly suppose that God created the universe for the sole purpose of making men happy. Appearances suggest that if there is an intelligent creator, he has other motives besides the happiness of mankind, or of sentient beings in general, and that these other motives, whatever they may be, are of greater importance to him.

In other words, natural theology does not carry us very far. It is not indeed unreasonable, at least in the present state of the evidence, to believe in an intelligent divine being of limited power. But the proper attitude to adopt is what Mill calls a rational scepticism, which is more than sheer agnosticism but less than firm assent.

This might be all very well if those who are really interested in the question of the existence of God were concerned simply and solely with finding an explanatory hypothesis. But it is quite evident that they are not. For a religious person belief in the existence of God is not quite like belief that the architect of St. Paul's Cathedral was Sir Christopher Wren. And Mill sees this to the limited extent of raising the question of the pragmatic value or utility of religion. While recognizing that much evil has been done in the name of religion and that some religious beliefs can be detrimental to human conduct, he is not prepared to subscribe to his father's view that religion is 'the greatest enemy of morality'.[113] For religion, like poetry, can supply man with ideals beyond those which we actually find realized in human life. 'The value, therefore, of religion to the individual, both in the past and present, as a source of personal satisfaction and of elevated feelings, is not to be disputed.'[114] And in Christianity we find a conception of ideal goodness embodied in the figure of Christ.

To be sure, some people look on any suggestion that the pragmatic value of religion provides a reason for believing in God as an immoral suggestion, a betrayal of our duty to pay attention simply to the weight of the empirical evidence. But though this point of view is understandable, Mill does at any rate see that the function of religion in human history is something more than the solving of an intellectual puzzle in terms of an inductive hypothesis.

At the same time Mill raises the question whether the moral uplift of the higher religions cannot be preserved without belief in a supernatural Being. And as far as the provision of an ideal object of emotion and desire is concerned, he suggests that the 'need is fulfilled by the Religion of Humanity in as eminent a degree, and in as high a sense, as by the supernatural religions even in their best manifestations, and far more so than in any of the others'.[115] True, some religions have the advantage of holding out the prospect of immortality. But as the conditions of this life improve and men grow happier and more capable of deriving happiness from unselfish action, human beings, Mill thinks, 'will care less and less for this flattering expectation'.[116] However, if we include in the religion of humanity that belief in the existence of a God of limited power which natural theology justifies as a probable truth, it superadds to other inducements for working for the welfare of our fellow men the conviction that 'we may be co-operating with the unseen Being to whom we owe all that is enjoyable in life'.[117] Hence even if the religion of humanity is destined to be the religion of the future, this does not necessarily exclude belief in God.

Mill is thus in agreement with Auguste Comte that the so-called religion of humanity is the religion of the future, though he has no sympathy with Comte's fantastic proposals for the organization of this religion. At the same time he does not rule out belief in a finite God with whom man can co-operate. And though his idea of religion is clearly not such as to satisfy Kierkegaard or indeed anyone who understands religion as involving absolute self-commitment to the personal Absolute, he does not think, like some empiricists before him, that religion can be disposed of either by a psychological account of the way in which religious belief could have arisen or by drawing attention to the evils which have been done in the name of religion. Though his empiricist premisses actually determine his evaluation of the force of the arguments for God's existence, he endeavours to keep an open mind. And though he regarded the evidence as amounting 'only to one of the lower degrees of probability',[118] when the *Three Essays on Religion* were published posthumously in 1874 some surprise was felt in positivist circles at the extent to which Mill made concessions to theism. He had travelled at any rate a modest distance beyond the point at which his father had stopped.

Chapter Four

EMPIRICISTS, AGNOSTICS, POSITIVISTS

Alexander Bain and the associationist psychology – Bain on utilitarianism – Henry Sidgwick's combination of utilitarianism and intuitionism – Charles Darwin and the philosophy of evolution – T. H. Huxley; evolution, ethics and agnosticism – Scientific materialism and agnosticism; John Tyndall and Leslie Stephen – G. J. Romanes and religion – Positivism; the Comtist groups, G. H. Lewes, W. K. Clifford, K. Pearson – B. Kidd; concluding remarks.

1. The associationist psychology was further developed by Alexander Bain (1818–1903), who occupied the chair of logic in the University of Aberdeen from 1860 until 1880. He was of some help to J. S. Mill in the preparation of his *System of Logic,*[1] and prepared some of the psychological notes for Mill's edition of his father's *Analysis of the Phenomena of the Human Mind.* But though he is sometimes described as a disciple of Mill, Mill himself remarks that the younger man did not really stand in need of any predecessor except the common precursors of them both.

Bain was primarily interested in developing empirical psychology as a separate science, rather than in employing the principle of the association of ideas to solve specifically philosophical problems. Further, he was particularly concerned with correlating psychical processes with their physiological bases, and in this respect he continued the interests of Hartley rather than of the two Mills.[2] While, however, his thought remained within the general framework of the associationist psychology,[3] the titles of his chief works, *The Senses and the Intellect* (1855) and *The Emotions and the Will* (1859), show that he extended his field of study from sensation and intellectual activity to the emotive and volitional aspects of human nature.[4] And this shift of emphasis enabled him to surmount, to some extent at least, the tendency of associationist psychologists to depict man's mental life as the result of a purely mechanical process.

Bain's emphasis on human activity shows itself, for example, in his account of the genesis of our belief in an external, material world. If we were simply subjects of purely passive sensations, of sensations or impressions, that is to say, considered apart from any activity or putting forth of energy on our part, our waking state of consciousness would resemble the dream-state. In point of fact, however, 'in us sensation is never wholly passive, and in general is much the reverse. Moreover, the tendency to movement exists before the stimulus of sensation; and movement gives a new character to our whole percipient existence'.[5] Impressions received from without arouse movement, activity, the display of energy or force; and 'it is in this exercise of force that we must look for the peculiar feeling of externality of objects'.[6] For instance, in the case of touch, the sense which is the first to make us clearly aware of an external world, 'it is hard contact that suggests externality; and the reason is that in this contact we put forth force of our own'.[7] Reacting to a sensation of touch by muscular exertion, we have a sense of resistance, 'a feeling which is the principal foundation of our notion of externality'.[8] In fine, 'the sense of the external is the consciousness of particular energies and activities of our own';[9] and our external world, the external world as it is presented to our minds, can be described as 'the sum total of all the occasions for putting forth active energy, or for conceiving this as possible to be put forth'.[10] Bain thus defines the external world, as it exists for our consciousness,[11] in terms of possible active responses to sensations rather than, as Mill defined it, of possible sensations.

It is not surprising, therefore, that Bain emphasizes the intimate connection between belief in general and action. 'Belief has no meaning, except in reference to our actions.'[12] Whenever a man, or an animal for the matter of that, performs an action as a means to an end, the action is sustained by a primitive belief or credulity which can be described 'as expectation of some contingent future about to follow on an action'.[13] It is this primitive credulity which leads a sentient being to repeat its successful experiment, say of running to a brook to quench its thirst. It does not follow, however, that the force of belief rises gradually from zero to a state of full development in proportion to the length and uniformity of experience. For there is a primitive impulse or tendency to belief, which is derived from the natural activity of the organic system, and the strength of which is proportionate to the strength of the 'will'. 'The creature that wills strongly believes strongly at the origin of its career.'[14] What experience does is to determine the particular forms taken by a primitive impulse which it does not itself generate. And the factor which is of most importance in establishing sound belief is absence of contradiction or factual invariability of sequence, between, that is, expectation and its fulfilment.

If we assume, therefore, our instinctive responses in action to pleasure and pain, we can say that experience, with the inferences which follow on it, is the cardinal factor in stabilizing beliefs. But it is certainly not the only factor which is influential in shaping particular beliefs. For though feeling and emotion do not alter the objective facts, they may, and often do, affect our way of seeing and interpreting the facts. Evidence and feeling: 'the nature of the subject, and the character of the individual mind, determine which is to predominate; but in this life of ours, neither is the exclusive master'.[15]

If one wished to draw general conclusions about Bain's philosophical position, one could draw different conclusions from different groups of statements. On the one hand the emphasis which he lays on the physiological correlates of psychical processes might suggest a materialistic position. On the other hand a position of subjective idealism is suggested when he speaks, for example, of 'the supposed perception of an external and independent material world'[16] and adds that 'what is here said to be perceived is a convenient fiction, which by the very nature of the case transcends all possible experience'.[17] In point of fact, however, Bain tries to steer clear of metaphysics and to devote himself to empirical and genetic psychology, even if some of his statements have philosophical implications.

Bain's psychological investigations were continued by James Sully (1842–1923), who occupied the chair of philosophy at University College, London, from 1892 until 1903. In his *Outlines of Psychology* (1884) and in his two-volume work *The Human Mind* (1892) he followed Bain in emphasizing the physiological correlates of psychical processes and in employing the principle of the association of ideas. Further, he extended his reflections into the field of the theory of education and applied himself to child-psychology in his *Studies of Childhood* (1895).

Already in Bain's lifetime, however, the associationist psychology was subjected to attack by James Ward and others. It is doubtless true that the emphasis laid by Bain on the emotive and volitional aspects of man gave to his thought a rather more modern tone than one finds in his predecessors. But it can also be argued that his introduction of fresh ideas into the old psychology helped to prepare the way for the lines of thought which supplanted it. Obviously, association continued to be recognized as a factor in mental life. But it could no longer be taken as a key to unlock all doors to the understanding of psychical processes, and the old atomistic associationist psychology had had its day.

2. In the ethical field Bain introduced into utilitarianism important modifications or supplementary considerations. These modifications doubtless impaired the simple unity of the utilitarian ethics. But Bain considered them necessary if an adequate account was to be given of the moral consciousness as it actually exists, that is, as Bain saw it in himself and in the members of the society or culture to which he belonged.

Utilitarianism, Bain remarks, has this great advantage over the moral sense theory, that it provides an external standard of morality, substituting 'a regard to consequences for a mere unreasoning sentiment, or feeling'.[18] It is also opposed to the theory that all human actions are the result of selfish impulses, a theory which is committed to misinterpreting affection and sympathy, 'the main foundations of disinterestedness'.[19] To be sure, these impulses belong to the self. But it does not follow that they can properly be described as 'selfish' impulses. In point of fact selfishness has never been the sole foundation of men's ideas of what is right. And it certainly is not the present sole foundation of men's moral convictions. This is recognized by the utilitarians, who connect the notion of utility with that of the common good.

At the same time utilitarianism cannot constitute the whole truth about morality. For one thing, we must find room for a distinction between 'utility made compulsory and what is left free'.[20] After all, there are many actions which are useful to the community but which are not regarded as obligatory. For another thing, it is clear that the moral rules which prevail in most communities are grounded partly on sentiment, and not only on the idea of utility. Hence, even though the principle of utility is an essential feature of ethics, we must add sentiment and also tradition, 'which is the continuing influence of some former Utility or Sentiment'.[21] That is to say, we must add them if we wish to give a comprehensive account of existing moral practices.

Bain is not concerned, therefore, with working out an *a priori* theory of ethics. He is concerned with exhibiting the empirical foundations of morality as it exists. He approaches morality very much from the point of view of a psychologist. And if we bear this approach in mind, we can understand his genetic treatment of conscience and the feeling of obligation. In contrast to the view of Dugald Stewart that conscience is 'a primitive and independent faculty of the mind, which would be developed in us although we never had any experience of external authority',[22] Bain holds that 'conscience is an imitation within us of the government without us'.[23] In other words, conscience is an interior reflection of the voices of parents, educators and external authority in general. And the sense of obligation and duty arises out of the association established in the infant mind between the performance of actions forbidden by external authority and the sanctions imposed by this authority.

Now, if we interpret J. S. Mill as offering utilitarianism as an adequate description of the existing moral consciousness, Bain is doubtless right in saying that for an adequate description other factors have to be taken into account besides the principle of utility. But if we interpret Mill as recommending a particular system of ethics and as preferring this system to the moral sense theory on the ground that the principle of utility provides a criterion of moral conduct which is lacking in any pure moral sense theory, it is arguable that Bain is really more of a positivist than Mill. For though, as we have seen, he recognizes the advantage which utilitarianism possesses in having an external standard, he tends to emphasize the relativity of moral convictions. If someone asks, what is the moral standard? the proper answer would be that it is 'the enactments of the existing society, as derived from some one clothed in his day with a moral legislative authority'.[24] Instead of treating morality as if it were one indivisible whole, we ought to consider particular codes and moral rules separately. And then we shall see that behind the phenomena of conscience and obligation there lies authority. Bain allows for the influence of outstanding individuals; but the assent of the community at large, whatever it may be, is required to complete the legislative process. And once it is completed, the external authority is present which shapes conscience and the sense of duty in the individual.

Bain would have done well to reflect on his own admission that outstanding individuals are capable of moulding afresh the moral outlook of a society. That is to say, he might well have asked himself whether this admission was really consistent with an ethics of social pressure. Some have concluded that there is a field of objective values into which different degrees of insight are possible, while Bergson thought it necessary to make a distinction between what he called 'closed' and 'open' morality. But the problem does not seem to have troubled Bain, even though the data for the raising of the problem were present in his account of morality.

3. A much more radical change in the utilitarian ethics was made by Henry Sidgwick (1838–1900), Fellow of Trinity College, Cambridge, who was elected to the chair of moral philosophy in that university in 1883. His reputation rests principally on *The Methods of Ethics* (1874). Other writings include his *Outlines of the History of Ethics for English Readers* (1886) and his posthumously published *Lectures on the Ethics of Green, Spencer and Martineau* (1902).

In Sidgwick's account of the development of his ethical

views, which was printed in the sixth edition (1901) of
The Methods of Ethics, he remarked that 'my first adhesion
to a definite Ethical system was to the Utilitarianism of
Mill'.[25] But he soon came to see a discrepancy between psychological hedonism, the thesis that every man seeks his own
pleasure, and ethical hedonism, the thesis that every man
ought to seek the general happiness. If psychological hedonism is taken to mean that as a matter of fact every man
seeks exclusively his own pleasure, the thesis is questionable,
or, rather, false. But in any case a purely psychological thesis
cannot establish an ethical thesis. As Hume maintained, we
cannot deduce an 'ought' from an 'is', an ought-statement
from a purely factual descriptive statement. James Mill may
have tried to show how it is psychologically possible for a
person who by nature pursues his own pleasure or happiness
to act altruistically. But even if his account of the matter
were valid from a psychological point of view, this would not
show that we *ought* to act altruistically. If, therefore, ethical
or universalistic hedonism is to have a philosophical basis,
we must look elsewhere for it than in psychology.

Sidgwick came to the conclusion that this philosophical
basis could be found only in the intuition of some fundamental moral principle or principles. He was thus drawn
away from the utilitarianism of Bentham and J. S. Mill to
intuitionism. But further reflection convinced him that the
principles which were implicit in the morality of common
sense, as distinct from philosophical theories about morality,
were either utilitarian in character or at any rate compatible
with utilitarianism. 'I was then a Utilitarian again, but on an
Intuitional basis.'[26]

In Sidgwick's view, therefore, there are certain moral principles which are self-evidently true. Thus it is evident that
one should prefer a future greater good to a present lesser
one.[27] This is the principle of prudence. It is also self-
evident that as rational beings we ought to treat others in
the way in which we think that we ought to be treated, unless there is some difference 'which can be stated as a reasonable ground for difference of treatment'.[28] This is the
principle of justice. It is also self-evident both that from the
point of view of the Universe the good of any one individual

is of no more importance than the good of any other individual, and that as a rational being I ought to aim at the general good, so far as it is attainable by my efforts. From these two propositions we can deduce the principle of benevolence, namely that 'each one is morally bound to regard the good of any other individual as much as his own, except in so far as he judges it to be less, when impartially viewed, or less certainly knowable or attainable by him'.[29]

The principle of prudence or of 'rational egoism', as mentioned above, implies that a man ought to seek his own good. And Sidgwick is in fact convinced, with Butler, that this is a manifest obligation. The principle of rational benevolence, however, states that we ought to seek for the good of others, under certain conditions at any rate. If therefore we combine them, we have the command to seek the good of all, including one's own, or to seek one's own good as a constituent part of the general good. For the general good is made up of individual goods. Now, the general good can be equated with universal happiness, provided that we do not understand by happiness simply the pleasures of sense, and provided that we do not intend to imply that happiness is always best attained by aiming at it directly. Hence 'I am finally led to the conclusion that the Intuitional method rigorously applied yields as its final result the doctrine of pure Universalistic Hedonism—which it is convenient to denote by the single word, Utilitarianism'.[30]

If we look at Sidgwick's moral philosophy in the light of the utilitarian tradition, we naturally tend to focus our attention on his rejection of the claims of genetic psychology to provide an adequate basis for our moral convictions, especially of the consciousness of obligation, and on his use of the idea of intuitively perceived moral axioms, a use which was encouraged by his reading of Samuel Clarke and other writers.[31] He can be described as an intuitionist utilitarian or as an utilitarian intuitionist, if such descriptions do not involve a contradiction in terms. Sidgwick, indeed, maintained that there is no real incompatibility between utilitarianism and intuitionism. At the same time he was too honest a thinker to assert that he had given a definitive solution to the problem of reconciling the claims of interest and duty, of prudence or rational egoism and of benevolence, a be-nevolence capable of expressing itself not only in altruistic conduct but also in complete self-sacrifice in the service of others or in the pursuit of some ideal end.

If, however, we look at Sidgwick's moral philosophy in relation to what was to come later instead of in relation to what went before, we shall probably lay more stress on his method. He laid emphasis on the need for examining what he called the morality of common sense; and he attempted to discover the principles which are implicit in the ordinary moral consciousness, to state them precisely and to deter-mine their mutual relations. His method was analytic. He selected a problem, considered it from various angles, pro-posed a solution and raised objections and counter-objections. He may have tended to lose himself in details and to suspend final judgment because he was unable to see his way clearly through all difficulties. To say this, however, is in a sense to commend his thoroughness and careful honesty. And though his appeal to self-evident truths may not appear very convincing, his devotion to the analysis and clarification of the ordinary moral consciousness puts one in mind of the later analytic movement in British philosophy.

4. The associationist psychology, the phenomenalism of J. S. Mill and the utilitarian ethics, all had their roots in the eighteenth century. Soon after the middle of the nineteenth century, however, a new idea began to colour the empiricist current of thought. This was the idea of evolution. We can-not indeed fix on a certain date and say that after this date empiricism became a philosophy of evolution. Herbert Spencer, the great philosopher of evolution in nineteenth-century England, had started publishing his *System of Phi-losophy* before J. S. Mill published his work on Hamilton, and Bain, who died in the same year as Spencer, continued the tradition represented by the two Mills. Moreover, it is less a question of the empiricist movement as a whole coming under the domination of the idea of evolution than of the idea becoming prominent in certain representatives of the movement. We can, however, say that in the second half of the century the theory of evolution invaded and occupied

not only the relevant parts of the scientific field but also a considerable part of the field of empiricist philosophy.

The idea of biological evolution was not, of course, an invention of the middle of the nineteenth century. As a purely speculative idea it had appeared even in ancient Greece. In the eighteenth century the way had been prepared for it by Georges-Louis de Buffon (1707–88), while Jean-Baptiste Pierre Lamarck (1744–1829) had proposed his theories that in response to new needs brought about by changes in the environment changes take place in the organic structure of animals, some organs falling into disuse and others being evolved and developed, and that acquired habits are transmitted by heredity. Moreover, when the idea of evolution was first publicized in Britain, the publicist was a philosopher, Spencer, rather than a scientist. At the same time this does not affect the importance of Darwin's writings in setting the theory of evolution on its feet and in giving an enormously powerful impetus to its propagation.

Charles Robert Darwin (1809–82) was a naturalist, not a philosopher. During his famous voyage on the 'Beagle' (1831–6), observation of variations between differently situated animals of the same species and reflection on the differences between living and fossilized animals led him to question the theory of the fixity of species. In 1838 study of Malthus's *Essay on the Principle of Population* helped to lead him to the conclusions that in the struggle for existence favourable variations tend to be preserved and unfavourable variations to be destroyed, and that the result of this process is the formation of new species, acquired characteristics being transmitted by heredity.

Similar conclusions were reached independently by another naturalist, Alfred Russel Wallace (1823–1913), who, like Darwin, was influenced by a reading of Malthus in arriving at the idea of the survival of the fittest in the struggle for existence. And on July 1st, 1858, a joint communication by Wallace and Darwin was presented at a meeting of the Linnean Society in London. Wallace's contribution was a paper *On the Tendency of Varieties to Depart Indefinitely from the Original Type*, while Darwin contributed an abridgment of his own ideas.

Darwin's famous work on the *Origin of Species by Means of Natural Selection, or The Preservation of Favoured Races in the Struggle for Life* was published in November 1859, all copies being sold out on the day of publication. This was followed in 1868 by *The Variation of Animals and Plants under Domestication*. And the year 1871 saw the publication of *The Descent of Man, and Selection in Relation to Sex*. Darwin published a number of further works, but he is chiefly known for *The Origin of Species* and *The Descent of Man*.

Being a naturalist, Darwin was sparing of philosophical speculation and devoted himself primarily to working out a theory of evolution based on the available empirical evidence. He did indeed interpret morality as evolving out of the purposiveness of animal instinct and as developing through changes in social standards which confer survival value on societies. And he was obviously well aware of the flutter in theological dovecotes which was caused by his theory of evolution, particularly in its application to man. In 1870 he wrote that while he could not look on the universe as the product of blind chance, he could see no evidence of design, still less of beneficent design, when he came to consider the details of natural history. And though he was originally a Christian, he arrived in the course of time at an agnostic suspension of judgment. He tended, however, to avoid personal involvement in theological controversy.

Unless perhaps we happen to live in one of the few surviving pockets of fundamentalism, it is difficult for us now to appreciate the ferment which was caused in the last century by the hypothesis of organic evolution, particularly in its application to man. For one thing, the idea of evolution is now common coin and is taken for granted by very many people who would be quite unable either to mention or to weigh the evidence adduced in its favour. For another thing, the hypothesis is no longer an occasion for bitter theological controversy. Even those who question the sufficiency of the evidence to prove the evolution of the human body from some other species commonly recognize that the first chapters of *Genesis* were not intended to solve scientific problems, and that the matter is one which has to be settled according to

the available empirical evidence. Again, if we except the
Marxists, who are in any case committed to materialism,
reflective unbelievers do not generally maintain that the hypothesis of organic evolution, taken by itself, disproves Christian theism or is incompatible with religious belief. After
all, the presence of evil and suffering in the world, which
constitutes one of the main objections to Christian theism,
remains an indubitable fact whether the hypothesis is accepted or rejected. Further, we have seen philosophers such
as Bergson developing a spiritualistic philosophy within the
framework of the general idea of creative evolution, and,
more recently, a scientist such as Teilhard de Chardin making an enthusiastic use of the same idea in the service of a
religious world-view. Hence the controversies of the last century naturally seem to many people to have accumulated a
great deal of dust and cobwebs in the interval.

We have to remember, however, that in the middle of
the last century the idea of the evolution of species, especially as applied to man himself, was for the general educated
public a complete novelty. Moreover, the impression was
commonly given, not only by exponents of the idea but also
by some of its critics, that the Darwinian theory rendered
superfluous or, rather, positively excluded any teleological
interpretation of the cosmic process. For example, T. H. Huxley wrote as follows. 'That which struck the present writer
most forcibly on his first perusal of the *Origin of Species*
was the conviction that Teleology, as commonly understood,
had received its deathblow at Mr. Darwin's hands.'[32] Those
species survive which are the best fitted for the struggle for
existence; but the variations which make them the best fitted
are fortuitous.

Our concern here is with the impact of the theory of evolution on philosophy rather than with the theological controversies to which it gave rise. Herbert Spencer, the foremost
philosopher of evolution in the nineteenth century, merits a
chapter to himself. Meanwhile we can consider briefly two or
three writers who contributed to publicizing the idea of evolution and to developing some philosophical theories based
on or connected with this idea. It is to be noted, however,
that they were scientists who made excursions into philos-

ophy, rather than professional philosophers. Generally speaking, the academic or university philosophers held aloof from the topic and maintained a reserved attitude. As for Spencer, he never occupied an academic post.

5. The name which immediately suggests itself in this context is that of Thomas Henry Huxley (1825–95). As a naval surgeon aboard the 'Rattlesnake' Huxley had opportunity for studying the marine life of the tropical seas, and as a result of his researches he was elected a Fellow of the Royal Society in 1851. In 1854 he was appointed lecturer in natural history at the School of Mines. In the course of time he became more and more involved in public life, serving on some ten royal commissions and taking an active part in educational organization. From 1883 to 1885 he was president of the Royal Society.

In Huxley's opinion Darwin had placed the theory of evolution on a sound footing by following a method in accordance with the rules of procedure laid down by J. S. Mill. 'He has endeavoured to determine great facts inductively, by observation and experiment; he has then reasoned from the data thus furnished; and lastly, he has tested the validity of his ratiocination by comparing his deductions with the observed facts of Nature.'[33] It is true that the origin of species by natural selection has not been proved with certainty. The theory remains an hypothesis which enjoys only a high degree of probability. But it is 'the only extant hypothesis which is worth anything in a scientific point of view'.[34] And it is a marked improvement on Lamarck's theory.[35]

But though Huxley accepted the view that organic evolution proceeds by natural selection or the survival of the fittest in the struggle for existence, he made a sharp distinction between the evolutionary process and man's moral life. Those who expound an ethics of evolution, according to which man's moral life is a continuation of the evolutionary process, are probably right in maintaining that what we call the moral sentiments have evolved like other natural phenomena. But they forget that the immoral sentiments are also the result of evolution. 'The thief and the murderer follow nature just as much as the philanthropist.'[36]

In fine, morality involves going against the evolutionary process. In the struggle for existence the strongest and most self-assertive tend to trample down the weaker, whereas 'social progress means a checking of the cosmic process at every step and the substitution for it of another, which may be called the ethical process'.[37] Originally, human society was probably just as much a product of organic necessity as the societies of bees and ants. But in the case of man social progress involves strengthening the bonds of mutual sympathy, consideration and benevolence, and self-imposed restrictions on anti-social tendencies. True, in so far as this process renders a society more fitted for survival in relation to Nature or to other societies, it is in harmony with the cosmic progress. But in so far as law and moral rules restrict the struggle for existence between members of a given society, the ethical process is plainly at variance with the cosmic process. For it aims at producing quite different qualities. Hence we can say that 'the ethical progress of society depends, not on imitating the cosmic process, still less in running away from it, but in combating it'.[38]

There is thus a marked difference between the views of T. H. Huxley and his grandson, Sir Julian Huxley, on the relation between evolution and ethics. I do not mean to imply, of course, that Sir Julian Huxley rejects the moral qualities and ideals which his grandfather considered desirable. The point is that whereas Sir Julian Huxley emphasizes the element of continuity between the general movement of evolution and moral progress, T. H. Huxley emphasized the element of discontinuity, maintaining that 'the cosmic process has no sort of relation to moral ends'.[39] T. H. Huxley might, of course, have called for a new type of ethics, involving a Nietzschean exaltation of Nature's strong men, which could have been interpreted as a continuation of what he called the cosmic process. But he did not aim at any such transvaluation of values. Rather did he accept the values of sympathy, benevolence, consideration for others, and so on; and in the cosmic process he found no respect for such values.

Though, however, man's moral life formed for Huxley a world of its own within the world of Nature, it does not follow that he looked on man as possessing a spiritual soul which cannot be accounted for in terms of evolution. He maintained that 'consciousness is a function of the brain'.[40] That is to say, consciousness is an epiphenomenon which arises when matter has developed a special form of organization. And this theory, together with his defence of determinism, led to his being described as a materialist.

Huxley, however, stoutly denied the applicability to himself of this description. One reason which he gave for this denial is perhaps not very impressive, because it involved a very narrow interpretation of materialism. Materialism, according to Huxley, maintains that there is nothing in the universe but matter and force, whereas the theory of the epiphenomenal nature of consciousness neither denies the reality of consciousness nor identifies it with the physical processes on which it depends.[41] But Huxley went on to remark, with a rather charming unexpectedness, that 'the arguments used by Descartes and Berkeley to show that our certain knowledge does not extend beyond our states of consciousness, appear to me to be as impregnable now as they did when I first became acquainted with them some half-century ago. . . . Our one certainty is the existence of the mental world, and that of *Kraft und Stoff* falls into the rank of, at best, a highly probable hypothesis.'[42] Further, if material things are resolved into centres of force, one might just as well speak of immaterialism as of materialism.

It is not perhaps very easy to understand how the doctrine that we can never really know anything with certainty but our states of consciousness can be harmonized with the doctrine that consciousness is a function of the brain. But the first doctrine enables Huxley to say that 'if I were forced to choose between Materialism and Idealism, I should elect for the latter'.[43]

It must be added, however, that Huxley has no intention of letting himself be forced to choose between materialism and idealism. And the same applies to the issue between atheism and theism. Huxley proclaims himself an agnostic, and in his work on David Hume he expresses agreement with the Scottish philosopher's suspension of judgment about metaphysical problems. We have our scientific knowledge, and 'the man of science has learned to believe in justification, not by faith, but by verification'.[44] In regard to that which lies beyond the scope of verification we must remain agnostic, suspending judgment.

As one might expect in the case of a naturalist who makes excursions into philosophy, Huxley's philosophical theories are not well worked out. Nor is their mutual consistency clearly exhibited, to put it mildly. At the same time they manifest the not uncommon English attitude which shows itself in a dislike of extremes and a reluctance to submit to the imposition of restrictive labels. Huxley was quite prepared to defend evolution against attack, as he did in his famous encounter with Bishop Samuel Wilberforce in 1860. And he was prepared to criticize orthodox theology. But though he clearly did not believe in the Christian doctrine of God, he refused to commit himself either to atheism or to materialism. Behind the veil of phenomena lies the unknowable. And in regard to the unknowable agnosticism is, by definition, the appropriate attitude.

6. (i) The label 'materialist', repudiated by Huxley, was accepted by John Tyndall (1820–93), who in 1853 was appointed professor of natural philosophy in the Royal Institution, where he was a colleague of Faraday.[45] Tyndall was chiefly concerned with inorganic physics, particularly with the subject of radiant heat; and he was much less inclined than Huxley to make prolonged excursions into the field of philosophy. But he did not hesitate to profess openly what he called 'scientific materialism'.

The scientific materialism accepted by Tyndall was not, however, the same thing as the materialism which was rejected by Huxley. For it meant in large part the hypothesis that every state of consciousness is correlated with a physical process in the brain. Thus in his address to the British Association in 1868 on the *Scope and Limit of Scientific Materialism* Tyndall explained that 'in affirming that the growth of the body is mechanical, and that thought, as exercised by us, has its correlative in the physics of the brain, I think that the position of the "Materialist" is stated, as far as that position is a tenable one'.[46] In other words, the materialist asserts that two sets of phenomena, mental processes and physical processes in the brain, are associated, though he is 'in absolute ignorance'[47] of the real bond of union between them. Indeed, in his so-called Belfast Address, delivered before the British Association in 1874, Tyndall asserted roundly that 'man the *object* is separated by an impassable gulf from man the *subject*. There is no motor energy in the human intellect to carry it, without logical rupture, from the one to the other.'[48]

Tyndall did indeed understand scientific materialism as involving 'a provisional assent'[49] to the hypothesis that the mind and all its phenomena 'were once latent in a fiery cloud'[50] and that they are 'a result of the play between organism and environment through cosmic ranges of time'.[51] But the conclusion which he drew from the theory of evolution was that matter could not properly be looked on as mere 'brute' matter. It had to be regarded as potentially containing within itself life and mental phenomena. In other words, scientific materialism demanded a revision of the concept of matter as something essentially dead and opposed to biological and mental life.

Beyond the phenomena of matter and force, which form the object of scientific inquiry, 'the real mystery of the universe lies unsolved, and, as far as we are concerned, is incapable of solution'.[52] But this acknowledgment of mystery in the universe was not intended by Tyndall as a support for belief in God as conceived by Christians. In his *Apology for the Belfast Address* (1874), he spoke of the idea of creative activity by 'a Being standing outside the nebula'[53] not only as based on no empirical evidence but also as 'opposed to the very spirit of science'.[54] Further, when answering a Catholic critic he remarked, in the same *Apology*, that he would not disavow the charge of atheism, as far as any concept of the Supreme Being was concerned which his critics would be likely to accept.

Tyndall's scientific materialism was not confined, therefore, to a methodological point of view presupposed by scientific inquiry. He was not simply saying, for example, that the scientific psychologist should pursue his inquiries into the relation between mind and body on the assumption that we shall find a correlation between any given mental phenomenon and a physical process. He was saying that as far as

knowledge is concerned, science is omnicompetent. Problems
which cannot be answered by science are unanswerable in
principle. Religion, for example, is immune from disproof
as long as it is regarded simply as a subjective experience.[55]
But if it is regarded as claiming to extend our knowledge,
its claim is bogus. In a general sense of the term, therefore,
Tyndall was a positivist. By admitting a sphere for agnosticism, mysteries or enigmas, that is to say, which cannot be
solved, he stopped short of the position to be adopted later
by the neopositivists or logical positivists. But this does not
alter the fact that scientific materialism involved for him a
positivist view of the omnicompetence of science in the field
of knowledge.

(ii) The view that agnosticism is the only attitude which
is really in harmony with the genuinely scientific spirit was
also maintained by Sir Leslie Stephen (1832–1904), author
of a two-volume *History of English Thought in the Eighteenth Century* (1876) and of a three-volume work on *The
English Utilitarians* (1900). At first a clergyman, he came
successively under the influence of J. S. Mill, Darwin and
Spencer, and in 1875 he finally abandoned his clerical status.

In a discussion of the nature of materialism Stephen maintains that it 'represents the point of view of the physical
inquirer. A man is a materialist for the time being so long
as he has only to do with that which may be touched, handled, seen or otherwise perceived through the senses'.[56] In
other words, scientific inquiry demands a methodical materialism. It does not demand acceptance of the doctrine
that matter is the ultimate reality.

It by no means follows, however, that we are entitled to
assert spiritualism, the doctrine that mind is the ultimate
reality. The truth of the matter is that 'we cannot get behind the curtain, which is reality'.[57] If we try to do so, we
are at once plunged into 'the transcendental region of antinomies and cobwebs of the brain'.[58] The unknowable
which lies beyond 'reality' is 'a mere blank':[59] it is not itself
converted into a reality by being spelt with a capital letter.
'The ancient secret is a secret still; man knows nothing of
the Infinite and Absolute.'[60]

One would have thought that if the phenomenal world

is once equated with 'reality', there is no good reason for supposing that there is any unknowable beyond it. What is the reason for supposing that there *is* a secret which always remains a secret? Conversely, if there is good reason for supposing that there is an unknowable Absolute, there is no good reason for equating the phenomenal world with reality. But Stephen's agnosticism represents less a carefully thought out position than a general attitude. Science alone provides us with definite knowledge. Science knows nothing of any meta-empirical Absolute. But we feel that even if all scientific problems were answered, the universe would still be mysterious, enigmatic. The enigma, however, is insoluble.

Needless to say, scientific materialism and agnosticism were by no means regarded as entailing the rejection of moral values. Tyndall insisted that moral values are independent of religious creeds, and that scientific materialism must not be understood as involving or implying a belittlement of man's highest ideals. As for Sir Leslie Stephen, in his work *The Science of Ethics* (1882) he tried to continue and develop Spencer's attempt to ground morals on evolution. Abstractly considered, the function of morality is to further the health and vitality of the social organism. Historically considered, moral principles undergo a process of natural selection, and those which are most effective in furthering the good of the social organism prevail over the less effective. That is to say, they are approved by the society in question. Thus even morality is brought under the law of the survival of the fittest. Obviously, Stephen's point of view was different from that of T. H. Huxley.

7. Agnosticism was not, of course, the only attitude adopted by those who embraced the theory of evolution. Henry Drummond (1851–97), for example, a writer whose books once enjoyed great popularity, tried to bring together science and religion, Darwinism and Christianity, in terms of the operation of one law of continuing evolution. More interesting, however, is the case of George John Romanes (1848–94), biologist and author of a number of works on evolution, who passed from early religious belief to agnosticism and from agnosticism by way of pantheism back in the direction of Christian theism.

The agnostic phase in Romanes's thought found expression
in *A Candid Examination of Theism*, which he published in
1878 under the pseudonym of *Physicus*. There is, he maintained, no real evidence for the existence of God, though it
may possibly be true, for all we know, that there would be no
universe unless there were a God. Some years later, however, in a lecture entitled *Mind, Motion and Monism*
(1885), Romanes proposed a form of pantheism, while his
adoption of a more sympathetic attitude towards Christian
theism was represented by *Thoughts on Religion* (1895),
edited by Charles Gore, later Bishop of Oxford. This work
comprises some articles which Romanes wrote for the *Nineteenth Century* but did not publish, together with notes for
a second *Candid Examination of Theism* which was to
have been signed *Metaphysicus*.

In the articles on the influence of science on religion, which
form part of *Thoughts on Religion*, Romanes argues that this
influence has been destructive in the sense that it has progressively revealed the invalidity of appeals to direct inter-
vention in Nature or to alleged evidence of special cases of
design. At the same time science necessarily presupposes the
idea of Nature as a system, as exemplifying universal order;
and theism provides a reasonable explanation of this universal order. If, however, we wish to speak of the postulated
creator of universal order as a divine Mind, we must remember that none of the qualities which characterize the
minds with which we are acquainted can be properly attributed to God. Hence 'the word Mind, as applied to the
supposed agency, stands for a blank'.[61] In this sense, therefore, the argument for theism leads to agnosticism.

In his notes for the proposed second version of his *Candid
Examination of Theism* Romanes adopts a somewhat different point of view by arguing that the advance of science,
'far from having weakened religion, has immeasurably
strengthened it. For it has proved the uniformity of natural
causation'.[62] But the question whether one is to look on the
universal causal order as a continuing expression of the divine
will or simply as a natural fact, is not one which can be
settled by the human understanding alone. Science provides
an empirical basis, as it were, for a religious vision of the

world, but the transition to this vision requires an act of faith. True, 'no one is entitled to deny the possibility of what may be termed an organ of spiritual discernment',[63] manifested in the religious consciousness; and 'reason itself tells me it is not unreasonable to expect that the heart and will should be required to join with reason in seeking God'.[64] The way to become a Christian is to act as one, 'and if Christianity be true, the verification will come, not indeed immediately through any course of speculative reason, but immediately by spiritual intuition'.[65] At the same time faith, definite self-commitment to a religious view of the world, demands 'a severe effort of the will',[66] an effort which Romanes himself is not prepared to make.

It is thus a mistake to say that Romanes came to commit himself definitely to a theistic position. In a sense he not only begins but also ends with agnosticism. At the same time there is a considerable difference between the initial and the terminal agnosticism. For whereas in one period of his life Romanes was evidently convinced that his scientific conscience demanded of him an agnostic position, in later years he came to insist that the religious view of the world may be justified, though it would be justified by something of the nature of spiritual intuition. The agnostic has no right to rule out this possibility or to say that the venture of faith is a fool's venture. For the experiment of faith may well have its own peculiar mode of verification, about which science cannot pronounce judgment. In other words, Romanes was neither satisfied with agnosticism nor fully prepared to reject it. He developed a sympathy with religious belief which Tyndall did not share. But he did not feel able to commit himself to it by that effort of the will which he considered necessary before the internal validation of the religious consciousness could manifest itself.

8. (i) As we have seen, J. S. Mill admired Auguste Comte and was prepared to talk in a general way about the religion of humanity. But he had no use for Comte's proposals for organizing a cult for the new religion or for his dreams of a spiritual and intellectual domination to be exercised by the positivist philosophers. Again, Spencer, who also derived stimulus from Comte, adopted a critical attitude towards

some of the Frenchman's theories,[67] while T. H. Huxley described the philosophy of Comte as Catholicism minus Christianity. For real disciples of Comte we have to turn to Richard Congreve (1818–99), Fellow of Wadham College, Oxford, who translated Comte's positivist catechism into English and to his circle. This included John Henry Bridges (1832–1906), Frederic Harrison (1831–1923) and Edward Spencer Beesley (1831–1915).

The London Positivist Society was founded in 1867, and in 1870 it opened a positivist temple in Chapel Street. But after some years a split occurred in the ranks of the Comtists, and those who accepted the leadership of Pierre Laffitte (1823–1903), friend and successor of Comte as high priest of positivism, formed the London Positivist Committee which opened a centre of its own in 1881. Bridges was the first president of the new Committee (1878–80), and he was succeeded by Harrison. The original group was led by Congreve. In 1916 the two groups were reunited.[68]

(ii) The independent thinkers are obviously of more interest than those who were primarily engaged in spreading the pure word of Comtism. One of these independent thinkers was George Henry Lewes (1817–78), author of the once popular but long superseded two-volume *Biographical History of Philosophy* (1845–6). In his earlier years Lewes was an enthusiastic follower of Comte, and in 1853 he published *Comte's Philosophy of the Positive Sciences*. But though he remained a positivist in the sense of holding that philosophy consists in the widest generalizations from the results of the particular sciences and should abstain from any treatment of the meta-empirical, he moved away from Comte and came more under the influence of Spencer. In 1874–9 he published five volumes of *Problems of Life and Mind*.

Lewes made a distinction between the phenomenon which is understandable simply in terms of its constituent factors and the phenomenon which emerges from its constituent factors as something new, a novelty. The former he called a 'resultant', the latter an 'emergent'. The idea of this distinction was not Lewes's invention, but he appears to have coined the term 'emergent', which was later to play a conspicuous role in the philosophy of evolution.

(iii) A more interesting figure was William Kingdon Clifford (1845–79), who from 1871 was professor of applied mathematics in University College, London. An eminent mathematician, he was also extremely interested in philosophical topics. And he was a fervent preacher of the religion of humanity.

Clifford's best known philosophical idea is probably that of 'mind-stuff', which he proposed as a means of solving the problem of the relation between the psychical and the physical and of avoiding the necessity of postulating the emergence of mind from a completely heterogeneous matter. Like other defenders of the ancient theory of panpsychism, Clifford did not mean to imply that all matter enjoys consciousness. His thesis was that the relation between the psychical and the physical is comparable to that between a read sentence and the same sentence as written or printed. There is a complete correspondence, and every atom, for example, has a psychical aspect. Emergence is not indeed excluded. For consciousness arises when a certain organization of mind-stuff has developed. But any leap from the physical to the psychical, which might seem to imply the causal activity of a creative agent, is avoided.[69]

In the field of ethics Clifford emphasized the idea of the tribal self. The individual has indeed his egoistic impulses and desires. But the concept of the human atom, the completely solitary and self-contained individual, is an abstraction. In actual fact every individual is by nature, in virtue of the tribal self, a member of the social organism, the tribe. And moral progress consists in subordinating the egoistic impulses to the interests or good of the tribe, to that which, in Darwinian language, makes the tribe most fit for survival. Conscience is the voice of the tribal self; and the ethical ideal is to become a public-spirited and efficient citizen. In other words, morality as described by Clifford corresponds pretty well to what Bergson was later to call 'closed morality'.

On the subject of religion Clifford was something of a fanatic. Not only did he speak of the clergy as enemies of humanity, and of Christianity as a plague, but he also attacked all belief in God. He was thus more akin to some of the writers of the French Enlightenment than to the nineteenth-century English agnostics, who were generally polite in what they said about religion and its official representatives. And he has been compared not inaptly with Nietzsche. At the same time he proclaimed a substitute religion, that of humanity, though he looked to the progress of science to establish the kingdom of man rather than to any organization on the lines proposed by Comte. Clifford did indeed speak of the 'cosmic emotion' which man can feel for the universe; but it was not his intention to replace theism by pantheism. He was concerned rather with substituting man for God, as he thought that belief in God was inimical to human progress and morality.

(iv) Clifford's successor in his chair of applied mathematics was Karl Pearson (1857–1936), who was later (1911–33) Galton professor of eugenics in the University of London.[70] In Pearson's writings we find a clear exposition of the positivist spirit. He was not indeed the man to look with a kindly eye on Comte's ideas about religious cult, but he was a firm believer in the omnicompetence of science. And his attitude towards metaphysics and theology was very similar to that advanced later by the neopositivists.

According to Pearson, the function of science is 'the classification of facts, the recognition of their sequence and relative significance',[71] while the scientific frame of mind is the habit of forming impersonal judgments upon the facts, judgments, that is to say, which are unbiased by personal feeling and by the idiosyncrasies of the individual temperament. This is not, however, a frame of mind which is characteristic of the metaphysician. Metaphysics, in fact, is poetry which masquerades as something else. 'The poet is a valued member of the community, for he is known to be a poet. . . . The metaphysician is a poet, often a very great one, but unfortunately he is not known to be a poet, because he strives to clothe his poetry in the language of reason, and hence it follows that he is liable to be a dangerous member of the community.'[72] Rudolf Carnap was to expound exactly the same point of view.

What, then, are the facts which form the basis for scientific judgment? Ultimately they are simply sense-impressions or sensations. These are stored up in the brain, which acts as a kind of telephone exchange; and we project groups of impressions outside ourselves and speak of these as external objects. 'As such we call it [a group thus projected] a *phenomenon*, and in practical life term it *real*.'[73] What lies behind sense-impressions, we do not and cannot know. The claims of philosophers to have penetrated to things-in-themselves are completely bogus. Indeed, we cannot with propriety even raise the question what causes sense-impressions. For the causal relation is simply a relation of regular sequence between phenomena. Pearson therefore prefers the term 'sensations' to 'sense-impressions', as the latter term naturally suggests the causal activity of an unknown agent.

Obviously, Pearson does not intend to say that science consists simply of noting sensations or sense-impressions. Concepts are derived from sensations; and deductive inference is an essential feature of scientific method. But science is grounded in sensations and it also terminates in them, in the sense that we test the conclusions of an inference by the process of verification. As a body of propositions science is a mental construction, but it rests at either end, so to speak, on sense-impressions.

The statement that science is a mental construction is to be taken literally. On the level of pre-scientific thought the permanent physical object is, as we have seen, a mental construct. And on the level of scientific thought both laws and scientific entities are both mental constructs. The descriptive laws of science[74] are general formulas constructed for economy of thought, and 'the logic man finds in the universe is but the reflection of his own reasoning faculty'.[75] As for postulated entities such as atoms, the term 'atom' denotes neither an observed object nor a thing-in-itself. 'No physicist ever saw or felt an individual atom. Atom and molecule are intellectual conceptions by aid of which physicists classify phenomena, and formulate the relationships between their sequences.'[76] In other words, it is not sufficient to write off metaphysics as a possible source of knowledge about things-in-themselves. Science itself needs to be purified of its superstitions and of the tendency to think that its useful concepts refer to hidden entities or forces.

The beneficent social effects of science are strongly emphasized by Pearson. In addition to the technical application of scientific knowledge and its use in special departments such as that of eugenics, there is the general educative effect of scientific method. 'Modern science, as training the mind to an exact and impartial analysis of facts, is an education specially fitted to promote sound citizenship.'[77] Indeed, Pearson goes so far as to quote with approval a remark by Clifford to the effect that scientific thought is human progress itself, and not simply an accompaniment to or condition of such progress.

On the basis, therefore, of a phenomenalism which stood in the tradition of Hume and J. S. Mill Pearson developed a theory of science akin to that of Ernst Mach.[78] In fact, Mach dedicated to Pearson his *Beiträge zur Analyse der Empfindungen*. Common to both men is the idea of science as enabling us to predict and as practising, for this purpose, a policy of economy of thought by linking phenomena in terms of the fewest and simplest concepts possible. And both men interpret unobserved scientific entities as mental constructions. Further, as both Pearson and Mach resolve phenomena ultimately into sensations, we seem to arrive at the odd conclusion that though science is purely descriptive, there is really no world to be described, apart from the contents of consciousness. Thus empiricism, which began by stressing the experimental foundations of all knowledge, ends, through its phenomenalistic analysis of experience, in having no world left, outside the sphere of sensations. To put the matter in another way, empiricism started with the demand for respect for facts and then went on to resolve facts into sensations.

9. Generally speaking, the thinkers mentioned in this chapter can be said to have given expression to a vivid recognition of the part played by scientific method in the enormous increase in man's knowledge of the world. And it is understandable that this recognition was accompanied by the conviction that scientific method was the only means of acquiring anything that could properly be called knowledge. Science, they thought, continually extends the frontiers of human knowledge; and if there is anything which lies beyond the reach of science, it is unknowable. Metaphysics and theology

claim to make true statements about the metaphenomenal; but their claims are bogus.

In other words, the growth of a genuinely scientific outlook is necessarily accompanied by a growth of agnosticism. Religious belief belongs to the childhood of the human race, not to a truly adult mentality. We cannot indeed prove that there is no reality beyond the phenomena, the relations between which are studied by the scientist. Science is concerned with description, not with ultimate explanations. And there may be, for all we know, such an explanation. Indeed, the more phenomena are reduced to sensations or sense-impressions, the more difficult it is to avoid the concept of a metaphenomenal reality. But in any case a reality of this kind could not be known. And the adult mind simply accepts this fact and embraces agnosticism.

With Romanes, it is true, agnosticism came to mean something much more than a mere formal acknowledgment of the impossibility of proving the non-existence of God. But with the more positivist-minded thinkers religion, as far as the adult man was concerned, was deprived of intellectual content. That is to say, it would not comprise belief in the truth of propositions about God. In so far as religion could be retained by the adult mind, it would be reduced to an emotive element. But the emotive attitude would be directed either to the cosmos, as the object of cosmic emotion or feeling, or to humanity, as in the so-called religion of humanity. In fine, the emotive element in religion would be detached from the concept of God and re-directed elsewhere, traditional religion being something that should be left behind in the onward march of scientific knowledge.

We can say, therefore, that a large number of thinkers considered in this chapter were forerunners of the so-called scientific humanists of today, who look on religious belief as lacking any rational support and tend to emphasize the alleged detrimental effect of religion on human progress and morality. Obviously, if one is convinced that man is essentially related to God as his last end, one will question the propriety of the use of the term 'humanism' for any atheistic philosophy of man. But if one regards the movement of evolution in human society as simply an advance in the scientific knowledge and control by man both of his environment and of himself, one can hardly keep any room for religion in so far as it directs man's attention to the transcendent. Scientism is necessarily opposed to traditional religion.

A rather different point of view was advanced by Benjamin Kidd (1858–1916), author of the once popular works *Social Evolution* (1894), *The Principles of Western Civilization* (1902), and *The Science of Power* (1918). In his opinion natural selection in human society tends to favour the growth of man's emotional and affective rather than of his intellectual qualities. And as religion is grounded on the emotive aspects of human nature, it is not surprising if we find that religious peoples tend to prevail over communities in the struggle for existence. For religion encourages, in a way that science can never do, altruism and devotion to the interests of the community. In its ethical aspects especially religion is the most potent of social forces. And the highest expression of the religious consciousness is Christianity, on which Western civilization is built.

In other words, Kidd belittled the reason as a constructive force in social evolution and laid the emphasis on feeling. And as he deprived religion of its intellectual content and interpreted it as the most powerful expression of the emotive aspect of man's nature, he depicted it as an essential factor in human progress. Hostile criticism of religion by the destructive reason was thus for him an attack on progress.

Kidd's recognition of the influence of religion in human history was obviously quite justified. But the emphasis which he placed on the emotive aspects of religion laid him open to the retort that religious beliefs belong to the class of emotively-sustained myths which have as a matter of fact exercised a great influence but the need of which should be outgrown by the adult mentality. Kidd would answer, of course, that such a retort presupposes that progress is secured by the exercise of the critical reason, whereas in his view progress is secured by the development of the emotional and affective aspects of man, not by the development of a reason which is destructive rather than constructive. It seems, however, to be obvious that though the emotive aspects of man are essential to his nature, reason should retain control. And if religion has no rational warrant at all, it is necessarily suspect. Further, though the influence exercised by religions on human societies is an undoubted fact, it by no means necessarily follows that this influence has been invariably beneficial. We need rational principles of discrimination.

There is, however, one main belief which is common to both Kidd and those whom he attacked, namely the belief that in the struggle for existence the principle of natural selection works automatically for progress.[79] And it is precisely this dogma of progress which has been called in question in the course of the twentieth century. In view of the cataclysmic events of this century we can hardly retain a serene confidence in the beneficent effects of collective emotion. But, equally, we find it difficult to suppose that the advance of science, taken by itself, is synonymous with social progress. There is the all-important question of the purposes to be realized by scientific knowledge. And consideration of this question takes us outside the sphere of descriptive science. Obviously, we should all agree that science should be used in the service of man. But the question arises, how are we to interpret man? And our answer to this question will involve metaphysics, either explicit or implicit. The attempt to by-pass or exclude metaphysics will often be found to involve a concealed metaphysical assumption, an unavowed theory of being. In other words, the idea that scientific advance pushes metaphysics out of the picture is mistaken. Metaphysics simply reappears in the form of concealed assumptions.

Chapter Five

THE PHILOSOPHY OF HERBERT SPENCER

Life and writings – The nature of philosophy and its basic concepts and principles – The general law of evolution: the alternation of evolution and dissolution – Sociology and politics – Relative and absolute ethics – The Unknowable in religion and science – Final comments.

1. In 1858, the year preceding that of the publication of Darwin's *The Origin of Species*, Herbert Spencer mapped out a plan for a system which was to be based on the law of evolution or, as he expressed it, the law of progress. He is one of the few British thinkers who have deliberately attempted the construction of a comprehensive philosophical system. He is also one of the few British philosophers who have acquired a world-wide reputation during their lifetime. Seizing on an idea which was already in the air and to which Darwin gave an empirical basis in a restricted field, Spencer turned it into the key-idea of a synoptic vision of the world and of human life and conduct, an optimistic vision which appeared to justify nineteenth-century belief in human progress and which made of Spencer one of the major prophets of an era.

Though, however, Spencer remains one of the great figures of the Victorian age, he now gives the impression of being one of the most dated of philosophers. Unlike Mill, whose writings well repay study, whether one agrees or not with the views expressed. Spencer is little read nowadays. It is not merely that the idea of evolution has become common coin and no longer arouses much excitement. It is rather that after the brutal challenges of the twentieth century we find it difficult to see how the scientific hypothesis of evolution, taken by itself, can provide any adequate basis for that optimistic faith in human progress which was, generally speaking, a characteristic feature of Spencer's thought. On the one hand positivism has changed its character and fights shy of explicit and comprehensive world-visions. On the other hand those philosophers who believe that the trend of evolution is in some real sense beneficent to man generally appeal to metaphysical theories which were foreign to the mind of Spencer. Moreover, while Mill not only dealt with many problems which are still examined by British philosophers but also treated them in a way which is still considered relevant, Spencer is notable for his large-scale exploration of one leading idea rather than for any detailed analyses. However, though Spencer's thought is so closely wedded to the Victorian era that it can scarcely be described as a living influence today, the fact remains that he was one of the leading representative members of the nineteenth century. Hence he cannot be passed over in silence.

Herbert Spencer was born at Derby on April 27th, 1820. Whereas Mill began Greek at the age of three, Spencer admits that at the age of thirteen he knew nothing worth mentioning of either Latin or Greek. By the age of sixteen, however, he had at any rate acquired some knowledge of mathematics; and after a few months as a schoolmaster at Derby he became a civil engineer employed by the Birmingham and Gloucester Railway. When the line was completed in 1841, Spencer was discharged. 'Got the sack—very glad', as he noted in his diary. But though in 1843 he moved to London to take up a literary career, he returned for a short while to the service of the railways and also tried his hand at inventions.

In 1848 Spencer became sub-editor of the *Economist*, and he entered into relations of friendship with G. H. Lewes, Huxley, Tyndall and George Eliot. With Lewes in particular he discussed the theory of evolution; and among the articles which he wrote anonymously for Lewes's *Leader* there was one on 'The Development Hypothesis', in which the idea of evolution was expounded on Lamarckian lines. In 1851 he published *Social Statics* and in 1855, at his own expense, *The Principles of Psychology*. At this time the state of his health was causing him serious concern, and he made several excursions to France, where he met Auguste Comte. He was able, however, to publish a collection of his essays in 1857.

At the beginning of 1858 Spencer drew up a scheme for *A System of Synthetic Philosophy*; and the prospectus, distributed in 1860, envisaged ten volumes. *First Principles* appeared in one volume in 1862, and *The Principles of Biology* in two volumes in 1864–7. *The Principles of Psychology*, originally published in one volume in 1855, appeared in two volumes in 1870–2, while the three volumes of *The Principles of Sociology* were published in 1876–96. *The Data of Ethics* (1879) was subsequently included with two other parts to form the first volume of *The Principles of Ethics* (1892), while the second volume of this work (1893) utilized *Justice* (1891). Spencer also published new editions of several volumes of the *System*. For example, the sixth edition of *First Principles* appeared in 1900, while a revised and enlarged edition of *The Principles of Biology* was published in 1898–9.

Spencer's *System of Synthetic Philosophy* constituted a remarkable achievement, carried through in spite of bad health and, at first at any rate, of serious financial difficulties. Intellectually, he was a self-made man; and the composition of his great work involved writing on a number of subjects which he had never really studied. He had to collect his data from various sources, and he then interpreted them in the light of the idea of evolution. As for the history of philosophy, he knew little about it, except from secondary sources. He did indeed make more than one attempt to read Kant's first *Critique*; but when he came to the doctrine of the subjectivity of space and time, he laid the book aside. He had little appreciation or understanding of points of view other than his own. However, if he had not practised what we might call a rigid economy of thought, it is unlikely he would ever have completed his self-imposed task.

Of Spencer's other publications we can mention *Education* (1861), a small but very successful book, *The Man Versus the State* (1884), a vigorous polemic against what the author regarded as the threatening slavery, and the posthumous *Autobiography* (1904). In 1885 Spencer published in America *The Nature and Reality of Religion*, comprising a controversy between himself and the positivist Frederic Harrison. But the work was suppressed, as Harrison protested against the re-publication of his articles without permission, especially as an introduction in support of Spencer's position by a Professor Yeomans had been included in the volume.

With the exception of membership of the Athenaeum Club (1868) Spencer consistently refused all honours. When invited to stand for the chair of mental philosophy and logic at University College, London, he refused; and he also declined membership of the Royal Society. He seems to have felt that when he had really had need of such offers they had not been made, and that when they were made, he no longer had need of them, his reputation being already established. As for honours offered by the government, his opposition to social distinctions of this kind militated against acceptance, quite apart from his annoyance at the lateness of the offers.

Spencer died on December 8th, 1903. At the time of his death he was extremely unpopular in his own country, mainly because of his opposition to the Boer War (1899–1902), which he regarded as an expression of the militaristic spirit that he so much hated.[1] Abroad, however, there was considerable criticism of English indifference to the passing of one of the country's outstanding figures. And in Italy the Chamber adjourned on receiving the news of Spencer's death.

2. Spencer's general account of the relation between philosophy and science bears a marked resemblance to that given by the classical positivists such as Auguste Comte. Both science and philosophy treat of phenomena, of, that is to say, the finite, conditioned and classifiable. True, in Spencer's opinion phenomena are manifestations to consciousness of infinite, unconditioned Being. But as knowledge involves relating and classification, whereas infinite, unconditional Being is by its very nature unique and unclassifiable, to say that such Being transcends the sphere of phenomena is to say that it transcends the sphere of the knowable.[2] Hence it cannot be investigated by the philosopher any more than by the scientist. Metaphenomenal or 'ultimate' causes lie outside the reach of both philosophy and science.

If, therefore, we are to distinguish between philosophy and science, we cannot do so simply in terms of the objects of

which they treat. For both are concerned with phenomena.
We have to introduce the idea of degrees of generalization.
'Science' is the name of the family of particular sciences.
And though every science, as distinct from the unco-ordinated
knowledge of particular facts, involves generalization, even
the widest of such generalizations are partial in comparison
with those universal truths of philosophy which serve to unify
the sciences. 'The truths of Philosophy thus bear the same
relation to the highest scientific truths, that each of these
bears to lower scientific truths. . . . Knowledge of the lowest
kind is un-unified knowledge; Science is *partially-unified*
knowledge; Philosophy is *completely-unified* knowledge.'[3]

The universal truths or widest generalizations of philosophy can be considered in themselves, as 'products of exploration'.[4] And we are then concerned with general philosophy. Or the universal truths can be considered according to
their active role as 'instruments of exploration'.[5] That is to
say, they can be considered as truths in the light of which
we investigate different specific areas of phenomena, such as
the data of ethics and sociology. And we are then concerned
with special philosophy. Spencer's *First Principles* is devoted
to general philosophy, while subsequent volumes of the *System* deal with the parts of special philosophy.

Taken by itself, Spencer's account of the relation between
science and philosophy in terms of degrees of unification
tends to suggest that in his view the basic concepts of philosophy are derived by generalization from the particular
sciences. But this is not the case. For he insists that there
are fundamental concepts and assumptions which are involved in all thinking. Let us suppose that a philosopher
decides to take one particular datum as the point of departure for his reflections, and that he imagines that by acting in this way he is making no assumptions. In actual fact
the choice of one particular datum implies that there are
other data which the philosopher might have chosen. And
this involves the concept of existence other than the existence
actually asserted. Again, no particular thing can be known
except as like some other things, as classifiable in virtue of
a common attribute, and as different from or unlike other
things. In fine, the choice of one particular datum involves

a number of 'unacknowledged postulates',[6] which together provide the outlines of a general philosophical theory. 'The developed intelligence is framed upon certain organized and consolidated conceptions of which it cannot divest itself; and which it can no more stir without using than the body can stir without help of its limbs.'[7]

It can hardly be claimed that Spencer makes his position crystal clear. For he speaks of 'tacit assumptions',[8] 'unavowed data',[9] 'unacknowledged postulates',[10] 'certain organized and consolidated conceptions',[11] and 'fundamental intuitions',[12] as though the meanings of these phrases stood in no need of further elucidation and as though they all meant the same thing. It is indeed clear that he does not intend to assert a Kantian theory of the *a priori*. The fundamental concepts and assumptions have an experimental basis. And sometimes Spencer speaks as though it were a question of the individual experience or consciousness. He says, for example, that 'we cannot avoid accepting as true the verdict of consciousness that some manifestations are like one another and some are unlike one another'.[13] The situation is complicated, however, by the fact that Spencer accepts the idea of a relative *a priori*, that is, of concepts and assumptions which are, from the genetic point of view, the product of the accumulated experience of the race[14] but which are *a priori* in relation to a given individual mind, in the sense that they came to it with the force of 'intuitions'.

The basic assumptions of the process of thought have to be taken provisionally as unquestionable. They can be justified or validated only by their results, that is, by showing the agreement or congruity between the experience which the assumptions logically lead us to expect and the experiences which we actually have. Indeed, 'the complete establishment of the congruity becomes the same thing as the complete unification of knowledge in which Philosophy reaches its goal'.[15] Thus general philosophy makes explicit the basic concepts and assumptions, while special philosophy shows their agreement with the actual phenomena in distinct fields or areas of experience.

Now, according to Spencer 'knowing is classifying, or grasping the like and separating the unlike'.[16] And as likeness and unlikeness are relations, we can say that all thinking is relational, that 'relation is the universal form of thought'.[17] We can distinguish, however, between two kinds of relations, those of sequence and those of co-existence.[18] And each gives rise to an abstract idea. 'The abstract of all sequences is Time. The abstract of all co-existences is Space.'[19] Time and Space are not indeed original forms of consciousness in an absolute sense. But as the generation of these ideas takes place through an organization of experiences which proceeds throughout the entire evolution of mind or intelligence, they can have a relatively *a priori* character, as far as a given individual mind is concerned.

Our concept of Space is fundamentally that of co-existent positions which offer no resistance. And it is derived by abstraction from the concept of Matter, which in its simplest form is that of co-existent positions which offer resistance. In turn, the concept of Matter is derived from an experience of force. For 'forces, standing in certain co-relations, form the whole content of our idea of Matter'.[20] Similarly, though the developed concepts of Motion involve the ideas of Space, Time and Matter, the rudimentary consciousness of Motion is simply that of 'serial impressions of force'.[21]

Spencer argues, therefore, that psychological analysis of the concepts of Time, Space, Matter and Motion shows that they are all based on experiences of Force. And the conclusion is that 'we come down, then, finally to Force, as the ultimate of ultimates'.[22] The principle of the indestructibility of matter is really that of the indestructibility of force. Similarly, all proofs of the principle of the continuity of motion 'involve the postulate that the quantity of Energy is constant',[23] energy being the force possessed by matter in motion. And in the end we arrive at the principle of the persistence of Force, 'which, as being the basis of science, cannot be established by science',[24] but transcends demonstration, a principle which has as its corollary that of the uniformity of law, the persistence of relations between forces.

It may be objected that such principles as that of the indestructibility of matter belong to science rather than to philosophy. But Spencer answers that they are 'truths which unify concrete phenomena belonging to all divisions of Nature, and so must be components of that all-embracing conception of things which Philosophy seeks'.[25] Further, though the word 'force' ordinarily signifies 'the consciousness of muscular tension',[26] the feeling of effort which we have when we set something in motion or resist a pressure is a symbol of Absolute Force. And when we speak of the persistence of Force, 'we really mean the persistence of some Cause which transcends our knowledge and conception'.[27] How we can intelligibly predicate persistence of an unknowable reality is not perhaps immediately evident. But if the assertion of the persistence of Force really means what Spencer says that it means, it clearly becomes a philosophical principle, even apart from the fact that its character as a universal truth would in any case qualify it for inclusion among the truths of philosophy according to Spencer's account of the relation between philosophy and science.

3. Though, however, such general principles as the indestructibility of matter, the continuity of motion and the persistence of force are components of the synthesis which philosophy seeks to achieve, they do not, even when taken together, constitute this synthesis. For we require a formula or law which specifies the course of the transformations undergone by matter and motion, and which thus serves to unify all the processes of change which are examined in the several particular sciences. That is to say, if we assume that there is no such thing as absolute rest or permanence but that every object is constantly undergoing change, whether by receiving or losing motion or by changes in the relations between its parts, we need to ascertain the general law of the continuous redistribution of matter and motion.

Spencer finds what he is looking for in what he calls indiscriminately a 'formula', 'law' or 'definition' of evolution. 'Evolution is an integration of matter and concomitant dissipation of motion; during which the matter passes from a relatively indefinite, incoherent homogeneity to a relatively definite, coherent heterogeneity; and during which the retained motion undergoes a parallel transformation.'[28] This law can be established deductively, by deduction from the persistence of force. It can also be established or confirmed inductively. For whether we contemplate the development of solar systems out of the nebular mass, or that of more highly organized and complex living bodies out of more primitive organisms, or that of man's psychological life, or the growth of language, or the evolution of social organization, we find everywhere a movement from relative indefiniteness to relative definiteness, from incoherence to coherence, together with a movement of progressive differentiation, the movement from relative homogeneity to relative heterogeneity. For example in the evolution of the living body we see a progressive structural and functional differentiation.

But this is only one side of the picture. For the integration of matter is accompanied by a dissipation of motion. And the process of evolution tends towards a state of equilibrium, of a balance of forces, which is succeeded by dissolution or disintegration. For example, the human body dissipates and loses its energies, dies and disintegrates; any given society loses its vigour and decays; and the heat of the sun is gradually dissipated.

Spencer is careful to avoid claiming that we can legitimately extrapolate what is true of a relatively closed system to the totality of things, the universe as a whole. We cannot, for example, argue with certainty from the running-down, so to speak, of our solar system to the running-down of the universe. And it is possible, for all we know, that when life has been extinguished on our planet through the dissipation of the sun's heat, it will be in process of development in some other part of the universe. In fine, we are not entitled to argue that what happens to a part *must* happen to the whole.

At the same time, if there is an alternation of evolution and dissolution in the totality of things, we must 'entertain the conception of Evolutions that have filled an immeasurable past and Evolutions that will fill an immeasurable future'.[29] And if this represents Spencer's personal opinion, we can say that he gives an up-to-date version of certain early Greek cosmologies, with their ideas of a cyclic process. In any case there is a rhythm of evolution and dissolution in the parts, even if we are not in a position to make dogmatic assertions about the whole. And though at first Spencer spoke about the law of evolution as the law of progress, his belief in alternations of evolution and dissolution evidently set limits to his optimism.

4. Spencer's ideal of a complete philosophical synthesis demands the inclusion of a systematic treatment of the inorganic world in the light of the idea of evolution. And he remarks that if this topic had been treated in the *System of Philosophy*, it 'would have occupied two volumes, one dealing with Astrogeny and the other with Geogeny'.[30] In point of fact, however, Spencer confines himself, in special philosophy, to biology, psychology, sociology and ethics. He alludes, of course, to astronomical, physical and chemical topics, but the *System* contains no systematic treatment of evolution in the inorganic sphere.

As limitations of space exclude a recapitulation of all the parts of Spencer's system, I propose to pass over biology and psychology and to make some remarks in this section about his sociological and political ideas, devoting the following section to the subject of ethics.

The sociologist is concerned with the growth, structures, functions and products of human societies.[31] The possibility of a science of sociology follows from the fact that we can find regular sequences among social phenomena, which permit prediction; and it is not excluded by the fact that social laws are statistical and predictions in this field approximate. 'Only a moiety of science is exact science.'[32] It is the possibility of generalization which is required, not quantitative exactitude. As for the utility of sociology, Spencer claims in a somewhat vague way that if we can discern an order in the structural and functional changes through which societies pass, 'knowledge of that order can scarcely fail to affect our judgments as to what is progressive and what retrograde—what is desirable, what is practicable, what is Utopian'.[33]

When we consider the struggle for existence in the general process of evolution, we find obvious analogies between the inorganic, organic and super-organic (social) spheres. The behaviour of an inanimate object depends on the relations between its own forces and the external forces to which it is exposed. Similarly, the behaviour of an organic body is the product of the combined influences of its intrinsic nature and of its environment, both inorganic and organic. Again,

every human society 'displays phenomena that are ascribable
to the character of its units and to the conditions under
which they exist'.[34]

It is indeed true that the two sets of factors, intrinsic and
extrinsic, do not remain static. For example, man's powers,
physical, emotional and intellectual, have developed in the
course of history, while evolving society has produced remarkable changes in its organic and inorganic environment.
Again, the products of evolving society, its institutions and
cultural creations, bring fresh influences into being. Further,
the more human societies develop, so much the more do they
react on one another, so that the super-organic environment
occupies a position of even greater importance. But in spite
of the growing complexity of the situation an analogous inter-
play of forces, intrinsic and extrinsic, is discernible in all
three spheres.

Though, however, there is continuity between the inorganic, organic and super-organic spheres, there is also discontinuity. If there is similarity, there is also dissimilarity.
Consider, for example, the idea of a society as an organism.
As in the case of an organic body in the proper sense, the
growth of society is accompanied by a progressive differentiation of structures, which results in a progressive differentiation of functions. But this point of similarity between the
organic body and human society is also a point of dissimilarity between them both and the inorganic body. For according to Spencer the actions of the different parts of an inorganic thing cannot properly be regarded as functions.
Further, there is an important difference between the process
of differentiation in an organic body and that in the social
organism. For in the latter we do not find that kind of differentiation which in the former results in one part alone
becoming the organ of intelligence and in some parts becoming sense-organs while others do not. In the organic body
'consciousness is concentrated in a small part of the aggregate', whereas in the social organism 'it is diffused throughout the aggregate: all the units possess the capacity for happiness and misery, if not in equal degrees, still in degrees that
approximate'.[35]

An enthusiast for the interpretation of political society as an organism might, of course, try to find detailed analogies between differentiation of functions in the organic body and in society. But this might easily lead him into speaking, for example, as though the government were analogous to the brain and as though the other parts of society should leave all thinking to the government and simply obey its decisions. And this is precisely the sort of conclusion which Spencer wishes to avoid. Hence he insists on the relative independence of the individual members of a political society and denies the contention that society is an organism in the sense that it is more than the sum of its members and possesses an end which is different from the ends of the members. 'As, then, there is no social sensorium, it results that the welfare of the aggregate, considered apart from that of the members, is not an end to be sought. The society exists for the benefit of its members; not its members for the benefit of society.'[36] In other words, we can say that the arms and the legs exist for the good of the whole body. But in the case of society we have to say that the whole exists for the parts. Spencer's conclusion at any rate is clear. And even if his arguments are sometimes obscure and perplexing, it is also clear that in his opinion the analogy of an organism, as applied to a political society, is not only misleading but also dangerous.

The situation is in fact this. Spencer's determination to use the idea of evolution throughout all fields of phenomena leads him to speak of political society, the State, as a super-organism. But as he is a resolute champion of individual liberty against the claims and encroachment of the State, he tries to deprive this analogy of its sting by pointing out essential differences between the organic body and the body political. And he does this by maintaining that while political development is a process of integration, in the sense that social groups become larger and individual wills are merged together, it is also a movement from homogeneity to heterogeneity, so that differentiation tends to increase. For example, with the advance of civilization towards the modern industrialized State the class-divisions of relatively more primitive societies tend, so Spencer believes, to become less rigid and even to break down. And this is a sign of progress.

Spencer's point depends in part on his thesis that 'the state of homogeneity is an unstable state; and where there is already some heterogeneity, the tendency is towards greater heterogeneity'.[37] Given this idea of the movement of evolution, it obviously follows that a society in which differentiation is relatively greater is more evolved than one in which there is relatively less differentiation. At the same time it is clear that Spencer's point of view also depends on a judgment of value, namely that a society in which individual liberty is highly developed is intrinsically more admirable and praiseworthy than a society in which there is less individual liberty. True, Spencer believes that a society which embodies the principle of individual liberty possesses a greater survival-value than societies which do not embody the principle. And this can be understood as a purely factual judgment. But it seems obvious to me at any rate that Spencer considers the first type of society to be more deserving of survival because of its greater intrinsic value.

If we pass over Spencer's account of primitive societies and their development, we can say that he concentrates most of his attention on the transition from the militaristic or militant type of society to the industrial type. The militant society is basically 'one in which the army is the nation mobilized while the nation is the quiescent army, and which, therefore, acquires a structure common to army and nation'.[38] There can indeed be development within this kind of society. For example, the military leader becomes the civil or political head, as in the case of the Roman emperor; and in the course of time the army becomes a specialized professional branch of the community instead of being coextensive with the adult male population. But in the militant society in general integration and cohesion are dominant features. The primary aim is the preservation of the society, while the preservation of individual members is a matter for concern only as a means to the attainment of the primary aim. Again, in this kind of society there is constant regulation of conduct, and 'the individuality of each member has to be so subordinated in life, liberty, and property, that he is largely, or completely *owned* by the State'.[39] Further, as the militant type of society aims at self-sufficiency, political autonomy tends to be accompanied by economic autonomy.[40] The Germany of National Socialism would doubtless have represented for Spencer a good example of a revival of the militant type of society in the modern industrial era.

Spencer does not deny that the militant type of society had an essential role to play in the process of evolution considered as a struggle for existence in which the fittest survive. But he maintains that though inter-social conflict was necessary for the formation and growth of societies, the development of civilization renders war increasingly unnecessary. The militant type of society thus becomes an anachronism, and a transition is required to what Spencer calls the industrial type of society. This does not mean that the struggle for existence ceases. But it changes its form, becoming 'the industrial struggle for existence',[41] in which that society is best fitted to survive which produces 'the largest number of the best individuals—individuals best adapted for life in the industrial state'.[42] In this way Spencer tries to avoid the accusation that when he has arrived at the concept of the industrial type of society, he abandons the ideas of the struggle for existence and of the survival of the fittest.

It would be a great mistake to suppose that by the industrial type of society Spencer means simply a society in which the citizens are occupied, exclusively or predominantly, in the economic life of production and distribution. For an industrial society in this narrow sense would be compatible with a thorough-going regulation of labour by the State. And it is precisely this element of compulsion which Spencer is concerned to exclude. On the economic level, he is referring to a society dominated by the principle of *laissez-faire*. Hence in his view socialist and communist States would be very far from exemplifying the essence of the industrial type of society. The function of the State is to maintain individual freedom and rights, and to adjudicate, when necessary, between conflicting claims. It is not the business of the State to interfere positively with the lives and conduct of the citizens, except when interference is required for the maintenance of internal peace.

In other words, in the ideal type of industrial society, as Spencer interprets the term, emphasis is shifted from the totality, the society as a whole, to its members considered as individuals. 'Under the industrial *régime* the citizen's individuality, instead of being sacrificed by the society, has to be defended by the society. Defence of his individuality becomes the society's essential duty.'[43] That is to say, the cardinal function of the State becomes that of equitably adjusting conflicting claims between individual citizens and preventing the infringement of one man's liberty by another.

Spencer's belief in the universal applicability of the law of evolution obviously committed him to maintaining that the movement of evolution tends to the development of the industrial type of State, which he regarded, rather over-optimistically, as an essentially peaceful society. But the tendencies to interference and regulation by the State which were showing themselves in the last decades of his life led him to express his fear of what he called 'the coming slavery'[44] and to attack violently any tendency on the part of the State or of one of its organs to regard itself as omni-competent. 'The great political superstition of the past was the divine right of kings. The great political superstition of the present is the divine right of parliaments.'[45] Again, 'the function of Liberalism in the past was that of putting a limit to the powers of kings. The function of true Liberalism in the future will be that of putting a limit to the powers of Parliaments.'[46]

Obviously, in this resolute attack on 'the coming slavery' Spencer could not appeal simply to the automatic working-out of any law of evolution. His words are clearly inspired by a passionate conviction in the value of individual liberty and initiative, a conviction which reflected the character and temperament of a man who had never at any period of his life been inclined to bow before constituted authority simply because it was authority. And it is a notorious fact that Spencer carried his attack on what he regarded as encroachments by the State on private liberty to the extent of condemning factory legislation, sanitary inspection by government officials, State management of the Post Office, poor relief by the State and State education. Needless to say, he did not condemn reform as such or charitable relief work or the running of hospitals and schools. But his insistence was always on voluntary organization of such projects, as opposed to State action, management and control. In short, his ideal was that of a society in which, as he put it, the individual would be everything and the State nothing, in contrast with the militant type of society in which the State is everything and the individual nothing.

Spencer's equation of the industrial type of society with peace-loving and anti-militaristic society is likely to strike us as odd, unless we make the equation true by definition. And his extreme defence of the policy of *laissez-faire* is likely to appear to us as eccentric, or at least as a hangover from a bygone outlook. He does not seem to have understood, as Mill came to understand, at least in part, and as was understood more fully by an idealist such as T. H. Green, that social legislation and so-called interference by the State may very well be required to safeguard the legitimate claims of every individual citizen to lead a decent human life.

At the same time Spencer's hostility to social legislation which nowadays is taken for granted by the vast majority of citizens in Great Britain should not blind us to the fact that he, like Mill, saw the dangers of bureaucracy and of any exaltation of the power and functions of the State which tends to stifle individual liberty and originality. To the present writer at any rate it seems that concern with the common good leads to an approval of State action to a degree far beyond what Spencer was prepared to endorse. But it should never be forgotten that the common good is not something entirely different from the good of the individual. And Spencer was doubtless quite right in thinking that it is for the good both of individuals and of society in general that citizens should be able to develop themselves freely and show initiative. We may well think that it is the business of the State to create and maintain the conditions in which individuals can develop themselves, and that this demands, for example, that the State should provide for all the means of education according to the individual's capacity for profiting by it. But once we accept the principle that the State should concern itself with positively creating and maintaining the conditions which will make it possible for every individual to lead a decent human life in accordance with his or her capacities, we expose ourselves to the danger of sub-sequently forgetting that the common good is not an abstract entity to which the concrete interests of individuals have to be ruthlessly sacrificed. And Spencer's attitude, in spite of its eccentric exaggerations, can serve to remind us that the State exists for man and not man for the State. Further, the State is but one form of social organization: it is not the only legitimate form of society. And Spencer certainly understood this fact.

As has already been indicated, Spencer's political views were partly the expression of factual judgments, connected with his interpretation of the general movement of evolution, and partly an expression of judgments of value. For example, his assertion that what he calls the industrial type of society possesses a greater survival value than other types was partly equivalent to a prediction that it would in fact survive, in virtue of the trend of evolution. But it was also partly a judgment that the industrial type of society deserved to survive, because of its intrinsic value. Indeed, it is clear enough that with Spencer a positive evaluation of personal liberty was the really determining factor in his view of modern society. It is also clear that if a man is resolved that, as far as depends on him, the type of society which respects individual freedom and initiative *will* survive, this resolution is based primarily on a judgment of value rather than on any theory about the automatic working-out of a law of evolution.

5. Spencer regarded his ethical doctrine as the crown of his system. In the preface to *The Data of Ethics* he remarks that his first essay, on *The Proper Sphere of Government* (1842), vaguely indicated certain general principles of right and wrong in political conduct. And he adds that 'from that time onwards my ultimate purpose, lying behind all proximate purposes, has been that of finding for the principles of right and wrong in conduct at large, a scientific basis'.[47] Belief in supernatural authority as a basis for ethics has waned. It thus becomes all the more imperative to give morality a scientific foundation, independent of religious beliefs. And for Spencer this means establishing ethics on the theory of evolution.

Conduct in general, including that of animals, consists of acts adjusted to ends.[48] And the higher we proceed in the scale of evolution, the clearer evidence do we find of purposeful actions directed to the good either of the individual or of the species. But we also find that teleological activity of this kind forms part of the struggle for existence between different individuals of the same species and between different species. That is to say, one creature tries to preserve itself at the expense of another, and one species maintains itself by preying on another.

This type of purposeful conduct, in which the weaker goes to the wall, is for Spencer imperfectly evolved conduct. In perfectly evolved conduct, ethical conduct in the proper sense, antagonisms between rival groups and between individual members of one group will have been replaced by co-operation and mutual aid. Perfectly evolved conduct, however, can be achieved only in proportion as militant societies give place to permanently peaceful societies. In other words it cannot be achieved in a stable manner except in the perfectly evolved society, in which alone can the clash between egoism and altruism be overcome and transcended.

This distinction between imperfectly and perfectly evolved conduct provides the basis for a distinction between relative and absolute ethics. Absolute ethics is 'an ideal code of conduct formulating the behaviour of the completely adapted man in the completely evolved society',[49] while relative ethics is concerned with the conduct which is the nearest approximation to this ideal in the circumstances in which we find ourselves, that is, in more or less imperfectly evolved societies. According to Spencer, it is simply not true that in any set of circumstances which call for purposeful action on our part we are always faced with a choice between an action which is absolutely right and one which is absolutely wrong. For example, it may happen that circumstances are such that, however I act, I shall cause some pain to another person. And an action which causes pain to another cannot be absolutely right. In such circumstances, therefore, I have to try to estimate which possible course of action is relatively right, that is, which possible course of action will probably cause the greatest amount of good and the least amount of evil. I cannot expect to make an infallible judgment. I can only act as seems to me best, after devoting to the matter the amount of reflection which appears to be demanded by the relative importance of the issue. I can indeed bear in mind the ideal code of conduct of absolute ethics; but I cannot legitimately assume that this standard will serve as a premiss from which I can infallibly deduce what action would be relatively best in the circumstances in which I find myself.

Spencer accepts the utilitarian ethics in the sense that he takes happiness to be the ultimate end of life and measures the rightness or wrongness of actions by their relation to this end. In his opinion the 'gradual rise of a utilitarian ethic has, indeed, been inevitable'.[50] True, there was from the start a nascent utilitarianism, in the sense that some actions were always felt to be beneficial and others injurious to man and society. But in past societies ethical codes were associated with authority of some sort or another, or with the idea of divine authority and divinely imposed sanctions, whereas in the course of time ethics has gradually become independent of non-ethical beliefs, and there has been growing up a moral outlook based simply on the ascertainable natural consequences of actions. In other words, the trend of evolution in the moral sphere has been towards the development of utilitarianism. It must be added, however, that utilitarianism must be understood in such a way that room is found for the distinction between relative and absolute ethics. Indeed, the very idea of evolution suggests progress towards an ideal limit. And in this progress advance in virtue cannot be separated from social advance. 'The co-existence of a perfect man and an imperfect society is impossible.'[51]

As Spencer regards utilitarianism as the scientifically-based ethics, it is understandable that he wishes to show that it is not simply one among many mutually exclusive systems, but that it can find room for the truths contained in other systems. Thus he maintains, for example, that utilitarianism, when rightly understood, finds room for the point of view which insists on the concepts of right, wrong and obligation rather than on the attainment of happiness. Bentham may have thought that happiness is to be aimed at directly, by applying the hedonistic calculus. But he was wrong. He would indeed have been right if the attainment of happiness did not depend on the fulfilment of conditions. But in this case any action would be moral if it produced pleasure. And this notion is incompatible with the moral consciousness. In point of fact the attainment of happiness depends on the fulfilment of certain conditions, that is, on the observance of certain moral precepts or rules.[52] And it is at the fulfilment of these conditions that we ought to aim directly. Bentham thought that everyone knows what happiness is, and that it is more intelligible than, say, the principles of justice. But this view is the reverse of the truth. The principles of justice are easily intelligible, whereas it is far from easy to say what happiness is. Spencer advocates, therefore, what he calls a 'rational' utilitarianism, one which 'takes for its immediate object of pursuit conformity to certain principles which, in the nature of things, causally determine welfare'.[53]

Again, the theory that moral rules can be inductively established by observing the natural consequences of actions does not entail the conclusion that there is no truth at all in the theory of moral intuitionism. For there are indeed what can be called moral intuitions, though they are not something mysterious and inexplicable but 'the slowly organized results of experiences received by the race'.[54] What was originally an induction from experience can come in later generations to have for the individual the force of an intuition. The individual may see or feel instinctively that a certain course of action is right or wrong, though this instinctive reaction is the result of the accumulated experience of the race.

Similarly, utilitarianism can perfectly well recognize truth in the contention that the perfection of our nature is the object for which we should seek. For the trend of evolution is towards the emergence of the highest form of life. And though happiness is the supreme end, it is 'the concomitant of that highest life which every theory of moral guidance has distinctly or vaguely in view'.[55] As for the theory that virtue is the end of human conduct, this is simply one way of expressing the doctrine that our direct aim should be that of fulfilling the conditions for the attainment of the highest form of life to which the process of evolution tends. If it were attained, happiness would result.

Needless to say, Spencer could not reasonably claim to ground his ethical theory on the theory of evolution without admitting a continuity between evolution in the biological sphere and that in the moral sphere. And he maintains, for example, that 'human justice must be a further development of sub-human justice'.[56] At the same time, in a preface, subsequently withdrawn, to the fifth and sixth parts of The Principles of Ethics he admits that the doctrine of evolution has not furnished guidance to the hoped-for extent. He seems, however, never to have understood clearly that the process of evolution, considered as an historical fact, could not by itself establish the value-judgments which he brought to bear upon its interpretation. For example, even if we grant that evolution is moving towards the emergence of a certain type of human life in society and that this type is therefore shown to be the most fitted for survival, it does not necessarily follow that it is morally the most admirable type. As T. H. Huxley saw, factual fitness for survival in the struggle for existence and moral excellence are not necessarily the same thing.

Of course, if we assume that evolution is a teleological process directed towards the progressive establishment of a moral order, the situation is somewhat different. But though an assumption of this kind may have been implicit in Spencer's outlook, he did not profess to make any such metaphysical assumptions.

6. The explicit metaphysical element in Spencer's thought is, somewhat paradoxically, his philosophy of the Unknowable. This topic is introduced in the context of a discussion about the alleged conflict between religion and science. 'Of all antagonisms of belief the oldest, the widest, the most profound, and the most important is that between Religion and Science.'[57] Of course, if religion is understood simply as a subjective experience, the question of a conflict between it and science hardly arises. But if we bear in mind religious beliefs, the case is different. In regard to particular events supernatural explanations have been superseded by scientific or natural explanations. And religion has had to confine

itself more or less to offering an explanation of the existence of the universe as a totality.[58] But the arguments are unacceptable to anyone who possesses a scientific outlook. In this sense, therefore, there is a conflict between the religious and scientific mentalities. And it can be resolved, according to Spencer, only through a philosophy of the Unknowable.

If we start from the side of religious belief, we can see that both pantheism and theism are untenable. By pantheism Spencer understands the theory of a universe which develops itself from potential to actual existence. And he contends that this idea is inconceivable. We do not really know what it means. Hence the question of its truth or falsity hardly arises. As for theism, understood as the doctrine that the world was created by an external agent, this too is untenable. Apart from the fact that the creation of space is inconceivable, because its non-existence cannot be conceived, the idea of a self-existent Creator is as inconceivable as that of a self-existent universe. The very idea of self-existence is inconceivable. 'It is not a question of probability, or credibility, but of conceivability.'[59]

It is true, Spencer concedes, that if we inquire into the ultimate cause or causes of the effects produced on our senses, we are led inevitably to the hypothesis of a First Cause. And we shall find ourselves driven to describe it as both infinite and absolute. But Mansel[60] has shown that though the idea of a finite and dependent First Cause involves manifest contradictions, the idea of a First Cause which is infinite and absolute is no more free from contradictions, even if they are not so immediately evident. We are unable, therefore, to say anything intelligible about the nature of the First Cause. And we are left in the end with nothing more than the idea of an inscrutable Power.

If, however, we start from the side of science, we are again brought face to face with the Unknowable. For science cannot solve the mystery of the universe. For one thing, it cannot show that the universe is self-existent, for the idea of self-existence is, as we have seen, inconceivable or unintelligible. For another thing, the ultimate ideas of science itself 'are all representative of realities that cannot be comprehended'.[61] For example, we cannot understand what force is 'in itself'. And in the end 'ultimate religious ideas and ultimate scientific ideas alike turn out to be merely symbols of the actual, not cognitions of it'.[62]

This point of view is supported by an analysis of human thought. All thinking, as we have seen, is relational. And that which is not classifiable by being related to other things through relations of similarity and dissimilarity is not a possible object of knowledge. Hence we cannot know the unconditioned and absolute. And this applies not only to the Absolute of religion but also to ultimate scientific ideas if considered as representing metaphenomenal entities or things-in-themselves. At the same time to assert that all knowledge is 'relative' is to assert implicitly that there exists a non-relative reality. 'Unless a real Non-relative or Absolute be postulated, the Relative itself becomes absolute, and so brings the argument to a contradiction.'[63] In fact, we cannot eliminate from our consciousness the idea of an Absolute behind appearances.

Thus whether we approach the matter through a critical examination of religious beliefs or through reflection on our ultimate scientific ideas or through an analysis of the nature of thought and knowledge, we arrive in the end at the concept of an unknowable reality. And a permanent state of peace between religion and science will be achieved 'when science becomes fully convinced that its explanations are proximate and relative, while Religion becomes fully convinced that the mystery it contemplates is ultimate and absolute'.[64]

Now, the doctrine of the Unknowable forms the first part of *First Principles* and thus comes at the beginning of Spencer's system of philosophy as formally arranged. And this fact may incline the unwary reader to attribute to the doctrine a fundamental importance. When, however, he discovers that the inscrutable Absolute or Power of religion is practically equiparated with Force, considered in itself, he may be led to conclude that the doctrine is not much more, if anything, than a sop politely offered to the religious-minded by a man who was not himself a believer in God and who was buried, or rather cremated, without any religious ceremony. It is thus easy to understand how some writers have dismissed the first part of *First Principles* as an unhappy excrescence. Spencer deals with the Unknowable at considerable length. But the total result is not impressive from the metaphysical point of view, as the arguments are not well thought out, while the scientist is likely to demur at the notion that his basic ideas pass all understanding.

The fact remains, however, that Spencer recognizes a certain mystery in the universe. His arguments for the existence of the Unknowable are indeed somewhat confused. Sometimes he gives the impression of accepting a Humian phenomenalism and of arguing that the modifications produced on our senses must be caused by something which transcends our knowledge. At other times he seems to have at the back of the mind a more or less Kantian line of thought, derived from Hamilton and Mansel. External things are phenomena in the sense that they can be known only in so far as they conform to the nature of human thought. Things-in-themselves or noumena cannot be known; but as the idea of the noumenon is correlative to that of the phenomenon, we cannot avoid postulating it.[65] Spencer also relies, however, on what he calls an all-important fact, namely that besides 'definite' consciousness 'there is also an *indefinite* consciousness which cannot be formulated'.[66] For example, we cannot have a definite consciousness of the finite without a concomitant indefinite consciousness of the infinite. And this line of argument leads to the assertion of the infinite Absolute as a positive reality of which we have a vague or indefinite consciousness. We cannot know *what* the Absolute is. But even though we deny each successive definite interpretation or picture of the Absolute which presents itself, 'there ever remains behind an element which passes into new shapes'.[67]

This line of argument appears to be intended seriously. And though it might be more convenient to turn Spencer into a complete positivist by dismissing the doctrine of the Unknowable as a patronizing concession to religious people, there does not seem to be any adequate justification for this summary dismissal. When Frederic Harrison, the positivist, exhorted Spencer to transform the philosophy of the Unknowable into the Comtist religion of humanity, Spencer turned a deaf ear. It is easy to poke fun at him for using a capital letter for the Unknowable, as though, as it has been said, he expected one to take off one's hat to it. But he seems to have been genuinely convinced that the world of science is the manifestation of a reality which transcends human knowledge. The doctrine of the Unknowable is unlikely to satisfy many religious people. But this is another question. As far as Spencer himself is concerned, he appears to have sincerely believed that the vague consciousness of an Absolute or Unconditioned is an uneliminable feature of human thought, and that it is, as it were, the heart of religion, the permanent element which survives the succession of different creeds and different metaphysical systems.

7. Needless to say, Spencer's philosophy contains a good deal of metaphysics. Indeed, it is difficult to think of any philosophy which does not. Is not phenomenalism a form of metaphysics? And when Spencer says, for example, that 'by reality we mean *persistence* in consciousness',[68] it is arguable that this is a metaphysical assertion. We might, of course, try to interpret it as being simply a definition or as a declaration about the ordinary use of words. But when we are told that 'persistence is our ultimate test of the real whether as existing under its unknown form or under the form known to us',[69] it is reasonable to classify this as a metaphysical assertion.

Obviously, Spencer cannot be described as a metaphysician if we mean by this a philosopher who undertakes to disclose the nature of ultimate reality. For in his view it cannot be disclosed. And though he is a metaphysician, to the extent of asserting the existence of the Unknowable, he then devotes himself to constructing a unified overall interpretation of the knowable, that is, of phenomena. But if we like to call this general interpretation 'descriptive metaphysics', we are, of course, free to do so.

In developing this interpretation Spencer adheres to the empiricist tradition. It is true that he is anxious to reconcile conflicting points of view. But when he is concerned with showing that his own philosophy can recognize truth in non-empiricist theories, his method of procedure is to give an empiricist explanation of the data on which the theories

are based. As has already been mentioned, he is quite prepared to admit that there are what can be called moral intuitions. For an individual may very well feel a quasi-instinctive approval or disapproval of certain types of action and
may 'see', as though intuitively and without any process of
reasoning, that such actions are right or wrong. But in
Spencer's opinion moral intuitions in this sense are 'the results of accumulated experiences of Utility, gradually organized and inherited'.[70] Whether there are such things as
inherited experiences of utility, is open to question. But in
any case it is abundantly clear that Spencer's way of showing
that there is truth in moral intuitionism is to give an empiricist explanation of the empirical data to which this theory
appeals.

Similarly, Spencer is prepared to admit that there is something which can be called an intuition of space, in the sense
that as far as the individual is concerned it is practically a
form independent of experience. But it by no means follows
that Spencer is trying to incorporate into his own philosophy
the Kantian doctrine of the *a priori*. What he does is to argue
that this theory is based on a real fact, but that this fact can
be explained in terms of the 'organized and consolidated experiences of all antecedent individuals who bequeathed to
him [a given subsequent individual] their slowly-developed
nervous organizations'.[71]

Though, however, we are not entitled to conclude from
Spencer's concern with reconciling conflicting points of view
that he throws empiricism overboard, he is, we can say, an
empiricist with a difference. For he does not simply tackle individual problems separately, as many empiricists are apt
to do. In his autobiography he speaks of his architectonic instinct, his love for system-building. And in point of fact his
philosophy was designed as a system: it did not simply become a system in the sense that different lines of investigation and reflection happened to converge towards the formation of an overall picture. Spencer's general principle of
interpretation, the so-called law of evolution, was conceived
at an early stage and then used as an instrument for the
unification of the sciences.

It can hardly be claimed that Spencer's architectonic instinct, his propensity for synthesis, was accompanied by an outstanding gift for careful analysis or for the exact statement of his meaning. But his weak health and the obstacles which he had to face in the fulfilment of his self-imposed mission did not in any case leave him the time or the energy for much more than he was able in fact to achieve. And though most readers probably find his writings extremely dull, his ambitions and pertinacious attempt to unify our knowledge of the world and of man, as well as our moral consciousness and social life, in the light of one all-pervading idea demands the tribute of our admiration. He has relapsed, as it were, into the Victorian era; and, as has already been remarked, in regard to living influence there is no comparison between Spencer and J. S. Mill. But though Spencer's philosophy may be covered with dust it deserves something better than the contemptuous attitude adopted by Nietzsche, who regarded it as a typical expression of the tame and limited mentality of the English middle class.

PART II

THE IDEALIST MOVEMENT IN GREAT BRITAIN

Chapter Six

THE BEGINNINGS OF THE MOVEMENT

Introductory historical remarks – Literary pioneers; Coleridge and Carlyle – Ferrier and the subject-object relation – John Grote's attack on phenomenalism and hedonism – The revival of interest in Greek philosophy and the rise of interest in Hegel; B. Jowett and J. H. Stirling.

1. In the second half of the nineteenth century idealism became the dominant philosophical movement in the British universities. It was not, of course, a question of subjective idealism. If this was anywhere to be found, it was a logical consequence of the phenomenalism associated with the names of Hume in the eighteenth century and J. S. Mill in the nineteenth century. For the empiricists who embraced phenomenalism tended to reduce both physical objects and minds to impressions or sensations, and then to reconstruct them with the aid of the principle of the association of ideas. They implied that, basically, we know only phenomena, in the sense of impressions, and that, if there are metaphenomenal realities, we cannot know them. The nineteenth-century idealists, however, were convinced that things-in-themselves, being expressions of the one spiritual reality which manifests itself in and through the human mind, are essentially intelligible, knowable. Subject and object are correlative because they are both rooted in one ultimate spiritual principle. It was thus a question of objective rather than subjective idealism.[1]

Nineteenth-century British idealism thus represented a revival of explicit metaphysics.[2] That which is the manifestation of Spirit can in principle be known by the human spirit. And the whole world is the manifestation of Spirit. Science is simply one level of knowledge, one aspect of the complete knowledge to which the mind tends, even if it cannot fully actualize its ideal. Metaphysical philosophy endeavours to complete the synthesis.

The idealist metaphysics was thus a spiritualist metaphysics, in the sense that for it ultimate reality was in some sense spiritual. And it follows that idealism was sharply opposed to materialism. In so far indeed as the phenomenalists tried to go beyond the dispute between materialism and spiritualism by reducing both minds and physical objects to phenomena which cannot properly be described either as spiritual or as material, we cannot legitimately call them materialists. But these phenomena were evidently something very different from the one spiritual reality of the idealists. And in any case we have seen that on the more positivistic side of the empiricist movement there appeared an at least methodological materialism, the so-called scientific materialism, a line of thought for which the idealists had no sympathy.

With its emphasis on the spiritual character of ultimate reality and on the relation between the finite spirit and infinite Spirit idealism stood for a religious outlook as against materialistic positivism and the tendency of empiricism in general to by-pass religious problems or to leave room, at best, for a somewhat vague agnosticism. Indeed, a good deal of the popularity of idealism was due to the conviction that it stood firmly on the side of religion. To be sure, with Bradley, the greatest of the British idealists, the concept of God passed into that of the Absolute, and religion was depicted as a level of consciousness which is surpassed in metaphysical philosophy, while McTaggart, the Cambridge idealist, was an atheist. But with the earlier idealists the religious motive was much in evidence, and idealism seemed to be the natural home of those who were concerned with preserving a religious outlook in face of the threatening incursions of agnostics, positivists and materialists.[3] Further, after Bradley and Bosanquet idealism turned from absolute to personal idealism and was once again favourable to Christian theism, though by that time the impetus of the movement was already spent.

It would, however, be a mistake to conclude that British idealism in the nineteenth century represented simply a retreat from the practical concerns of Bentham and Mill into the metaphysics of the Absolute. For it had a part to play in the development of social philosophy. Generally speaking, the ethical theory of the idealists emphasized the idea of self-realization, of the perfecting of the human personality as an organic whole, an idea which had more in common with Aristotelianism than with Benthamism. And they looked on the function of the State as that of creating the conditions under which individuals could develop their potentialities as persons. As the idealists tended to interpret the creation of such conditions as a removal of hindrances, they could, of course, agree with the utilitarians that the State should interfere as little as possible with the liberty of the individual. They had no wish to replace freedom by servitude. But as they interpreted freedom as freedom to actualize the potentialities of the human personality, and as the removal of hindrances to freedom in this sense involved in their opinion a good deal of social legislation, they were prepared to advocate a measure of State-activity which went beyond anything contemplated by the more enthusiastic adherents of the policy of *laissez faire*. We can say, therefore, that in the latter part of the nineteenth century idealist social and political theory was more in tune with the perceived needs of the time than the position defended by Herbert Spencer. Benthamism or philosophical radicalism doubtless performed a useful task in the first part of the century. But the revised liberalism expounded by the idealists later in the century was by no means 'reactionary'. It looked forward rather than backward.

The foregoing remarks may appear to suggest that nineteenth-century idealism in Great Britain was simply a native reaction to empiricism and positivism and to *laissez faire* economic and political theory. In point of fact, however, German thought, especially that of Kant and Hegel successively, exercised an important influence on the development of British idealism. Some writers, notably J. H. Muirhead,[4] have maintained that the British idealists of the nineteenth century were the inheritors of a Platonic tradition which had manifested itself in the thought of the Cambridge Platonists in the seventeenth century and in the philosophy of Berkeley in the eighteenth century. But though it is useful to draw attention to the fact that British philosophy has not been exclusively empiricist in character, it would be difficult to show that nineteenth-century idealism can legitimately be considered as an organic development of a native Platonic tradition. The influence of German thought, particularly of Kant and Hegel,[5] cannot be dismissed as a purely accidental factor. It is indeed true that no British idealist of note can be described as being in the ordinary sense a disciple of either Kant or Hegel. Bradley, for example, was an original thinker. But it by no means follows that the stimulative influence of German thought was a negligible factor in the development of British idealism.

A limited knowledge of Kant was provided for English readers even during the philosopher's lifetime. In 1795 a disciple of Kant, F. A. Nitzsch, gave some lectures on the critical philosophy at London, and in the following year he published a small work on the subject. In 1797 J. Richardson published his translation of *Principles of Critical Philosophy* by J. J. Beck, and in 1798 A. F. M. Willich published *Elements of Critical Philosophy*. Richardson's translation of Kant's *Metaphysic of Morals* appeared in 1799; but the first translation of the *Critique of Pure Reason*, by F. Haywood, did not appear until 1838. And the serious studies of Kant, such as E. Caird's great work, *A Critical Account of the Philosophy of Kant* (1877), did not appear until a considerably later date. Meanwhile the influence of the German philosopher, together with a host of other influences, was felt by the poet Coleridge, whose ideas will be discussed presently, and in a more obvious way by Sir William Hamilton, though the element of Kantianism in Hamilton's thought was most conspicuous in his doctrine about the limits of human knowledge and in his consequent agnosticism in regard to the nature of ultimate reality.

Among the British idealists proper, Kant's influence may be said to have been felt particularly by T. H. Green and E. Caird. But it was mixed with the influence of Hegel. More accurately, Kant was seen as looking forward to Hegel or was read, as it has been put, through Hegelian spectacles. Indeed, in J. H. Stirling's *The Secret of Hegel* (1865) the view was explicitly defended that the philosophy of Kant, if properly understood and evaluated, leads straight to Hegelianism. Hence, though we can say with truth that the influence of Hegel is more obvious in the absolute idealism of Bradley and Bosanquet than in the philosophy of Green, there is no question of suggesting that we can divide up the British idealists into Kantians and Hegelians. Some pioneers apart, the influence of Hegel was felt from the beginning of the movement. And it is thus not altogether unreasonable to describe British idealism, as is often done, as a Neo-Hegelian movement, provided at least that it is understood that it was a question of receiving stimulus from Hegel rather than of following him in the relation of pupil to master.

In its earlier phases the British idealist movement was characterized by a marked concentration on the subject-object relationship. In this sense idealism can be said to have had an epistemological foundation, inasmuch as the subject-object relationship is basic in knowledge. The metaphysics of the Absolute was not indeed absent. For subject and object were regarded as grounded in and manifesting one ultimate spiritual reality. But the point of departure affected the metaphysics in an important way. For the emphasis placed in the first instance on the finite subject militated against any temptation to interpret the Absolute in such a manner as to entail the conclusion that the finite is no more than its 'unreal' appearance. In other words, the earlier idealists tended to interpret the Absolute in a more or less theistic, or at any rate in a panentheistic, sense, the monistic aspect of metaphysical idealism remaining in the background. And this, of course, made it easier to represent idealism as an intellectual support for traditional religion.

Gradually, however, the idea of the all-comprehensive organic totality came more and more into the foreground. Thus with Bradley the self was depicted as a mere 'appearance' of the Absolute, as something which is not fully real when regarded in its *prima facie* independence. And this explicit metaphysics of the Absolute was understandably accompanied by a greater emphasis on the State in the field of social philosophy. While Herbert Spencer on the one hand was engaged in asserting an opposition between the interests of the free individual and those of the State, the idealists were engaged in representing man as achieving true freedom through his participation in the life of the totality.

In other words, we can see in the idealist movement up to Bradley and Bosanquet the increasing influence of Hegelianism. As has already been indicated, the influence of Kant was never unmixed. For the critical philosophy was seen as looking forward to metaphysical idealism. But if we make allowances for this fact and also for the fact that there were very considerable differences between Bradley's theory of the Absolute and that of Hegel, we can say that the change from emphasis on the subject-object relationship to emphasis on the idea of the organic totality represented a growing predominance of the stimulative influence of Hegelianism over that of the critical philosophy of Kant.

In the final phase of the idealist movement emphasis on the finite self became once again prominent, though it was a question this time of the active self, the human person, rather than of the epistemological subject. And this personal idealism was accompanied by a reapproximation to theism, except in the notable case of McTaggart, who depicted the Absolute as the system of finite selves. But though this phase of personal idealism is of some interest, inasmuch as it represents the finite self's resistance to being swallowed up in some impersonal Absolute, it belongs to a period when idealism in Britain was giving way to a new current of thought, associated with the names of G. E. Moore, Bertrand Russell, and, subsequently, Ludwig Wittgenstein.

2. As far as the general educated public was concerned, the influence of German thought first made itself felt in Great Britain through the writings of poets and literary figures such as Coleridge and Carlyle.

(i) Samuel Taylor Coleridge (1772–1834) seems to have made his first acquaintance with philosophy through the writings of Neo-Platonists, when he was a schoolboy at Christ's Hospital. This early attraction for the mystical philosophy of Plotinus was succeeded, however, by a Voltairean phase, during which he was for a short time a sceptic in regard to religion. Then at Cambridge Coleridge developed a perhaps somewhat surprising enthusiasm for David Hartley and his associationist psychology.[6] Indeed, Coleridge claimed to be more consistent than Hartley had been. For whereas Hartley, while maintaining that psychical processes depend on and are correlated with vibrations in the brain, had not asserted the corporeality of thought, Coleridge wrote to Southey in 1794 that he believed thought to be corporeal, that is, motion. At the same time Coleridge combined his enthusiasm for Hartley with religious faith.[7] And he came to think that the scientific understanding is inadequate as a key to reality, and to speak of the role of intuition and the importance of moral experience. Later on he was to declare that Hartley's system, in so far as it differs from that of Aristotle, is untenable.[8]

Coleridge's distinction between the scientific understanding and the higher reason or, as the Germans would put it, between *Verstand* and *Vernunft* was one expression of his revolt against the spirit of the eighteenth-century Enlightenment. He did not, of course, mean to imply that the scientific and critical understanding should be rejected in the name of a higher and intuitive reason. His point was rather that the former is not an omnicompetent instrument in the interpretation of reality, but that it needs to be supplemented and balanced by the latter, namely the intuitive reason. It can hardly be claimed that Coleridge made his distinction between understanding and reason crystal clear. But the general line of his thought is sufficiently plain. In *Aids to Reflection* (1825) he describes the understanding as the faculty which judges according to sense. Its appropriate sphere is the sensible world, and it reflects and generalizes on the basis of sense-experience. Reason, however, is the vehicle of ideas which are presupposed by all experience, and in this sense it predetermines and governs experience. It also perceives truths which are incapable of verification in sense-experience, and it intuitively apprehends spiritual realities. Further, Coleridge identifies it with the practical reason, which comprises the will and the moral aspect of the human personality. J. S. Mill is thus perfectly justified in saying in his famous essay on Coleridge that the poet dissents from the 'Lockian' view that all knowledge consists of generalizations from experience, and that he claims for the reason, as distinct from the understanding, the power to perceive by direct intuition realities and truths which transcend the reach of the senses.[9]

In his development of this distinction Coleridge received stimulus from the writings of Kant, which he began to study shortly after his visit to Germany in 1798–9.[10] But he tends to speak as though Kant not only limited the scope of the understanding to knowledge of phenomenal reality but also envisaged an intuitive apprehension of spiritual realities by means of the reason, whereas in point of fact in attributing this power to the reason, identified moreover with the practical reason, Coleridge obviously parts company with the German philosopher. He is on firmer ground when he claims an affinity with Jacobi[11] in maintaining that the relation between reason and spiritual realities is analogous to that between the eye and material objects.

Nobody, however, would wish to maintain that Coleridge was a Kantian. It was a question of stimulus, not of discipleship. And though he recognized his debt to German thinkers, especially to Kant, it is clear that he regarded his own philosophy as being fundamentally Platonic in inspiration. In *Aids to Reflection* he asserted that every man is born either a Platonist or an Aristotelian. Aristotle, the great master of understanding, was unduly earthbound. He 'began with the sensual, and never received that which was above the senses, but by necessity, but as the only remaining hypothesis. . . .'[12] That is to say, Aristotle postulated spiritual reality only as a last resort, when forced to do so by the need of explaining physical phenomena. Plato, however, sought the supersensible reality which is revealed to us through reason and our moral will. As for Kant, Coleridge sometimes describes him as belonging spiritually to the ranks of the Aristotelians, while at other times he emphasizes the metaphysical aspects of Kant's thought and finds in him an approach to Platonism. In other words, Coleridge welcomes Kant's restriction of the reach of understanding to phenomenal reality and then tends to interpret his doctrine of reason in the light of Platonism, which is itself interpreted in the light of the philosophy of Plotinus.

These remarks should not be understood as implying any contempt for Nature on Coleridge's part. On the contrary, he disliked Fichte's 'boastful and hyperstoic hostility to Nature, as lifeless, godless, and altogether unholy'.[13] And he expressed a warm sympathy with Schelling's philosophy of Nature, as also with his system of transcendental idealism, in which 'I first found a genial coincidence with much that I had toiled out for myself, and a powerful assistance in what I had yet to do'.[14] Coleridge is indeed at pains to reject the charge of plagiarism, and he maintains that both he and Schelling have drunk at the same springs, the writings of Kant, the philosophy of Giordano Bruno and the speculations of Jakob Boehme. However, the influence of Schelling seems to be sufficiently evident in the line of thought which we can now briefly outline.

'All knowledge rests on the coincidence of an object with a subject.'[15] But though subject and object are united in the act of knowledge, we can ask which has the priority. Are we to start with the object and try to add to it the subject? Or are we to start with the subject and try to find a passage to the object? In other words, are we to take Nature as prior and try to add to it thought or mind, or are we to take thought as prior and try to deduce Nature? Coleridge answers that we can do neither the one nor the other. The ultimate principle is to be sought in the identity of subject and object.

Where is this identity to be found? 'Only in the self-consciousness of a spirit is there the required identity of object and of representation.'[16] But if the spirit is originally the identity of subject and object, it must in some sense dissolve this identity in order to become conscious of itself as object. Self-consciousness, therefore, cannot arise except through an act of will, and 'freedom must be assumed as a *ground* of philosophy, and can never be deduced from it'.[17] The spirit becomes a subject knowing itself as object only through 'the act of constructing itself objectively to itself'.[18]

This sounds as though Coleridge begins by asking the sort of question which Schelling asks, then supplies Schelling's answer, namely that we must postulate an original identity of subject and object, and finally switches to Fichte's idea of the ego as constituting itself as subject and object by an original act. But Coleridge has no intention of stopping short with the ego as his ultimate principle, especially if we mean by this the finite ego. Indeed, he ridicules the 'egoism' of Fichte.[19] Instead, he insists that to arrive at the absolute identity of subject and object, of the ideal and the real, as the ultimate principle not only of human knowledge but also of all existence we must 'elevate our conception to the absolute self, the great eternal I am'.[20] Coleridge criticizes Descartes's *Cogito, ergo sum* and refers to Kant's distinction between the empirical and the transcendental ego. But he then tends to speak as though the transcendental ego were the absolute *I am that I am* of *Exodus*[21] and the God in whom the finite self is called to lose and find itself at the same time.

All this is obviously cloudy and imprecise. But it is at any rate clear that Coleridge opposes a spiritualistic interpretation of the human self to materialism and phenomenalism. And it is clearly this interpretation of the self which in his view provides the basis for the claim that reason can apprehend supersensible reality. Indeed, in his essay on faith Coleridge describes faith as fidelity to our own being in so far as our being is not and cannot become an object of sense-experience. Our moral vocation demands the subordination of appetite and will to reason; and it is reason which apprehends God as the identity of will and reason, as the ground of our existence, and as the infinite expression of the ideal which we are seeking as moral beings. In other words, Coleridge's outlook was essentially religious, and he tried to bring together philosophy and religion. He may have tended, as Mill notes, to turn Christian mysteries into philosophical truths. But an important element in the mission of idealism, as conceived by its more religious adherents, was precisely that of giving a metaphysical basis to a Christian tradition which seemed to be signally lacking in any philosophical backbone.

In the field of social and political theory Coleridge was conservative in the sense that he was opposed to the iconoclasm of the radicals and desired the preservation and actualization of the values inherent in traditional institutions. At one time he was indeed attracted, like Wordsworth and Southey, by the ideas which inspired the French Revolution. But he came to abandon the radicalism of his youth, though his subsequent conservatism arose not from any hatred of change as such but from a belief that the institutions created by the national spirit in the course of its history embodied real values which men should endeavour to realize. As Mill put it, Bentham demanded 'the extinction of the institutions and creeds which had hitherto existed', whereas Coleridge demanded 'that they be made a reality'.[22]

(ii) Thomas Carlyle (1795–1881) belonged to a later generation than that of Coleridge; but he was considerably less systematic in the presentation of his philosophical ideas, and there are doubtless very many people today who find the turbulent prose of *Sartor Resartus* quite unreadable. However, he was one of the channels through which German thought and literature were brought to the attention of the British public.

Carlyle's first reaction to German philosophy was not exactly favourable, and he made fun both of Kant's obscurity and of the pretensions of Coleridge. But in his hatred of materialism, hedonism and utilitarianism he came to see in Kant the brilliant foe of the Enlightenment and of its derivative movements. Thus in his essay on the *State of German Literature* (1827) he praised Kant for starting from within and proceeding outwards instead of pursuing the Lockian path of starting with sense-experience and trying to build a philosophy on this basis. The Kantian, according to Carlyle, sees that fundamental truths are apprehended by intuition in man's inmost nature. In other words, Carlyle ranges himself with Coleridge in using Kant's restriction of the power and scope of the understanding as a foundation for asserting the power of reason to apprehend intuitively basic truths and spiritual realities.

Characteristic of Carlyle was his vivid sense of the mystery of the world and of its nature as an appearance of, or veil before, supersensible reality. In the *State of German Literature* he asserted that the ultimate aim of philosophy is to interpret phenomena or appearances, to proceed from the symbol to the reality symbolized. And this point of view found expression in *Sartor Resartus*,[23] under the label of the philosophy of clothes. It can be applied to man, the microcosm. 'To the eye of vulgar Logic what is man? An omnivorous Biped that wears Breeches. To the eye of Pure Reason what is he? A Soul, a Spirit, and divine Apparition. . . . Deep-hidden is he under that strange Garment.'[24] And the analogy is applicable also to the macrocosm, the world in general. For the world is, as Goethe divined, *'the living visible Garment of God'*.[25]

In the *State of German Literature* Carlyle explicitly connects his philosophy of symbolism with Fichte, who is regarded as having interpreted the visible universe as the symbol and sensible manifestation of an all-pervading divine Idea, the apprehension of which is the condition of all genuine virtue and freedom. And there is indeed no great difficulty in understanding Carlyle's predilection for Fichte. For seeing, as he does, human life and history as a constant struggle between light and darkness, God and the devil, a struggle in which every man is called to play a part and to make an all-important choice, he naturally feels an attraction for Fichte's moral earnestness and for his view of Nature as being simply the field in which man works out his moral vocation, the field of obstacles, so to speak, which man has to overcome in the process of attaining his ideal end.

This outlook helps to explain Carlyle's concern with the hero, as manifested in his 1840 lectures *On Heroes, Hero-Worship and the Heroic in History*. Over against materialism and what he calls profit-and-loss philosophy he sets the ideas of heroism, moral vocation and personal loyalty. Indeed, he is prepared to assert that 'the life-breath of all society [is] but an effluence of Hero-worship, submissive admiration for the truly great. Society is founded on Hero-worship.'[26] Again, 'Universal History, the history of what man has accomplished in the world, is at bottom the History of the Great Men who have worked here'.[27]

In his insistence on the role of history's 'great men' Carlyle resembles Hegel[28] and anticipates Nietzsche in some aspects, though hero-worship in the political field is an idea which we are likely to regard with mixed feelings nowadays. However, it is clear that what especially attracted Carlyle in his heroes was their earnestness and self-devotion and their freedom from a morality based on the hedonistic calculus. For example, while aware of Rousseau's shortcomings and faults of character, which made him 'a sadly *contracted* Hero',[29] Carlyle insists that this unlikely candidate for the title possessed 'the first and chief characteristic of a Hero: he is heartily *in earnest*. In earnest, if ever man was; as none of these French Philosophes were.'[30]

3. In spite of the fact that both men delivered lectures it would be idle to look either to Coleridge or Carlyle for a systematic development of idealism. For a pioneer in this field we have to turn rather to James Frederick Ferrier (1808–64), who occupied the chair of moral philosophy in the University of St. Andrews from 1845 until the year of his death, and who made a great point of systematic procedure in philosophy.

In 1838–9 Ferrier contributed a series of articles to *Blackwood's Magazine*, which was published with the title *Introduction to the Philosophy of Consciousness*. In 1854 he published his main work, *The Institutes of Metaphysics*, which is remarkable for the way in which the author develops his doctrine in a series of propositions, each of which, with the exception of the first fundamental proposition, is supposed to follow with logical rigour from its predecessor. In 1856 he published *Scottish Philosophy*, while his *Lectures on Greek Philosophy and Other Philosophical Remains* appeared posthumously in 1866.

Ferrier claimed that his philosophy was Scottish to the core. But this does not mean that he regarded himself as an adherent of the Scottish philosophy of common sense. On the contrary, he vigorously attacked Reid and his followers. In the first place a philosopher should not appeal to a multitude of undemonstrated principles, but should employ the deductive method which is essential to metaphysics and not an optional expository device. In the second place the Scottish philosophers of common sense tended to confuse metaphysics with psychology, trying to solve philosophical problems by psychological reflections, instead of by rigorous logical reasoning.[31] As for Sir William Hamilton, his agnosticism about the Absolute was quite misplaced.

When Ferrier said that his philosophy was Scottish to the core, he meant that he had not borrowed it from the Germans. Though his system was not uncommonly regarded as Hegelian, he claimed that he had never been able to understand Hegel.[32] Indeed, he expressed a doubt whether the German philosopher had been able to understand himself.

In any case Hegel starts with Being, whereas his own system took knowledge as its point of departure.[33]

Ferrier's first move is to look for the absolute starting-point of metaphysics in a proposition which states the one invariable and essential feature in all knowledge, and which cannot be denied without contradiction. This is that 'along with whatever any intelligence knows, it must, as the ground or condition of its knowledge, have some cognizance of itself'.[34] The object of knowledge is a variable factor. But I cannot know anything without knowing that I know. To deny this is to talk nonsense. To assert it is to admit that there is no knowledge without self-consciousness, without some awareness of the self.

It follows from this, Ferrier argues, that nothing can be known except in relation to a subject, a self. In other words, the object of knowledge is essentially object-for-a-subject. And Ferrier draws the conclusion that nothing is thinkable except in relation to a subject. From this it follows that the material universe is unthinkable as existing without any relation to subject.

The critic might be inclined to comment that Ferrier is really saying no more than that I cannot think of the universe without thinking of it, or know it without knowing it. If anything more is being said, if, in particular, a transition is being made from an epistemological point to the assertion of an ontological relation, a solipsistic conclusion seems to follow, namely that the existence of the material world is unthinkable except as dependent on myself as subject.

Ferrier, however, wishes to maintain two propositions. First, we cannot think of the universe as 'dissociated from *every* me. You cannot perform the abstraction.'[35] Secondly, each of us can dissociate the universe from himself in particular. And from these two propositions it follows that though 'each of us can unyoke the universe (so to speak) from himself, he can do this only by yoking it on, in thought, to some other self'.[36] This is an essential move for Ferrier to make, because he wishes to argue that the universe is unthinkable except as existing in synthesis with the divine mind.

The first section of the *Institutes of Metaphysics* thus purports to show that the absolute element in knowledge is the synthesis of subject and object. But Ferrier does not proceed at once to his final conclusion. Instead, he devotes the second section to 'agnoiology', the theory of 'ignorance'. We can be said to be in a state of nescience in regard to the contradictions of necessarily true propositions. But this is obviously no sign of imperfection in our minds. As for ignorance, we cannot properly be said to be ignorant except of what is in principle knowable. Hence we cannot be ignorant of, for example, matter 'in itself' (without relation to a subject). For this is unthinkable and unknowable. Further, if we assume that we are ignorant of the Absolute, it follows that the Absolute is knowable. Hence Hamilton's agnosticism is untenable.

But what is the Absolute or, as Ferrier expresses it, Absolute Existence? It cannot be either matter *per se* or mind *per se*. For neither is thinkable. It must be, therefore, the synthesis of subject and object. There is, however, only one such synthesis which is necessary. For though the existence of a universe is not conceivable except as object-for-a-subject, we have already seen that the universe can be unyoked or dissociated from any given finite subject. Hence 'there is one, but only one, Absolute Existence which is strictly *necessary*; and that existence is a supreme, and infinite, and everlasting Mind in synthesis with all things'.[37]

By way of comment it is not inappropriate to draw attention to the rather obvious fact, that the statement 'there can be no subject without an object and no object without a subject' is analytically true, if the terms 'subject' and 'object' are understood in their epistemological senses. It is also true that no material thing can be conceived except as object-for-a-subject, if we mean by this that no material thing can be conceived except by constituting it ('intentionally', as the phenomenologists would say) as an object. But this does not seem to amount to much more than saying that a thing cannot be thought of unless it is thought of. And from this it does not follow that a thing cannot exist unless it is thought of. Ferrier could retort, of course, that we cannot intelligibly speak of a thing as existing independently of being conceived. For by the mere fact that we speak of it, we conceive it. If I try to think of material thing X as existing outside the subject-object relationship, my effort is defeated by the very fact that I am thinking of X. In this case, however, the thing seems to be irrevocably yoked, as Ferrier puts it, to me as subject. And how can I possibly unyoke it? If I try to unyoke it from myself and yoke it to some other subject, whether finite or infinite, does not this other subject, on Ferrier's premisses, become object-for-a-subject, the subject in question being myself?

It is not my intention to suggest that in point of fact the material universe could exist independently of God. The point is rather that the conclusion that it cannot so exist does not really follow from Ferrier's epistemological premisses. The conclusion which does seem to follow is solipsism. And Ferrier escapes from this conclusion only by an appeal to common sense and to our knowledge of historical facts. That is to say, as I cannot seriously suppose that the material universe is simply object for me as subject, I must postulate an eternal, infinite subject, God. But on Ferrier's premisses it appears to follow that God Himself, as thought by me, must be object-for-a-subject, the subject being myself.

4. Among Ferrier's contemporaries John Grote (1813–66), brother of the historian, deserves mention. Professor of moral philosophy at Cambridge from 1855 until 1866, he published the first part of *Exploratio philosophica* in 1865. The second part appeared posthumously in 1900. His *Examination of Utilitarian Philosophy* (1870) and *A Treatise on the Moral Ideals* (1876) were also published after his death. It is true that nowadays Grote is even less known than Ferrier; but his criticism of phenomenalism and of hedonistic utilitarianism is not without value.

Grote's critique of phenomenalism can be illustrated in this way. One of the main features of positivistic phenomenalism is that it first reduces the object of knowledge to a series of phenomena and then proceeds to apply a similar reductive analysis to the subject, the ego or self. In effect, therefore, the subject is reduced to its own object. Or, if preferred, subject and object are both reduced to phenomena which are assumed to be the basic reality, the ultimate entities out of which selves and physical objects can be reconstructed by thought. But this reduction of the self or subject can be shown to be untenable. In the first place talk about phenomena is not intelligible except in relation to consciousness. For that which appears, appears to a subject, within the ambit, so to speak, of consciousness. We cannot go behind consciousness; and analysis of it shows that it essentially involves the subject-object relationship. In primitive consciousness subject and object are virtually or confusedly present; and they are progressively distinguished in the development of consciousness until there arises an explicit awareness of a world of objects on the one hand and of a self or subject on the other, this awareness of the self being developed especially by the experience of effort. As, therefore, the subject is present from the start as one of the essential poles even in primitive consciousness, it cannot be legitimately reduced to the object, to phenomena. At the same time reflection on the essential structure of consciousness shows that we are not presented with a self-enclosed ego from which we have to find a bridge, as in the philosophy of Descartes, to the non-ego.

In the second place it is important to notice the way in which the phenomenalists overlook the active role of the subject in the construction of an articulated universe. The subject or self is characterized by teleological activity; it has ends. And in pursuit of its ends it constructs unities among phenomena, not in the sense that it imposes *a priori* forms on a mass of unrelated, chaotic data,[38] but rather in the sense that it builds up its world in an experimental way by a process of auto-correction. On this count too, therefore, namely the active role of the self in the construction of the world of objects, it is clear that it cannot be reduced to a series of phenomena, its own immediate objects.[39]

In the sphere of moral philosophy Grote was strongly opposed to both egoistic hedonism and utilitarianism. He did not object to them for taking into account man's sensibility and his search for happiness. On the contrary, Grote himself admitted the science of happiness, 'eudaemonics' as he called it, as a part of ethics. What he objected to was an exclusive concentration on the search for pleasure and a consequent neglect of other aspects of the human personality, especially man's capacity for conceiving and pursuing ideals which transcend the search for pleasure and may demand self-sacrifice. Hence to 'eudaemonics' he added 'aretaics', the science of virtue. And he insisted that the moral task is to achieve the union of the lower and higher elements of man's nature in the service of moral ideals. For our actions become moral when they pass from the sphere of the merely spontaneous, as in following the impulse to pleasure, into the sphere of the deliberate and voluntary, impulse supplying the dynamic element and intellectually-conceived principles and ideals the regulative element.

Obviously, Grote's attack on utilitarianism as neglecting the higher aspects of man through an exclusive concentration on the search for pleasure was more applicable to Benthamite hedonism than to J. S. Mill's revised version of utilitarianism. But in any case it was a question not so much of suggesting that a utilitarian philosopher could not have moral ideals as of maintaining that the utilitarian ethics could not provide an adequate theoretical framework for such ideals. Grote's main point was that this could be provided only by a radical revision of the concept of man which Bentham inherited from writers such as Helvétius. Hedonism, in Grote's opinion, could not account for the consciousness of obligation. For this arises when man, conceiving moral ideals, feels the need of subordinating his lower to his higher nature.

5. We can reasonably see a connection between the idealists' perception of the inadequacy of the Benthamite view of human nature and the revival of interest in Greek philosophy which occurred in the universities, especially at Oxford, in the course of the nineteenth century. We have already seen that Coleridge regarded his philosophy as being fundamentally Platonic in inspiration and character. But the renewal of Platonic studies at Oxford can be associated in particular with the name of Benjamin Jowett (1817–93), who became a Fellow of Balliol College in 1838 and occupied the chair of Greek from 1855 to 1893. The defects in his famous translation of Plato's *Dialogues* are irrelevant here. The point is that in the course of his long teaching career he contributed powerfully to a revival of interest in Greek thought. And it is not without significance that T. H. Green

and E. Caird, both prominent in the idealist movement, were at one time his pupils. Interest in Plato and Aristotle naturally tended to turn their minds away from hedonism and utilitarianism towards an ethics of self-perfection, based on a theory of human nature within a metaphysical framework.

The revival of interest in Greek thought was accompanied by a growing appreciation of German idealist philosophy. Jowett himself was interested in the latter, particularly in the thought of Hegel;[40] and he helped to stimulate the study of German idealism at Oxford. The first large-scale attempt, however, to elucidate what Ferrier had considered to be the scarcely intelligible profundities of Hegel was made by the Scotsman, James Hutchison Stirling (1820–1909), in his two-volume work *The Secret of Hegel*, which appeared in 1865.[41]

Stirling developed an enthusiasm for Hegel during a visit to Germany, especially during a stay at Heidelberg in 1856; and the result was *The Secret of Hegel*. In spite of the comment that if the author knew the secret of Hegel, he kept it successfully to himself, the book marked the beginning of the serious study of Hegelianism in Great Britain. In Stirling's view Hume's philosophy was the culmination of the Enlightenment, while Kant,[42] who took over what was valuable in Hume's thought and used it in the development of a new line of reflection, fulfilled and at the same time overcame and transcended the Enlightenment. While, however, Kant laid the foundations of idealism, it was Hegel who built and completed the edifice. And to understand the secret of Hegel is to understand how he made explicit the doctrine of the concrete universal, which was implicit in the critical philosophy of Kant.

It is noteworthy that Stirling regarded Hegel not only as standing to modern philosophy in the relation in which Aristotle stood to preceding Greek thought but also as the great intellectual champion of the Christian religion. He doubtless attributed to Hegel too high a degree of theological orthodoxy; but his attitude serves to illustrate the religious interest which characterized the idealist movement before Bradley. According to Stirling, Hegel was concerned with proving, among other things, the immortality of the soul. And though there is little evidence that Hegel felt much interest in this matter, Stirling's interpretation can be seen as representing the emphasis placed by the earlier idealists on the finite spiritual self, an emphasis which harmonized with their tendency to retain a more or less theistic outlook.

Chapter Seven

THE DEVELOPMENT OF IDEALISM

T. H. Green's attitude to British empiricism and to German thought – Green's doctrine of the eternal subject, with some critical comments – The ethical and political theory of Green – E. Caird and the unity underlying the distinction between subject and object – J. Caird and the philosophy of religion – W. Wallace and D. G. Ritchie.

1. Philosophers are not infrequently more convincing when they are engaged in criticizing the views of other philosophers than when they are expounding their own doctrines. And this perhaps somewhat cynical remark seems to be applicable to Thomas Hill Green (1836–82), Fellow of Balliol College, Oxford, and White's professor of moral philosophy in that university from 1878 to the year of his death. In his *Introductions to Hume's Treatise of Human Nature*,[1] which he published in 1874 for the Green and Grose edition of Hume, he made an impressive broadside attack on British empiricism. But his own idealist system is no less open to criticism than the views against which he raised objections.

From Locke onwards, according to Green, empiricists have assumed that it is the philosopher's business to reduce our knowledge to its primitive elements, to the original data, and then to reconstruct the world of ordinary experience out of these atomic data. Apart, however, from the fact that no satisfactory explanation has ever been offered of the way in which the mind can go behind the subject-object relationship and discover the primitive data out of which both minds and physical objects are supposed to be constructed, the empiricist programme lands us in an impasse. On the one hand, to construct the world of minds and physical objects the mind has to relate the primitive atomic data, discrete phenomena. In other words, it has to exercise activity. On the other hand, the mind's activity is inexplicable on empiricist principles. For it is itself reduced to a series of phenomena. And how can it construct itself? Further, though empiricism professes to account for human knowledge, it does not in fact do anything of the kind. For the world of ordinary experience is interpreted as a mental construction out of discrete impressions; and we have no way of knowing that the construction represents objective reality at all. In other words, a consistent empiricism leads inevitably to scepticism.

Hume himself, as Green sees him, was an outstanding thinker who discarded compromise and carried the principles of empiricism to their logical conclusion. 'Adopting the premisses and method of Locke, he cleared them of all illogical adaptations to popular belief, and experimented with them on the basis of professed knowledge. . . . As the result of the experiment, the method, which began with professing to explain knowledge, showed knowledge to be impossible.'[2] 'Hume himself was perfectly cognizant of this result, but his successors in England and Scotland would seem so far to have been unable to look it in the face.'[3]

Some philosophers after Hume, and here Green is evidently referring to the Scottish philosophers of common sense, have thrust their heads back into the thicket of uncriticized belief. Others have gone on developing Hume's theory of the association of ideas, apparently oblivious of the fact that Hume himself had shown the insufficiency of the principle of association to account for anything more than natural or quasi-instinctive belief.[4] In other words, Hume represented both the culmination and the bankruptcy of empiricism. And the torch of inquiry 'was transferred to a more vigorous line in Germany'.[5]

Kant, that is to say, was the spiritual successor of Hume. 'Thus the *Treatise of Human Nature* and the *Critique of Pure Reason*, taken together, form the real bridge between the old world of philosophy and the new. They are the essential "Propaedeutik" without which no one is a qualified student of modern philosophy.'[6] It does not follow, however, that we can remain in the philosophy of Kant. For Kant looks forward to Hegel or at any rate to something resembling Hegelianism. Green agrees with Stirling that Hegel developed the philosophy of Kant in the right direction; but he is not prepared to say that Hegel's system as it stands is satisfactory. It is all very well for the Sundays of speculation, as Green puts it; but it is more difficult to accept on the weekdays of ordinary thought. There is need for reconciling the judgments of speculative philosophy with our ordinary judgments about matters of fact and with the sciences. Hegelianism, however, if taken as it stands, cannot perform this task of synthesizing different tendencies and points of view in contemporary thought. The work has to be done over again.

In point of fact the name of Hegel does not loom large in the writings of Green. The name of Kant is far more prominent. But Green maintained that by reading Hume in the light of Leibniz and Leibniz in the light of Hume, Kant was able to free himself from their respective presuppositions. And we can justifiably say that though Green derived a great deal of stimulus from Kant, he read him in the light of his conviction that the critical philosophy needed some such development, though not precisely the same, as that which it actually received at the hands of the German metaphysical idealists, and of Hegel in particular.

2. In the introduction to his *Prolegomena to Ethics*, which was published posthumously in 1883, Green refers to the temptation to treat ethics as though it were a branch of natural science. This temptation is indeed understandable. For growth in historical knowledge and the development of theories of evolution suggest the possibility of giving a purely naturalistic and genetic explanation of the phenomena of the moral life. But what becomes then of ethics considered as a normative science? The answer is that the philosopher who 'has the courage of his principles, having reduced the speculative part of them [our ethical systems] to a natural science, must abolish the practical or preceptive part altogether'.[7] The fact, however, that the reduction of ethics to a branch of natural science involves the abolition of ethics as a normative science should make us reconsider the presuppositions or conditions of moral knowledge and activity. Is man merely a child of Nature? Or is there in him a spiritual principle which makes knowledge possible, whether it be knowledge of Nature or moral knowledge?

Green thus finds it necessary to start his inquiry into morals with a metaphysics of knowledge. And he argues in the first place that even if we were to decide in favour of the materialists all those questions about particular facts which have formed the subject of debate between them and the spiritualists, the possibility of our explaining the facts at all still remain to be accounted for. 'We shall still be logically bound to admit that in a man who can know a Nature—for whom there is a "cosmos of experience"—there is a principle which is not natural and which cannot without a ὕστερον πρότερον be explained as we explain the facts of nature.'[8]

According to Green, to say that a thing is real is to say that it is a member in a system of relations, the order of Nature. But awareness or knowledge of a series of related events cannot itself be a series of events. Nor can it be a natural development out of such a series. In other words, the mind as an active synthesizing principle is irreducible to the factors which it synthesizes. True, the empirical ego belongs to the order of Nature. But my awareness of myself as an empirical ego manifests the activity of a principle which transcends that order. In fine, 'an understanding—for that term seems as fit as any other to denote the principle of consciousness in question—irreducible to anything else, "makes nature" for us, in the sense of enabling us to conceive that there is such a thing'.[9]

We have just seen that for Green a thing is real in virtue of its membership in a system of related phenomena. At the same time he holds that 'related appearances are impossible apart from the action of an intelligence'.[10] Nature is thus made by the synthesizing activity of a mind. It is obvious, however, that we cannot seriously suppose that Nature, as the system of related phenomena, is simply the product of the synthesizing activity of any given finite mind. Though, therefore, it can be said that each finite mind constitutes Nature in so far as it conceives the system of relations, we must also assume that there is a single spiritual principle, an eternal consciousness, which ultimately constitutes or produces Nature.

From this it follows that we must conceive the finite mind as participating in the life of an eternal consciousness or intelligence which 'partially and gradually reproduces itself in us, communicating piece-meal, but in inseparable correlation, understanding and the facts understood, experience and the experienced world'.[11] This amounts to saying that God gradually reproduces his own knowledge in the finite mind. And, if this is the case, what are we to say about the empirical facts relating to the origin and growth of knowledge? For these hardly suggest that our knowledge is imposed by God. Green's answer is that God reproduces his own knowledge in the finite mind by making use, so to speak, of the sentient life of the human organism and of its response to stimuli. There are thus two aspects to human consciousness. There is the empirical aspect, under which our consciousness appears to consist 'in successive modifications of the animal organism'.[12] And there is the metaphysical aspect, under which this organism is seen as gradually becoming 'the vehicle of an eternally complete consciousness'.[13]

Green thus shares with the earlier idealists the tendency to choose an epistemological point of departure, the subject-object relationship. Under the influence of Kant, however, he depicts the subject as actively synthesizing the manifold of phenomena, as constituting the order of Nature by relating appearances or phenomena. This process of synthesis is a gradual process which develops through the history of the human race towards an ideal term. And we can thus conceive the total process as an activity of one spiritual principle which lives and acts in and through finite minds. In other words, Kant's idea of the synthesizing activity of the mind leads us to the Hegelian concept of infinite Spirit.

At the same time Green's religious interests militate against any reduction of infinite Spirit to the lives of finite spirits considered simply collectively. It is true that he wishes to avoid what he regards as one of the main defects of traditional theism, namely the representation of God as a Being over against the world and the finite spirit. Hence he depicts the spiritual life of man as a participation in the divine life. But he also wishes to avoid using the word 'God' simply as a label either for the spiritual life of man considered universally, as something which develops in the course of the evolution of human culture, or for the ideal of complete knowledge, an ideal which does not yet exist but towards which human knowledge progressively approximates. He does indeed speak of the human spirit as 'identical' with God; but he adds, 'in the sense that He *is* all which the human spirit is capable of becoming'.[14] God is the infinite eternal subject; and His complete knowledge is reproduced progressively in the finite subject in dependence, from the empirical point of view, on the modifications of the human organism.

If we ask why God acts in this way, Green implies that no answer can be given. 'The old question, why God made the world, has never been answered, nor will be. We know not why the world should be; we only know that there it is. In like manner we know not why the eternal subject of that world should reproduce itself, through certain processes of the world, as the spirit of mankind, or as the particular self of this or that man in whom the spirit of mankind operates. We can only say that, upon the best analysis we can make of our experience, it seems that so it does.'[15]

In Green's retention of the idea of an eternal subject which 'reproduces itself' in finite subjects and therefore can not be simply identified with them it is not unreasonable to see the operation of a religious interest, a concern with the idea of a God in whom we live and move and have our being. But this is certainly not the explicit or formal reason for postulating an eternal subject. For it is explicitly postulated as the ultimate synthesizing agent in constituting the system of Nature. And in making this postulate Green seems to lay himself open to the same sort of objection that we brought against Ferrier. For if it is once assumed, at least for the sake of argument, that the order of Nature is constituted by the synthesizing or relating activity of intelligence, it is obvious that I cannot attribute this order to an eternal intelligence or subject unless I have myself first conceived, and so constituted, it. And it then becomes difficult to see how, in Ferrier's terminology, I can unyoke the conceived system of relations from the synthesizing activity of my own mind and yoke it on to any other subject, eternal or otherwise.

It may be objected that this line of criticism, though possibly valid in the case of Ferrier, is irrelevant in that of Green. For Green sees the individual finite subject as participating in a general spiritual life, the spiritual life of humanity, which progressively synthesizes phenomena in its advance towards the ideal goal of complete knowledge, a knowledge which would be itself the constituted order of Nature. Hence there is no question of unyoking my synthesis from myself and yoking it to any other spirit. My synthesizing activity is simply a moment in that of the human race as a whole or of the one spiritual principle which lives in and through the multiplicity of finite subjects.

In this case, however, what becomes of Green's eternal subject? If we wish to represent, say, the advancing scientific knowledge of mankind as a life in which all scientists participate and which moves towards an ideal goal, there is, of course, no question of 'unyoking' and 'yoking'. But a concept of this sort does not by itself call for the introduction of any eternal subject which reproduces its complete knowledge in a piecemeal manner in finite minds.

Further, how precisely, in Green's philosophy, are we to conceive the relation of Nature to the eternal subject or intelligence? Let us assume that the constitutive activity of intelligence consists in relating or synthesizing. Now if God can properly be said to create Nature, it seems to follow that Nature is reducible to a system of relations without terms. And this is a somewhat perplexing notion. If, however, the eternal subject only introduces relations, so to speak, between phenomena, we seem to be presented with a picture similar to that painted by Plato in the *Timaeus*, in the sense, that is to say, that the eternal subject or intelligence would bring order out of disorder rather than create the whole of Nature out of nothing. In any case, though it may be possible to conceive a divine intelligence as creating the world by thinking it, terms such as 'eternal subject' and 'eternal consciousness' necessarily suggest a correlative eternal object. And this would mean an absolutization of the subject-object relationship, similar to that of Ferrier.

Objections of this sort may appear to be niggling and to indicate an inability to appreciate Green's general vision of an eternal consciousness in the life of which we all participate. But the objections serve at any rate the useful purpose of drawing attention to the fact that Green's often acute criticism of other philosophers is combined with that rather vague and woolly speculation which has done so much to bring metaphysical idealism into disrepute.[16]

3. In his moral theory Green stands in the tradition of Plato and Aristotle, in the sense that for him the concept of good is primary, not that of obligation. In particular, his idea of the good for man as consisting in the full actualization of the potentialities of the human person in an harmonious and unified state of being recalls the ethics of Aristotle. Green does indeed speak of 'self-satisfaction' as the end of moral conduct, but he makes it clear that self-satisfaction signifies for him self-realization rather than pleasure. We must distinguish between 'the quest for self-satisfaction which all moral activity is rightly held to be, and the quest for pleasure which morally *good* activity is not'.[17] This does not mean that pleasure is excluded from the good for man. But the harmonious and integrated actualization of the human person's potentialities cannot be identified with the search for pleasure. For the moral agent is a spiritual subject, not simply a sensitive organism. And in any case pleasure is a concomitant of the actualization of one's powers rather than this actualization itself.

Now it is certain that it is only through action that a man can realize himself, in the sense of actualizing his potentialities and developing his personality towards the ideal state of harmonious integration of his powers. And it is also obvious that every human act, in the proper sense of the term, is motivated. It is performed in view of some immediate end or goal. But it is arguable that a man's motives are determined by his existing character, in conjunction with other circumstances, and that character is itself the result of empirical causes. In this case are not a man's actions determined in such a way that what he will be depends on what he is, what he is depending in turn on circumstances other than his free choice? True, circumstances vary; but the ways in which men react to varying circumstances seem to be determined. And if all a man's acts are determined, is there any room for an ethical theory which sets up a certain ideal of human personality as that which we ought to strive to realize through our actions?

Green is quite prepared to concede to the determinists a good deal of the ground on which they base their case. But at the same time he tries to take the sting out of these concessions. 'The propositions, current among "determinists", that a man's action is the joint result of his character and circumstances, is true enough in a certain sense, and, in that sense, is quite compatible with an assertion of human freedom.'[18] In Green's view, it is not a necessary condition for the proper use of the word 'freedom' that a man should be able to do or to become anything whatsoever. To justify our describing a man's actions as free, it is sufficient that they should be his own, in the sense that he is truly the author of them. And if a man's action follows from his character, if, that is to say, he responds to a situation which calls for action in a certain way because he is a certain sort of man, the action is his own; he, and nobody else, is the responsible author of it.

In defending this interpretation of freedom Green lays emphasis on self-consciousness. In the history of any man there is a succession of natural empirical factors of one kind or another, natural impulses for example, which the determinist regards as exercising a decisive influence on the man's conduct. Green argues, however, that such factors become morally relevant only when they are assumed, as it were, by the self-conscious subject, that is, when they are taken up into the unity of self-consciousness and turned into motives. They then become internal principles of action; and, as such, they are principles of free action.

This theory, which is in some respects reminiscent of Schelling's theory of freedom, is perhaps hardly crystal clear. But it is clear at least that Green wishes to admit all the empirical data to which the determinist can reasonably appeal,[19] and at the same time to maintain that this admission is compatible with an assertion of human freedom. Perhaps we can say that the question which he asks is this. Given all the empirical facts about human conduct, have we still a use for words such as 'freedom' and 'free' in the sphere of morals? Green's answer is affirmative. The acts of a self-conscious subject, considered precisely as such, can properly be said to be free acts. Actions which are the result of physical compulsion, for example, do not proceed from the self-conscious subject as such. They are not really his own actions; he cannot be considered the true author of them. And we need to be able to distinguish between actions of this type and those which are the expression of the man himself, considered not merely as a physical agent but also as a self-conscious subject or, as some would say, a rational agent.

Mention of the fact that for Green self-realization is the end of moral conduct may suggest that his ethical theory is individualistic. But though he does indeed lay emphasis on the individual's realization of himself, he is at one with Plato and Aristotle in regarding the human person as essentially social in character. In other words, the self which has to be realized is not an atomic self, the potentialities of which can be fully actualized and harmonized without any reference to social relations. On the contrary, it is only in society that we can fully actualize our potentialities and really live as human persons. And this means in effect that the particular moral vocation of each individual has to be interpreted within a social context. Hence Green can use a phrase which Bradley was afterwards to render famous, by remarking that 'each has primarily to fulfil the duties of his station'.[20]

Given this outlook, it is understandable that Green lays emphasis, again with Plato and Aristotle but also, of course, with Hegel, on the status and function of political society, the State, which is 'for its members the society of societies'.[21] It will be noted that this somewhat grandiloquent phrase itself indicates a recognition of the fact that there are other societies, such as the family, which are presupposed by the State. But Hegel himself recognized this fact, of course. And it is clear that among societies Green attributes a preeminent importance to the State.

Precisely for this reason, however, it is important to understand that Green is not recanting, either explicitly or implicitly, his ethical theory of self-realization. He continues to maintain his view that 'our ultimate standard of worth is an ideal of *personal* worth. All other values are relative to value for, of, or in a person.'[22] This ideal, however, can be fully realized only in and through a society of persons. Society is thus a moral necessity. And this applies to that larger form of social organization which we call political society or the State as well as to the family. But it by no means follows that the State is an end itself. On the contrary, its function is to create and maintain the conditions for the good life, that is, the conditions in which human beings can best develop themselves and live as persons, each recognizing the others as ends, not merely as means. In this sense the State is an instrument rather than an end in itself. It is indeed an error to say that a nation or a political society is *merely* an aggregate of individuals. For use of the word 'merely' shows that the speaker overlooks the fact that the individual's moral capacities are actualized only in concrete social relations. It implies that individuals could possess their moral and spiritual qualities and fulfil their moral vocation quite apart from membership of society. At the same time the premiss that the nation or the State is not 'merely' a collection of individuals does not entail the conclusion that it is a kind of self-subsistent entity over and above the individuals who compose it. 'The life of the nation has no real existence except as the life of the individuals composing the nation.'[23]

Green is therefore quite prepared to admit that in a certain sense there are natural rights which are presupposed by the State. For if we consider what powers must be secured for the individual with a view to the attainment of his moral end, we find that the individual has certain claims which should be recognized by society. It is true that rights in the full sense of the term do not exist until they have been accorded social recognition. Indeed, the term 'right', in its full sense, has little or no meaning apart from society.[24] At the same time, if by saying that there are natural rights which are antecedent to political society we mean that a man, simply because he is a man, has certain claims which ought to be recognized by the State as rights, it is then perfectly true to say that 'the State presupposes rights, and rights of individuals. It is a form which society takes in order to maintain them.'[25]

It is sufficiently obvious from what has been said that in Green's view we cannot obtain a philosophical understanding of the function of the State simply by conducting an historical investigation into the ways in which actual political societies have in fact arisen. We have to consider the nature of man and his moral vocation. Similarly, to have a criterion for judging laws we have to understand the moral end of man, to which all rights are relative. 'A law is not good because it enforces "natural rights", but because it contributes to the realization of a certain end. We only discover what rights are natural by considering what powers must be secured to a man in order to the attainment of this end. These powers a perfect law will secure to their full extent.'[26]

From this close association of political society with the attainment of man's moral end it follows that 'morality and political subjection have a common source, "*political* subjection" being distinguished from that of a slave, as a subjection which secures rights to a subject. That common source is the rational recognition by certain human beings—it may be merely by children of the same parent—of a common well-being which is their well-being, and which they conceive as their well-being, whether at any moment any one of them is inclined to it or no, . . .'[27] Obviously, any given individual may be disinclined to pursue what promotes this common well-being or good. Hence there is need for moral rules or precepts and, in the political sphere, for laws. Moral obligation and political obligation are thus closely linked by Green. The real basis of an obligation to obey the law of the State is neither fear nor mere expediency but man's moral obligation to avoid those actions which are incompatible with the attainment of his moral end and to perform those actions which are required for its attainment.

It follows that there can be no right to disobey or rebel against the State as such. That is to say, 'so far as the laws anywhere or at any time in force fulfil the idea of a State, there can be no right to disobey them'.[28] But, as Hegel admitted, the actual State by no means always measures up to the idea or ideal of the State; and a given law may be incompatible with the real interest or good of society as a whole. Hence civil disobedience in the name of the common good or well-being can be justifiable. Obviously, men have to take into account the fact that it is in the public interest that laws should be obeyed. And the claim of this public interest will usually favour working for the repeal of the objectionable law rather than downright disobedience to it. Further, men ought to consider whether disobedience to an objectionable law might result in some worse evil, such as anarchy. But the moral foundation of political obligation does not entail the conclusion that civil disobedience is never justified. Green sets rather narrow limits to the scope of civil disobedience by saying that to justify our practising it we ought to be able 'to point to some public interest, generally recognized as such'.[29] But from what he subsequently says it does not seem that the proviso 'generally recognized as such' is intended to exclude entirely the possibility of a right to civil disobedience in the name of an ideal higher than that shared by the community in general. The reference is rather to an appeal to a generally recognized public interest against a law which is promulgated not for the public good but in the private interest of a special group or class.

Given Green's view that the State exists to promote the common good by creating and maintaining the conditions in which all its citizens can develop their potentialities as persons, it is understandable that he has no sympathy with attacks on social legislation as violating individual liberty, when liberty signifies the power to do as one likes without regard to others. Some people, he remarks, say that their rights are being violated if they are forbidden, for example, to build houses without any regard to sanitary requirements or to send their children out to work without having received any education. In point of fact, however, no rights are being violated. For a man's rights depend on social recognition in view of the welfare of society as a whole. And when society comes to see, as it has not seen before, that the common good requires a new law, such as a law enforcing elementary education, it withdraws recognition of what may formerly have been accounted a right.

Clearly, in certain circumstances the appeal from a less to a more adequate conception of the common good and its requirements might take the form of insisting on a greater measure of individual liberty. For human beings cannot develop themselves as persons unless they have scope for the exercise of such liberty. But Green is actually concerned with opposing *laissez-faire* dogmas. He does not advocate curtailment of individual liberty by the State for the sake of such curtailment. Indeed, he looks on the social legislation of which he approves as a removal of obstacles to liberty, that is, the liberty of all citizens to develop their potentialities as human beings. For example, a law determining the minimum age at which children can be sent to work removes an obstacle to their receiving education. It is true that the law curtails the liberty of parents and prospective employers to do what they like without regard to the common good. But Green will not allow any appeal from the common good to liberty in this sense. Private, sectional and class interests, however hard they may mask themselves under an appeal to private liberty, cannot be allowed to stand in the way of the creation by the State of conditions in which all its citizens have the opportunity to develop themselves as human beings and to live truly human lives.

With Green, therefore, we have a conspicuous example of the revision of liberalism in accordance with the felt need for an increase in social legislation. He tries to interpret, we can say, the operative ideal of a movement which was developing during the closing decades of the nineteenth century. His formulation of a theory may be open to some criticism. But it was certainly preferable not only to *laissez-faire* dogmatism but also to attempts to retain this dogmatism in principle while making concessions which were incompatible with it.

In conclusion it is worth remarking that Green is not blind to the fact that fulfilment of our moral vocation by performing the duties of our 'station' in society may seem to be a rather narrow and inadequate ideal. For 'there may be reason to hold that there are capacities of the human spirit not realizable in persons under the conditions of any society that we know, or can positively conceive, or that may be capable of existing on the earth'.[30] Hence, unless we judge that the problem presented by unfulfilled capacities is insoluble, we may believe that the personal life which is lived on earth in conditions which thwart its full development is continued in a society in which man can attain his full perfection. 'Or we may content ourselves with saying that the personal self-conscious being, which comes from God, is for ever continued in God.'[31] Green speaks in a rather non-committal fashion. But his personal attitude seems to be much more akin to that of Kant, who postulated continued life after death as an unceasing progress in perfection, than to that of Hegel, who does not appear to have been interested in the question of personal immortality, whether he believed in it or not.

4. The idea of a unity underlying the distinction between subject and object becomes prominent in the thought of Edward Caird (1835–1908), Fellow of Merton College, Oxford (1864–6), professor of moral philosophy in the University of Glasgow (1866–93) and Master of Balliol College, Oxford (1893–1907). His celebrated work, A Critical Account of the Philosophy of Kant, appeared in 1877, a revised edition in two volumes being published in 1889 under the title The Critical Philosophy of Kant. In 1883 Caird published a small work on Hegel,[32] which is still considered one of the best introductions to the study of this philosopher. Of Caird's other writings we may mention The Social Philosophy and Religion of Comte (1885), Essays on Literature and Philosophy (two volumes, 1892), The Evolution of Religion (two volumes, 1893) and The Evolution of Theology in the Greek Philosophers (two volumes, 1904). The two last named works are the published versions of sets of Gifford Lectures.

Though Caird wrote on both Kant and Hegel, and though he used metaphysical idealism as an instrument in interpreting human experience and as a weapon for attacking materialism and agnosticism, he was not, and did not pretend to be, a disciple of Hegel or of any other German philosopher. Indeed, he considered that any attempt to import a philosophical system into a foreign country was misplaced.[33] It is idle to suppose that what satisfied a past generation in Germany will satisfy a later generation in Great Britain. For intellectual needs change with changing circumstances.

In the modern world, Caird maintains, we have seen the reflective mind questioning man's spontaneous certainties and breaking asunder factors which were formerly combined. For example, there is the divergence between the Cartesian point of departure, the self-conscious ego, and that of the empiricists, the object as given in experience. And the gulf between the two traditions has grown so wide that we are told that we must either reduce the physical to the psychical or the psychical to the physical. In other words, we are told that we must choose between idealism and materialism, as their conflicting claims cannot be reconciled. Again, there is the gulf which has developed between the religious consciousness and faith on the one hand and the scientific outlook on the other, a gulf which implies that we must choose between religion and science, as the two cannot be combined.

When oppositions and conflicts of this kind have once arisen in man's cultural life, we cannot simply return to the undivided but naïve consciousness of an earlier period. Nor is it sufficient to appeal with the Scottish School to the principles of common sense. For it is precisely these principles which have been called in question, as by Humian scepticism. Hence the reflective mind is forced to look for a synthesis in which opposed points of view can be reconciled at a higher level than that of the naïve consciousness.

Kant made an important contribution to the fulfilment of this task. But its significance has, in Caird's opinion, been misunderstood, the misunderstanding being due primarily to Kant himself. For instead of interpreting the distinction between appearance and reality as referring simply to different stages in the growth of knowledge, the German philosopher represented it as a distinction between phenomena and unknowable things-in-themselves. And it is precisely this notion of the unknowable thing-in-itself which has to be expelled from philosophy, as indeed Kant's successors have done. When we have got rid of this notion, we can see that the real significance of the critical philosophy lies in its insight into the fact that objectivity exists only for a self-conscious subject. In other words, Kant's real service was to show that the fundamental relationship is that between subject and object, which together form a unity-in-difference. Once we grasp this truth, we are freed from the temptation to reduce subject to object or object to subject. For this temptation has its origin in an unsatisfactory dualism which is overcome by the theory of an original synthesis. The distinction between subject and object emerges within the unity of consciousness, a unity which is fundamental.

According to Caird, science itself bears witness in its own

way to this unity-in-difference. True, it concentrates on the object. At the same time it aims at the discovery of universal laws and at correlating these laws; and it thus tacitly presupposes the existence of an intelligible system which cannot be simply heterogeneous or alien to the thought which understands it. In other words, science bears witness to the correlativity of thought and its object.

Though, however, one of the tasks allotted to the philosopher by Caird is that of showing how science points to the basic principle of the synthesis of subject and object as a unity-in-difference, he himself gives his attention chiefly to the religious consciousness. And in this sphere he finds himself driven to go behind subject and object to an underlying unity and ground. Subject and object are distinct. Indeed, 'all our life moves between these two terms which are essentially distinct from, and even opposed to, each other'.[34] Yet they are at the same time related to each other in such a way that neither can be conceived without the other.[35] And 'we are forced to seek the secret of their being in a higher principle, of whose unity they in their action and reaction are the manifestations, which they presuppose as their beginning and to which they point as their end'.[36]

This enveloping unity, which is described in Platonic phrases as being 'at once the source of being to all things that are, and of knowing to all beings that know',[37] is the presupposition of all consciousness. And it is what we call God. It does not follow, Caird insists, that all men possess an explicit awareness of God as the ultimate unity of being and knowing, of objectivity and subjectivity. An explicit awareness is in the nature of the case the product of a long process of development. And we can see in the history of religion the main stages of this development.[38]

The first stage, that of 'objective religion', is dominated by awareness of the object, not indeed as the object in the abstract technical sense of the term, but in the form of the external things by which man finds himself surrounded. At this stage man cannot form an idea of anything 'which he cannot body forth as an existence in space and time'.[39] We can assume that he has some dim awareness of a unity comprehending both himself and other things; but he cannot form an idea of the divine except by objectifying it in the gods.

The second stage in the development of religion is that of 'subjective religion'. Here man returns from absorption in Nature to consciousness of himself. And God is conceived as a spiritual being standing apart from both Nature and man, and as revealing Himself above all in the inner voice of conscience.

In the third stage, that of 'absolute religion', the self-conscious subject and its object, Nature, are seen as distinct yet essentially related, and at the same time as grounded in an ultimate unity. And God is conceived 'as the Being who is at once the source, the sustaining power, and the end of our spiritual lives'.[40] This does not mean, however, that the idea of God is completely indeterminate, so that we are forced to embrace the agnosticism of Herbert Spencer. For God manifests Himself in both subject and object; and the more we understand the spiritual life of humanity on the one hand and the world of Nature on the other, so much the more do we learn about God who is 'the ultimate unity of our life and of the life of the world'.[41]

Insofar as Caird goes behind the distinction between subject and object to an ultimate unity, we can say that he does not absolutize the subject-object relationship in the way that Ferrier does. At the same time his epistemological approach, namely by way of their relationship, seems to create a difficulty. For he explicitly recognizes that 'strictly speaking, there is but one object and one subject for each of us'.[42] That is to say, for me the subject-object relationship is, strictly, that between myself as subject and my world as object. And the object must include other people. Even if, therefore, it is granted that I have from the beginning a dim awareness of an underlying unity, it seems to follow that this unity is the unity of myself as subject and of my object, other persons being part of 'my object'. And it is difficult to see how it can then be shown that there are other subjects, and that there is one and only one common underlying unity. Common sense may suggest that these conclusions are correct. But it is a question not of common sense but rather of seeing how the conclusions can be established, once we have adopted

Caird's approach. Taken by itself, the idea of an underlying unity may well be of value.[43] But arrival at the conclusion at which Caird wishes to arrive is not facilitated by his point of departure. And it is certainly arguable that Hegel showed wisdom in starting with the concept of Being rather than with that of the subject-object relationship.

5. It has been said of John Caird (1820–98), brother of Edward, that he preached Hegelianism from the pulpit. A Presbyterian theologian and preacher, he was appointed professor of divinity in the University of Glasgow in 1862, becoming Principal of the University in 1873. In 1880 he published *An Introduction to the Philosophy of Religion*, and in 1888 a volume on Spinoza in Blackwood's Philosophical Classics. Some other writings, including his Gifford Lectures on *The Fundamental Ideas of Christianity* (1899), appeared posthumously.

In arguing against materialism John Caird maintains not only that it is unable to explain the life of the organism and of consciousness,[44] but also that the materialists, though undertaking to reduce the mind to a function of matter, tacitly and inevitably presuppose from the outset that the mind is something different from matter. After all, it is the mind itself which has to perform the reduction. In an analogous manner he argues that the agnostic who says that God is unknowable betrays by his very statement the fact that he has an implicit awareness of God. 'Even in maintaining that the human mind is incapable of absolute knowledge the sceptic presupposes in his own mind an ideal of absolute knowledge in comparison with which human knowledge is pronounced defective. The very denial of an absolute intelligence in us could have no meaning but for a tacit appeal to its presence. An implicit knowledge of God in this sense is proved by the very attempt to deny it.'[45]

As expressed in this particular quotation, Caird's theory is obscure. But it can be elucidated in this way. Caird is applying to knowledge in particular Hegel's thesis that we cannot be aware of finitude without being implicitly aware of infinity. Experience teaches us that our minds are finite and imperfect. But we could not be aware of this except in the light of an implicit idea of complete or absolute knowledge, a knowledge which would be in effect the unity of thought and being. It is this implicit or virtual idea of absolute knowledge which constitutes a vaguely-conceived standard in comparison with which our limitations become clear to us. Further, this idea draws the mind as an ideal goal. It thus operates in us as a reality. And it is in fact an absolute intelligence, in the light of which we participate.

Obviously, it is essential for Caird to maintain the view expressed in the last two sentences. For if he said simply that we strive after complete or absolute knowledge as an ideal goal, we should probably conclude that absolute knowledge does not yet exist, whereas Caird wishes to arrive at the conclusion that in affirming the limitations of our knowledge we are implicitly affirming a living reality. Hence he has to argue that in asserting the limitations of my intelligence I am implicitly asserting the existence of an absolute intelligence which operates in me and in whose life I participate. He thus utilizes the Hegelian principle that the finite cannot be understood except as a moment in the life of the infinite. Whether the employment of these Hegelian principles can really serve the purpose for which Caird employed them, namely to support Christian theism, is open to dispute. But he at any rate is convinced that they can.

John Caird also argues, in the same way as his brother, that the interrelation of subject and object reveals an ultimate unity underlying the distinction. As for the traditional proofs of God's existence, they are exposed to the customary objections, if they are taken as claiming to be strictly logical arguments. If, however, they are interpreted more as phenomenological analyses of ways 'by which the human spirit rises to the knowledge of God, and finds therein the fulfilment of its own highest nature, these proofs possess great value'.[46] It is not quite clear perhaps where this great value is supposed to lie. Caird can hardly mean that logically invalid arguments possess great value if they exhibit ways in which the human mind has as a matter of fact reached a conclusion by faulty reasoning. So presumably he means that the traditional arguments possess value as illustrating ways in which the human mind can become explicitly conscious of an awareness which they already possess in an implicit and obscure manner. This point of view would allow him to say both that the arguments beg the question by presupposing the conclusion from the start and that this does not really matter, inasmuch as they are really ways of making the implicit explicit.[47]

Like Hegel, John Caird insists on the need for advancing from the level of ordinary religious thought to a speculative idea of religion, in which 'contradictions' are overcome. For example, the opposed and equally one-sided positions of pantheism and deism are both overcome in a truly philosophical conception of the relation between the finite and the infinite, a conception which is characteristic of Christianity when rightly understood. As for specifically Christian doctrines, such as that of the Incarnation, Caird's treatment of them is more orthodox than Hegel's. He is, however, too convinced of the value of the Hegelian philosophy as an ally in the fight against materialism and agnosticism to consider seriously whether, as McTaggart was later to put it, the ally may not turn out in the long run to be an enemy in disguise, inasmuch as the use of Hegelianism in the interpretation of Christianity tends, by the very nature of the Hegelian system, to involve the subordination of the content of the Christian faith to speculative philosophy and, indeed, a tie-up with a particular system.

In point of fact, however, John Caird does not adopt the Hegelian system lock, stock and barrel. What he does is rather to adopt from it those general lines of thought which seem to him to possess intrinsic validity and to be of service in supporting a religious outlook in the face of contemporary materialist and positivist tendencies. He thus provides a good example of the religious interest which characterized a large part of the idealist movement in Great Britain.

6. Among those who contributed to spreading a knowledge of Hegelianism in Great Britain William Wallace (1844–97), Green's successor as White's professor of moral philosophy at Oxford, deserves a mention. In 1874 he published a translation, furnished with prolegomena or introductory material, of Hegel's *Logic* as contained in the *Encyclopaedia of the Philosophical Sciences*.[48] He later pub-

lished a revised and enlarged edition in two volumes, the translation appearing in 1892 and the greatly augmented *Prolegomena*[49] in 1894. Wallace also published in 1894 a translation, with five introductory chapters, of Hegel's *Philosophy of Mind*, again from the *Encyclopaedia*. In addition he wrote the volume on Kant (1882) for Blackwood's Philosophical Classics series and a *Life of Schopenhauer* (1890). His *Lectures and Essays on Natural Theology and Ethics*, which appeared posthumously in 1898, show clearly the affinity between his thought and John Caird's speculative interpretation of religion in general and of Christianity in particular.

Though we must refrain from multiplying brief references to philosophers who stood within the ambit of the idealist movement, there is a special reason for mentioning David George Ritchie (1853–1903), who was converted to idealism by Green at Oxford and who in 1894 became professor of logic and metaphysics in the University of St. Andrews. For while the idealists in general were unsympathetic to systems of philosophy based on Darwinism, Ritchie undertook to show that the Hegelian philosophy was perfectly capable of assimilating the Darwinian theory of evolution.[50] After all, he argued, does not Darwin's theory of the survival of the fittest harmonize very well with Hegel's doctrine that the real is the rational and the rational the real, and that the rational, representing a value, triumphs over the irrational? And does not the disappearance of the weaker and less fitted for survival correspond with the overcoming of the negative factor in the Hegelian dialectic?

It is true, Ritchie admitted, that the Darwinians were so concerned with the origin of species that they failed to understand the significance of the movement of evolution as a whole. We must recognize the facts that in human society the struggle for existence takes forms which cannot be properly described in biological categories, and that social progress depends on co-operation. But it is precisely at this point that Hegelianism can shed a light which is shed neither by the biological theory of evolution taken purely by itself nor by the empiricist and positivist systems of philosophy which are professedly based on this theory.

Though, however, Ritchie made a valiant attempt to reconcile Darwinism and Hegelianism, the construction of 'idealist' philosophies of evolution, in the sense of philosophies which endeavoured to show that the total movement of evolution is towards an ideal term or goal, was actually to take place outside rather than inside the Neo-Hegelian current of thought.

Chapter Eight

ABSOLUTE IDEALISM: BRADLEY

Introductory remarks – The Presuppositions of Critical History – *Morality and its self-transcending in religion* – *The relevance of logic to metaphysics* – *The basic presupposition of metaphysics* – *Appearance: the thing and its qualities, relations and their terms, space and time, the self* – *Reality: the nature of the Absolute* – *Degrees of truth and reality* – *Error and evil* – *The Absolute, God and religion* – *Some critical discussion of Bradley's metaphysics.*

1. It was in the philosophy of Francis Herbert Bradley (1846–1924) that emphasis on the subject-object relationship was decisively supplanted by the idea of the supra-relational One, the all-embracing Absolute. Of Bradley's life there is little which needs to be said. In 1870 he was elected a Fellow of Merton College, Oxford, and he retained this post until his death. He did not lecture. And the quantity of his literary output, though substantial, was not exceptional. But as a thinker he is of considerable interest, especially perhaps for the way in which he combines a radical criticism of the categories of human thought, when considered as instruments for apprehending ultimate reality, with a firm faith in the existence of an Absolute in which all contradictions and antinomies are overcome.

In 1874 Bradley published an essay on *The Presuppositions of Critical History*, to which reference will be made in the next section. *Ethical Studies* appeared in 1876, *The Principles of Logic* in 1883,[1] *Appearance and Reality* in 1893,[2] and *Essays on Truth and Reality* in 1914. Other essays and articles were collected and published posthumously in two volumes in 1935 under the title *Collected Essays*.[3] A small book of *Aphorisms* appeared in 1930.

Bradley's enemies were those of the idealists in general,

namely empiricists, positivists and materialists, though in his case we have to add the pragmatists. As a polemical writer he did not always represent his opponents' views in a manner which they considered fair; but he could be devastating, and on occasion none too polite. His own philosophy has often been described as Neo-Hegelian. But though he was undoubtedly influenced by Hegelianism, the description is not altogether appropriate. It is true that both Hegel and Bradley were concerned with the totality, the Absolute. But the two men held markedly different views about the capacity of the human reason to grasp the Absolute. Hegel was a rationalist, in the sense, that is to say, that he regarded reason (*Vernunft*), as distinct from understanding (*Verstand*), as capable of penetrating the inner life of the Absolute. He endeavoured to lay bare the essential structure of the self-developing universe, the totality of Being; and he showed an overwhelming confidence in the power of dialectical thought to reveal the nature of the Absolute both in itself and in its concrete manifestations in Nature and Spirit. Bradley's dialectic, however, largely took the form of a systematic self-criticism by discursive thought, a criticism which, in his opinion at least, made clear the incapacity of human thought to attain any adequate grasp of ultimate reality, of what is really real. The world of discursive thought was for him the world of appearance; and metaphysical reflection showed that it was precisely this, by revealing the antinomies and contradictions engendered by such thought. Bradley was indeed convinced that the reality which is distorted by discursive thought is in itself free from all contradictions, a seamless whole, an all-comprehensive and perfectly harmonious act of experience. The point is, however, that he did not pretend to be able to show dialectically precisely how antinomies are overcome and contradictions solved in the Absolute. To be sure, he did in fact say a good deal about the Absolute. And in view of his thesis that ultimate reality transcends human thought, it is arguable that in doing so he showed a certain inconsistency. But the point which is relevant here is that Bradley gave expression not so much to Hegelian rationalism as to a peculiar combination of scepticism and fideism; of scepticism through his depreciation of human thought as an instrument of grasping reality as it really is, and of fideism by his explicit assertion that belief in a One which satisfies all the demands of ideal intelligibility rests on an initial act of faith that is presupposed by all genuinely metaphysical philosophy.

In reaching this characteristic position Bradley was influenced to a certain extent by Herbart's view that contradictions do not belong to reality itself but emerge only through our inadequate ways of conceiving reality.[4] This is not to suggest that Bradley was an Herbartian. He was a monist, whereas the German philosopher was a pluralist. But the late Professor A. E. Taylor relates that when he was at Merton College, he was recommended by Bradley to study Herbart as a wholesome correction to undue absorption in Hegelian ways of thinking.[5] And an understanding of Herbart's influence on Bradley helps to correct any overemphasis on Hegelian elements in the latter's philosophy.

Bradley's philosophy, however, cannot be adequately described in terms of influence exercised by other thinkers. It was in fact an original creation, in spite of the stimulus derived from such different German philosophers as Hegel and Herbart. In some respects, for instance in the way in which the concept of 'God' is represented as transcended in that of the suprapersonal Absolute, Bradley's thought shows clear signs of the influence of German absolute idealism. And the way in which the tendency of earlier British idealists to absolutize the subject-object relationship gives way before the idea of the totality, the One, can be said to represent the triumph of the absolute idealism which is associated above all with the name of Hegel. But British absolute idealism, especially in the case of Bradley, was a native version of the movement. It may not be as impressive as the Hegelian system; but this is no good reason for depicting it as no more than a minor replica of Hegelianism.

2. In his essay on *The Presuppositions of Critical History* Bradley writes that the critical mind must provisionally suspect the reality of everything before it. At the same time 'critical history must have a presupposition, and this presupposition is the uniformity of law'.[6] That is to say, 'critical history assumes that its world is one',[7] this unity being that

of the universality of law and of 'what loosely may be termed causal connection'.[8] History does not start by proving this unity; it presupposes it as the condition of its own possibility, though developed history confirms the truth of the presupposition.

There is no mention here of the Absolute. Indeed, the world of causal connections is relegated by Bradley in his metaphysics to the sphere of appearance. But in the light of the later development of his thought we can see in the idea of the unity of the world of history as a presupposition of historiography a hint of the idea of a total organic unity as the presupposition of metaphysics. And this suggestion seems to be supported by Bradley's assertion in a note that 'the universe seems to be one system; it is an organism (it would appear) and more. It bears the character of the self, the personality to which it is relative, and without which it is as good as nothing. Hence any portion of the universe by itself cannot be a consistent system; for it refers to the whole, and has the whole present in it. Potentially the whole (since embodying that which is actually the whole), in trying to fix itself on itself, it succeeds only in laying stress on its character of relativity; it is carried beyond and contradicts itself'.[9] To be sure, this is not precisely a statement of the doctrine of the Absolute as we find it in *Appearance and Reality*, where the Absolute is certainly not depicted as a self. At the same time the passage serves to show how Bradley's mind was dominated by the idea of the universe as an organic whole.

3. Bradley's *Ethical Studies* is not a metaphysical work. Indeed, on reading the first essay one may receive the impression that the writer's line of thought has more affinity with the modern analytic movement than with what would naturally be expected from a metaphysical idealist. For Bradley concerns himself with examining what the ordinary man understands by responsibility and imputability, and he then shows how two theories of human action are incompatible with the conditions of moral responsibility which are implicitly presupposed by 'the vulgar'.

On the one hand, the ordinary man implicitly assumes that he cannot legitimately be held morally responsible for an action unless he is the same man who performed the action. And if this assumption is taken to be correct, it excludes that form of determination which is based on the associationist psychology and to all intents and purposes does away with any permanent self-identity. 'Without personal identity responsibility is sheer nonsense; and to the psychology of our Determinists personal identity (with identity in general) is a word without a vestige of meaning.'[10] On the other hand, the ordinary man assumes that he cannot legitimately be held morally responsible for an action unless he is truly the author of it, unless it proceeds from him as effect from cause. And this assumption rules out any theory of indeterminism which implies that human free actions are uncaused and does away with the relation between a man's action and his self or character. For the agent as described by this sort of theory is 'a person who is *not* responsible, who (if he is anything) is idiotic'.[11]

Bradley is, of course, the last man to suggest that we should take the beliefs of the ordinary man as a final court of appeal. But for the moment he is concerned not with expounding a metaphysical theory of the self but with arguing that both determinism and indeterminism, when understood in the senses mentioned above, are incompatible with the presuppositions of the moral consciousness. And the positive conclusion to be drawn is that the moral consciousness of the ordinary man implies a close relation between actions for which one can legitimately be held responsible and one's self in the sense of character.

Though, however, *Ethical Studies* is not a metaphysical work, either in the sense that Bradley sets out to derive ethical conclusions from metaphysical premisses or in the sense that he explicitly introduces his metaphysical system,[12] it certainly has a metaphysical bearing or significance. For the upshot of the work is that morality gives rise to contradictions which cannot be resolved on the purely ethical level, and that it points beyond itself. True, in this work morality is depicted as leading on to religion. But elsewhere religion is depicted as leading on to the philosophy of the Absolute.

For Bradley the end of morality, of moral action, is self-realization. And it follows that the good for man cannot be identified with 'the feeling of self-realizedness',[13] or indeed with any feeling. Hedonism therefore, which looks on the feeling of pleasure as the good for man, is ruled out. In Bradley's view, as in that of Plato, the hedonist should logically assert that any action is moral which produces greater pleasure in the agent. For consistent hedonism admits only of a quantitative standard of discrimination. Once we introduce, with J. S. Mill, a qualitative distinction between pleasures, we require a standard other than the feeling of pleasure and have thus in effect abandoned hedonism. The truth of the matter is that Mill's utilitarianism expresses a groping after the ethical idea of self-realization, and that it is hindered from arriving fully at this idea by its illogical attempt to retain hedonism at the same time. 'May we suggest, in conclusion, that of all our utilitarians there is perhaps not one who has not still a great deal to learn from Aristotle's *Ethics?*"[14]

In making pleasure the sole good hedonism is a hopelessly one-sided theory. Another one-sided theory is the Kantian ethics of duty for duty's sake. But here the trouble is the formalism of the theory. We are told to realize the good will, 'but as to that which the good will is, it [the ethics of duty for duty's sake] tells us nothing, and leaves us with an idle abstraction'.[15] Bradley safeguards himself from the charge of caricaturing the Kantian ethics by saying that he does not intend to give an exegesis of Kant's moral theory. At the same time he states his belief that the Kantian ethical system 'has been annihilated by Hegel's criticism'.[16] And Hegel's main criticism was precisely that the Kantian ethics was involved in an empty formalism.

Bradley does not disagree, any more than Hegel did, with the view that the end of morality is the realization of a good will. His point is that content must be given to this idea. And to do this we must understand that the good will is the universal will, the will of a social organism. For this means that one's duties are specified by one's membership of the social organism, and that 'to be moral, I must will my station and its duties'.[17]

At first sight this Hegelian point of view, with its reminiscences of Rousseau, may seem to be at variance with Bradley's doctrine that the end of morality is self-realization. But all depends, of course, on how the term 'self' is understood. For Bradley, as for Hegel, the universal will, which is a concrete universal existing in and through its particulars, represents the individual's 'true' self. Apart from his social relations, his membership of a social organism, the individual man is an abstraction. 'And individual man is what he is because of and by virtue of community.'[18] Hence to identify one's private will with the universal will is to realize one's true self.

What does this mean in less abstract terms? The universal will is obviously the will of a society. And as the family, the basic society, is at the same time preserved and taken up in political society, the State, the emphasis is placed by Bradley, as by Hegel, on the latter. To realize oneself morally, therefore, is to act in accordance with social morality, that is, with 'the morality already existing ready to hand in laws, institutions, social usages, moral opinions and feelings'.[19]

This view obviously gives content to the moral law, to the command of reason to realize the good will. But, equally obviously, morality becomes relative to this or that human society. Bradley does indeed try to maintain a distinction between lower and higher moral codes. It is true that the essence of man is realized, however imperfectly, at any and every stage of moral evolution. But 'from the point of view of a higher stage, we can see that lower stages failed to realize the truth completely enough, and also, mixed and one with their realization, did present features contrary to the true nature of man as we now see it'.[20] At the same time Bradley's view that one's duties are specified by one's station, by one's place and function in the social organism, leads him to assert that morality not only is but ought to be relative. That is to say, it is not simply a question of noting the empirical fact that moral convictions have differed in certain respects in different societies. Bradley maintains in addition that moral codes would be of no use unless they were relative to given societies. In fine, 'the morality of every stage is justified for that stage; and the demand for a code of right in itself, apart from any stage, is seen to be the asking for an impossibility'.[21]

It scarcely needs saying that the very idea of a moral code involves the idea of a relation to possible conduct, and that a code which had no relation at all to a man's historical and social situation would be useless to him. But it does not necessarily follow that I must identify morality with the existing moral standards and outlook of the society to which I happen to belong. Indeed if, as Bradley admits, a member of an existing society can see the defects in the moral code of a past society, there does not seem to be any adequate reason why an enlightened member of the past society should not have seen these defects for himself and have rejected social conformism in the name of higher moral standards and ideals. This is, after all, precisely what has happened in history.

In point of fact, however, Bradley does not reduce morality simply to social morality. For in his view it is a duty to realize the ideal self; and the content of this ideal self is not exclusively social. For example, 'it is a moral duty for the artist or the inquirer to lead the life of one, and a moral offence when he fails to do so'.[22] True, the activities of an artist or of a scientist can, and generally do, benefit society. But 'their social bearing is indirect, and does not lie in their very essence'.[23] This idea is doubtless in tune with Hegel's attribution of art to the sphere of absolute spirit, rather than that of objective spirit, where morality belongs. But the point is that Bradley's assertion that 'man is not man at all unless social, but man is not much above the beasts unless more than social'[24] might well have led him to revise such statements as that 'there is nothing better than my station and its duties, nor anything higher or more truly beautiful'.[25] If morality is self-realization, and if the self cannot be adequately described in purely social categories, morality can hardly be identified with conformity to the standards of the society to which one belongs.

Yet in a sense all this is simply grist to Bradley's mill. For, as has already been mentioned, he wishes to show that morality gives rise to antinomies or contradictions which cannot be overcome on the purely ethical level. For example, and this is the principal contradiction, the moral law demands the perfect identification of the individual will with the ideally good and universal will, though at the same time morality cannot exist except in the form of an overcoming of the lower self, a striving which presupposes that the individual will is not identified with the ideally good will. In other words, morality is essentially an endless process; but by its very nature it demands that the process should no longer exist but should be supplanted by moral perfection.

Obviously, if we deny either that overcoming of the lower or bad self is an essential feature of the moral life or that the moral law demands the cessation of this overcoming, the antinomy disappears. If, however, we admit both theses, the conclusion to be drawn is that morality seeks its own extinction. That is to say, it seeks to transcend itself. 'Morality is an endless process and therefore a self-contradiction; and, being such, it does not remain standing in itself, but feels the impulse to transcend its existing reality.'[26] If the moral law demands the attainment of an ideal which cannot be attained as long as there is a bad self to be overcome, and if the existence in some degree of a bad self is a necessary presupposition of morality, the moral law, we must conclude, demands the attainment of an ideal or end which can be attained only in a supra-ethical sphere.

As far as *Ethical Studies* is concerned, this sphere is that of religion. The moral ideal is 'not realized in the objective world of the State';[27] but it can be realized for the religious consciousness. It is true that 'for religion the world is alienated from God, and the self is sunk in sin'.[28] At the same time for the religious consciousness the two poles, God and the self, the infinite and the finite, are united in faith. For religious faith the sinner is reconciled with God and justified, and he is united with other selves in the community of the faithful. Thus in the sphere of religion man reaches the term of his striving and he fulfils the demand of morality that he should realize himself as 'an infinite whole',[29] a demand which can be only imperfectly fulfilled on the ethical level through membership in political society.

Morality, therefore, consists in the realization of the true self. The true self, however, is 'infinite'. This means that morality demands the realization of the self as a member of an infinite whole. But the demand cannot be fully met on the level of the ethics of my station and its duties. Ultimately, indeed, it can be met only by the transformation of the self in the Absolute. And in this sense Bradley's account of morality is pregnant with metaphysics, the metaphysics of the Absolute. But in *Ethical Studies* he is content to take the matter as far as the self-transcending of morality in religion. The self-transcending of religion is left to the explicit metaphysics of *Appearance and Reality*.

4. Turning to Bradley's logical studies, we must note in the first place his concern with separating logic from psychology. Needless to say, he does not question the legitimacy of inquiries into the origin of ideas and into the association between ideas, inquiries which had occupied so prominent a place in empiricist philosophy from Locke to J. S. Mill. But he insists that they belong to the province of psychology, and that if we confuse logical and psychological inquiries, we shall find ourselves giving psychological answers to logical questions, as the empiricists were inclined to do. 'In England at all events we have lived too long in the psychological attitude.'[30]

Bradley starts his logical studies with an examination of the judgment, considered not as a combination of ideas, which have to be previously treated, but as an act of judging that something is or is not the case. It is true, of course, that we can distinguish various elements within the judgment. But the logician is concerned not with the psychological origin of ideas or concepts nor with the influence of mental associations but with the symbolic function, the reference, which concepts acquire in the judgment. 'For logical purposes ideas are symbols, and they are nothing but symbols.'[31] Terms acquire a definite meaning or reference in the proposition; and the proposition says something which is either true or false. The logician should concern himself with these aspects of the matter, leaving psychological questions to the psychologist.

Bradley's anti-psychologizing attitude in logic has won him a good mark from modern logicians including those whose general philosophical outlook is more or less empiricist. But the connection between his logic and his metaphysics is generally regarded much less benevolently. On this point, however, we have to be careful. On the one hand Bradley does not identify logic with metaphysics. And he regards his inquiries into the forms, quantity and modality of judgments and into the characteristics and types of inference as pertaining to logic, not to metaphysics. On the other hand in the preface to the first edition of *The Principles of Logic* he implicitly admits that 'I am not sure where logic begins or ends'.[32] And some of his logical theories have an obvious connection with his metaphysics, a connection which I wish to illustrate briefly by one or two examples.

As every judgment is either true or false, we are naturally inclined to assume that it asserts or denies a fact, its truth or falsity depending on its correspondence or lack of correspondence with some factual state of affairs. But while a singular judgmnt such as 'I have a toothache' or 'This leaf is green' seems at first sight to mirror a particular fact, reflection shows that the universal judgment is the result of inference and that it is hypothetical in character. For example, if I say that all mammals are warm-blooded, I infer from a limited number of instances a universal conclusion; and what I am actually asserting is that if at any time there is something which possesses the other attributes of being a mammal, it also possesses that of warm-bloodedness.[33] The judgment is thus hypothetical; and a gap is introduced between ideal content and actual fact. For the judgment is asserted as being true even if at any given time there are no actually existing mammals.

According to Bradley, however, it is a mistake to assume that though the universal judgment is hypothetical, the singular affirmative judgment enjoys the privilege of being tied to a particular fact or experience, which it mirrors. If I say that I have a toothache, I am referring, of course, to a particular pain of my own; but the judgment which I enunciate could perfectly well be enunciated by someone else, who would obviously be referring to a different toothache, his own and not mine. True, we can try to pin down the reference of singular judgments by the use of words, such as 'this', 'that', 'here' and 'now'. But though this device serves very well for practical purposes, it is not possible to eliminate every element of generality from the meaning of these particularizing expressions.[34] If someone holds an apple in his hand and says 'This apple is unripe', I am obviously perfectly well aware what apple is being referred to. But the judgment 'This apple is unripe' is not tied to this particular apple: it could be uttered by someone else, or indeed by the same man, with reference to some other apple. The singular affirmative judgment, therefore, does not enjoy any special privilege of being a mirror of existent fact.

The conclusion which Bradley wishes to draw is that if the judgment is regarded as a synthesis or union of ideas, every judgment is general, and that a gap is thus introduced between ideal content and reality. 'Ideas are universal, and, no matter what it is that we try to say and dimly mean, what we really express and succeed in asserting is nothing individual.'[35] If, therefore, an abstract universal judgment is hypothetical and so divorced to some extent from actual reality, it is no use thinking that in the singular judgment we can find an unequivocal reference to a particular fact. All judgments are tarred with the same brush.

In point of fact, however, 'judgment is not the synthesis of ideas, but the reference of ideal content to reality'.[36] And it is Bradley's contention that the latent and ultimate subject of any judgment is reality as a whole, reality, we may say, with a capital letter. 'Not only (this is our doctrine) does all judgment affirm of Reality, but in every judgment we have the assertion that "Reality is such that S is P".'[37] If, for example, I assert that this leaf is green, I am asserting that reality as a whole, the universe, is such that this leaf is green. There is no such thing as an isolated particular fact. So-called particular facts are what they are only because reality as a whole is what it is.

This point of view has an evident bearing on the relative adequacy of different types of judgment. For if reality as a whole is the latent ultimate subject of every judgment, it follows that the more particular a judgment is, the less adequate is it as a description of its ultimate subject. Further, an analytic judgment, in the sense of one which analyses a particular given sense-experience, distorts reality by arbitrarily selecting elements from a complex whole and treating them as though they constituted a self-sufficient particular fact, whereas there are no such facts. The only self-sufficient fact is reality as a whole.

Bradley thus turns his back on the empiricist belief that the more we analyse, the closer we approach to truth.[38] It has been assumed that 'analysis is no alteration, and that, whenever we distinguish, we have to do with divisible existence'.[39] This assumption, however, is a 'cardinal principle of error and delusion'.[40] In reality truth, as Hegel saw, is the whole.

This may suggest that we shall come nearer to an apprehension of reality if we turn away from the immediate judgments of sense to the general hypotheses of the sciences. But though in this sphere there is less fragmentation, there is also a much higher degree of abstraction and of mental construction. If reality consists of what is presented to the senses, the abstractions of the sciences seem to be further removed from reality than the immediate judgments of sense. And if reality does not consist of the wealth of sensuous phenomena, can we really suppose that it consists of logical constructions and scientific abstractions? 'It may come from a failure in my metaphysics, or from a weakness of the flesh which continues to blind me, but the notion that existence could be the same as understanding strikes as cold and ghost-like as the dreariest materialism. That the glory of this world in the end is appearance leaves the world more glorious, if we feel it is a show of some fuller splendour; but the sensuous curtain is a deception and a cheat, if it hides some colourless movement of atoms, some spectral woof of impalpable abstractions, or unearthly ballet of bloodless categories.'[41]

This oft-quoted passage is directed not only against the reduction of reality to scientific generalizations which form a web through whose meshes there slips the whole wealth of sensible particulars, but also against the Hegelian idea that logical categories reveal to us the essence of reality and that the movement of dialectical logic represents the movement of reality.[42] And Bradley's general point of view is that the process of judgment and inference, or, better, the process of discursive thought, is unable to grasp and represent reality. To be sure, for the purposes of practical life and of the sciences discursive thought is a perfectly adequate instrument.

This is shown by its success. But it does not necessarily follow that it is a fit instrument for grasping ultimate reality as it is in itself.

When Bradley was writing *The Principles of Logic*, he tried to avoid metaphysics as much as he felt possible. In the second edition, published twenty-nine years after the publication of *Appearance and Reality*, there is naturally more reference to metaphysics, together with modifications or corrections of some of the logical views advanced in the first edition. In other words, Bradley's explicit metaphysics reacted on his logic. In any case, however, it is quite clear that his logical theories have from the start a metaphysical relevance, even if the main conclusion is perhaps a negative one, namely that discursive thought cannot comprehend reality. At the same time, as Bradley remarks in his additional notes, if reality is the whole, the totality, it must somehow include thought within itself.

5. In his introduction to *Appearance and Reality* Bradley remarks that 'we may agree, perhaps, to understand by metaphysics an attempt to know reality as against mere appearance, or the study of first principles or ultimate truths, or again the effort to comprehend the universe, not simply piecemeal or by fragments, but somehow as a whole'.[43] Most of us would probably accept his contention that a dogmatic and *a priori* assertion of the impossibility of metaphysics should be ruled out of court. And it is obviously reasonable to say that if we are going to make the attempt to understand reality as a whole, it should be made 'as thoroughly as our nature permits'.[44] But in view of what has been said in the last section about the shortcomings of discursive thought it may seem odd that Bradley is prepared to make the attempt at all. He insists, however, that it is natural for the reflective mind to desire to comprehend reality, and that even if comprehension in the full sense turns out to be unattainable, a limited knowledge of the Absolute is none the less possible.

Now, if we describe metaphysics from the start as an attempt to know reality as contrasted with appearance, we presuppose that this distinction is meaningful and valid. And if we say that metaphysics is an attempt to understand reality as a whole, we assume, at least by way of hypothesis, that reality is a whole, that there is in the same sense a One. But Bradley is perfectly prepared to admit that metaphysics rests on an initial presupposition. 'Philosophy demands, and in the end it rests on, what may fairly be termed faith. It has, we may say, to presuppose its conclusion in order to prove it.'[45]

What precisely is the content of this assumption or presupposition or initial act of faith? In the appendix which he added to the second edition of *Appearance and Reality* Bradley tells us that 'the actual starting-point and basis of this work is an assumption about truth and reality. I have assumed that the object of metaphysics is to find a general view which will satisfy the intellect, and I have assumed that whatever succeeds in doing this is real and true, and that whatever fails is neither. This is a doctrine which, so far as I can see, can neither be proved nor questioned.'[46]

The natural way of interpreting this passage, if it is taken simply by itself, seems to be this. The scientist assumes that there are uniformities to be discovered within his field of investigation. Otherwise he would never look for them. And he has to assume that the generalizations which satisfy his intellect are true. Further investigations may lead him to modify or change his conclusions. But he cannot proceed at all without making some presupposition. Similarly, we are free to pursue metaphysics or to leave it alone; but if we pursue it at all, we inevitably assume that a 'general view' of reality is possible, and therefore that reality as a whole is intelligible in principle. We further inevitably assume that we can recognize the truth when we find it. We assume, that is to say, that the general view which satisfies the intellect is true and valid. For our only way of discriminating between rival general views is by choosing the one which most adequately satisfies the demands of the intellect.

Considered in itself this point of view is reasonable enough. But difficulties arise when we bear in mind Bradley's doctrine about the shortcomings of discursive thought. And it is perhaps not surprising to find expression being given to a somewhat different view. Thus in a supplementary note to the sixth chapter of his *Essays on Truth and Reality*

Bradley maintains that the One which is sought in metaphysics is not reached simply by a process of inference but is given in a basic feeling-experience. 'The subject, the object, and their relation, are experienced as elements or aspects in a One which is there from the start.'[47] That is to say, on the pre-reflective level there is an experience 'in which there is no distinction between my awareness and that of which it is aware. There is an immediate feeling, a knowing and being in one, with which knowledge begins.'[48] Indeed, 'at no stage of mental development is the mere correlation of subject and object actually given'.[49] Even when distinctions and relations emerge in consciousness, there is always the background of 'a felt totality'.[50]

This point of view is possibly compatible with that previously mentioned, though one would not normally describe a basic immediate experience as an 'assumption'. In any case Bradley's thesis that there is such an experience enables him to give some content to the idea of the Absolute, in spite of the shortcomings of discursive thought. Metaphysics is really an attempt to think the One which is given in the alleged primitive feeling-experience. In a sense this attempt is foredoomed to failure. For thought is inevitably relational. But inasmuch as thought can recognize the 'contradictions' which emerge when reality is conceived as a Many, as a multiplicity of related things, it can see that the world of common sense and of science is appearance. And if we ask, 'Appearance of what?', reference to the basic experience of a felt totality enables us to have some inkling at any rate of what the Absolute, ultimate reality, must be. We cannot attain a clear vision of it. To do so, we should have to be the comprehensive unified experience which constitutes the Absolute. We should have to get outside our own skins, so to speak. But we can have a limited knowledge of the Absolute by conceiving it on an analogy with the basic sentient experience which underlies the emergence of distinctions between subject and object and between different objects. In this sense the experience in question can be regarded as an obscure, virtual knowledge of reality which is the 'presupposition' of metaphysics and which the metaphysician tries to recapture at a higher level.

In other words, Bradley admits the truth of the objection that metaphysics presupposes its own conclusion, but he regards it not as an objection but rather as a clarification of the nature of metaphysics. In view, however, of the importance of the theme it is regrettable that he does not develop his thesis more at length. As it is, he speaks in a variety of ways, employing terms such as presupposition, assumption, faith and immediate experience. And though these different ways of speaking may be compatible, we are left in some doubt about his precise meaning. However, we are probably justified in laying emphasis on Bradley's thesis that there is an immediate experience of 'a many felt in one',[51] and that this experience gives us an inkling of the nature of the Absolute.

6. By the nature of the case there is not much that can be said by way of positive description either about the alleged pre-reflective experience of a felt totality or about the infinite act of experience which constitutes the Absolute. And it is hardly surprising if Bradley concentrates his attention on showing that our ordinary ways of conceiving reality give rise to contradictions and cannot yield a 'general view' capable of satisfying the intellect. But it is not possible to enter here into all the details of his dialectic. We must confine ourselves to indicating some of the phases of his line of thought.

(i) We are accustomed to group the world's contents into things and their qualities, in Scholastic language into substances and accidents, or, as Bradley puts it, into the substantive and adjectival. But though this way of regarding reality is embedded in language and undoubtedly has a practical utility, it gives rise, Bradley maintains, to insoluble puzzles.

Consider, for example, a lump of sugar which is said to have the qualities of whiteness, hardness and sweetness. If we say that the sugar is white, we obviously do not mean that it is identical with the quality of whiteness. For if this were what we meant, we could not then say that the lump of sugar is hard, unless indeed we were prepared to identify whiteness and hardness. It is natural, therefore, to conceive the sugar as a centre of unity, a substance which possesses different qualities.

If, however, we try to explain what this centre of unity is in itself, we are entirely at a loss. And in our perplexity we are driven to say that the sugar is not an entity which possesses qualities, a substance in which accidents inhere, but simply the qualities themselves as related to one another. Yet what does it mean to say, for example, that the quality of whiteness is related to the quality of sweetness? If, on the one hand, being related to sweetness is identical with being white, to say that whiteness is related to sweetness is to say no more than that whiteness is whiteness. If, on the other hand, being related to sweetness is something different from being white, to say that whiteness is related to sweetness is to predicate of it something different from itself, that is, something which it is not.

Obviously, Bradley is not suggesting that we should cease to speak about things and their qualities. His contention is that once we try to explain the theory implied by this admittedly useful language, we find the thing dissolving into its qualities, while at the same time we are unable to give any satisfactory explanation of the way in which the qualities form the thing. In brief, no coherent account can be given either of the substance-accident theory or of phenomenalism.

(ii) Now let us rule out the substance-accident theory and confine our attention to qualities and relations. In the first place we can say that qualities without relations are unintelligible. For one thing, we cannot think of a quality without conceiving it as possessing a distinct character and so as different from other qualities. And this difference is itself a relation.

In the second place, however, qualities taken together with their relations are equally unintelligible. On the one hand qualities cannot be wholly reduced to their relations. For relations require terms. The qualities must support their relations; and in this sense qualities can be said to make their relations. On the other hand a relation makes a difference to what is related. Hence we can also say that qualities are made by their relations. A quality must be 'at once condition and result'.[52] But no satisfactory account of this paradoxical situation can be given.

Approaching the matter from the side of relations we can

say at once that without qualities they are unintelligible. For relations must relate terms. But we are also driven to say that relations are unintelligible even when they are taken together with their terms, namely qualities. For a relation must be either nothing or something. If it is nothing, it cannot do any relating. But if it is something, it must be related to each of its terms by another relation. And we are then involved in an endless series of relations.

A Scholastic reader of this ingenious piece of dialectic would probably be inclined to remark that a relation is not an 'entity' of the same logical category as its terms, and that it makes no sense to say that it requires to be related to its terms by other relations. But Bradley does not, of course, intend to say that it is sensible to talk about relations being related to their terms. His point is that they must either be so related or be nothing at all, and that both theses are unacceptable.[53] And his conclusion is that 'a relational way of thought—any one that moves by the machinery of terms and relations—must give appearance, and not truth. It is a makeshift, a device, a mere practical compromise, most necessary, but in the end most indefensible.'[54]

To say roundly that thinking which employs the categories of terms and relations does not give us truth, seems to be an exaggeration even on Bradley's premisses. For, as will be seen later, he expounds a theory of degrees of truth, a theory which does not admit any simple distinction between truth and error. It is clear, however, that what he means is that relational thinking cannot give us Truth with a capital letter. That is to say, it cannot disclose the nature of reality as contrasted with appearance. For if the concept of relations and their terms gives rise to insoluble puzzles, it cannot be an instrument for attaining the 'general view' which will satisfy the intellect.

Bradley's position can be clarified in this way. It has sometimes been said that he denied external relations and accepted only internal relations. But this statement can be misleading. It is true that in Bradley's view all relations make a difference to their terms. In this sense they are internal. At the same time they cannot be simply identified with the terms which they relate. And in this sense there not only can but also must be external relations, though there cannot indeed be a relation which exists entirely on its own, and to which it is purely accidental whether it happens to connect terms or not. Hence Bradley can say: 'External relations, if they are to be absolute, I in short cannot understand except as the supposed necessary alternative when internal relations are denied. But the whole "Either-Or", between external and internal relations, to me seems unsound.'[55]

At the same time it is precisely the rejection of 'Either-Or' and the assertion of 'Both-And' which gives rise to Bradley's critique of relational thought. Relations cannot be external in an absolute sense. But neither can they be wholly internal, completely merged with their terms. And it is the difficulty in combining these two points of view which leads Bradley to conclude that relational thought is concerned with the sphere of appearance, and that ultimate reality, the Absolute, must be supra-relational.

(iii) Bradley remarks that anyone who has understood the chapter in *Appearance and Reality* on relation and quality 'will have seen that our experience, where relational, is not true; and he will have condemned, almost without a hearing, the great mass of phenomena'.[56] We need not, therefore, say much about his critique of space, time, motion and causality. It is sufficient to illustrate his line of thought by reference to his critique of space and time.

On the one hand space cannot be simply a relation. For any space must consist of parts which are themselves spaces. And if space were merely a relation, we should thus be compelled to make the absurd statement that space is nothing but the relation which connects spaces. On the other hand, however, space inevitably dissolves into relations and cannot be anything else. For space is infinitely differentiated internally, consisting of parts which themselves consist of parts, and so on indefinitely. And these differentiations are clearly relations. Yet when we look for the terms, we cannot find them. Hence the concept of space, as giving rise to a contradiction, must be relegated to the sphere of appearance.

A similar critique is applied to the concept of time. On the one hand time must be a relation, namely that between 'before' and 'after'. On the other hand it cannot be a relation.

If it is a relation between units which have no duration, 'then the whole time has no duration, and is not time at all'.[57] If, however, time is a relation between units which themselves possess duration, the alleged units cannot be really units but dissolve into relations. And there are no terms. It may be said that time consists of 'now's'. But as the concept of time involves the ideas of before and after, diversity is inevitably introduced into the 'now'; and the game starts once more.

(iv) Some people, Bradley remarks, are quite prepared to see the external spatio-temporal world relegated to the sphere of appearance, but will assure us that the self at least is real. For his own part, however, he is convinced that the idea of the self, no less than the ideas of space and time, gives rise to insoluble puzzles. Obviously, the self exists in some sense. But once we start to ask questions about the nature of the self, we soon see how little value is to be attached to people's spontaneous conviction that they know perfectly well what the term means.

On the one hand a phenomenalistic analysis of the self cannot be adequate. If we try to equate a man's self with the present contents of his experience, our thesis is quite incompatible with our ordinary use of the word 'self'. For we obviously think and speak of the self as having a past and a future, and so as enduring beyond the present moment. If, however, we try to find a relatively enduring self by distinguishing between the relatively constant average mass of a man's psychical states and those states which are clearly transitory, we shall find that it is impossible to say where the essential self ends and the accidental self begins. We are faced with 'a riddle without an answer'.[58]

On the other hand, if we abandon phenomenalism and locate the self in a permanent unit or monad, we are again faced with insoluble difficulties. If all the changing states of consciousness are to be attributed to this unit, in what sense can it be called a unit? And how is personal identity to be defined? If, however, the unit or monad is depicted as underlying all these changing states, 'it is a mere mockery to call it the self of a man'.[59] It would be absurd to identify a man's self with a kind of metaphysical point.

Bradley's conclusion is that 'the self is no doubt the highest form of experience which we have, but, for all that, is not a true form'.[60] The earlier idealists may have thought that the subject-object relationship was a firm rock on which to build a philosophy of reality, but in Bradley's opinion the subject, no less than the object, must be relegated to the sphere of appearance.

7. Reality for Bradley is one. The splintering of reality into finite things connected by relations belongs to the sphere of appearance. But to say of something that it is appearance is not to deny that it exists. 'What appears, for that sole reason, most indubitably *is*; and there is no possibility of conjuring its being away from it.'[61] Further, inasmuch as they exist, appearances must be comprised within reality; they are real appearances. Indeed, 'reality, set on one side and apart from all appearance, would assuredly be nothing'.[62] In other words, the Absolute is the totality of its appearances: it is not an additional entity lying behind them.

At the same time appearances cannot exist in the Absolute precisely as appearances. That is to say, they cannot exist in the Absolute in such a way as to give rise to contradictions or antinomies. For the whole which we seek in metaphysics must be one which completely satisfies the intellect. In the Absolute, therefore, appearances must be transformed and harmonized in such a way that no contradictions remain.

What must the Absolute, or reality, be, for such a transformation of appearances to be possible? Bradley answers that it must be an infinite act of experience, and moreover, sentient experience. 'Being and reality are, in brief, one thing with sentience; they can neither be opposed to, nor even in the end distinguished from it.'[63] Again, 'the Absolute is one system, and its contents are nothing but sentient experience. It will hence be a single and all-inclusive experience, which embraces every partial diversity in concord.'[64]

Use of the term 'sentient experience' should not, of course, be taken to imply that according to Bradley the Absolute can be identified with the visible universe as animated by some kind of world-soul. The Absolute is spirit. 'We may fairly close this work then by insisting that Reality is spiritual. . . . Outside of spirit there is not, and there cannot be, any reality, and, the more that anything is spiritual, so much the more is it veritably real.'[65]

We may very well ask, however, what Bradley means by saying that reality is spiritual, and how this statement is compatible with describing reality as sentient experience. And to answer these questions we must recall his theory of an immediate basic feeling-experience or sentient experience in which the distinction between subject and object, with the consequent sundering of ideal content from that of which it is predicated, has not yet emerged. On the level of human reflection and thought this basic unity, a felt totality, breaks up and externality is introduced. The world of the manifold appears as external to the subject. But we can conceive as a possibility an experience in which the immediacy of feeling, of primitive sentient experience, is recovered, as it were, at a higher level, a level at which the externality of related terms such as subject and object ceases utterly. The Absolute is such an experience in the highest degree. In other words, the Absolute is not sentient experience in the sense of being below thought and infra-relational: it is above thought and supra-relational, including thought as transformed in such a way that the externality of thought to being is overcome.

When, therefore, the Absolute is described as sentient experience, this term is really being used analogically. 'Feeling, as we have seen, supplies us with a positive idea of non-relational unity. The idea is imperfect, but is sufficient to serve as a positive basis',[66] as a positive basis, that is to say, for conceiving ultimate reality. And reality or the Absolute can properly be described as spiritual inasmuch as spirit is definable as 'a unity of the manifold in which the externality of the manifold has utterly ceased'.[67] In the human mind we find a unification of the manifold; but the externality of the manifold has by no means utterly ceased. The human mind is thus only imperfectly spiritual. 'Pure spirit is not realized except in the Absolute.'[68]

It is important to understand that when Bradley describes the Absolute as spiritual, he does not mean to imply that it is a spirit, a self. Inasmuch as the Absolute *is* its appearances, as transformed, it must include within itself all the elements, so to speak, of selfhood. 'Every element of the universe, sensation, feeling, thought and will, must be included within one comprehensive sentience.'[69] But it would be extremely misleading to apply to the infinite universe a term such as 'self', which connotes finitude, limitation. The Absolute is supra-personal, not infra-personal; but it is not a person, and it should not be described as a personal being.

In other words, the Absolute is not a sentient life below consciousness. But consciousness involves externality; and though it must be comprised within the Absolute, it must be comprised within it as transformed in such a way that it is no longer what it appears to us to be. Hence we cannot properly speak of the Absolute as conscious. All that we can say is that it includes and at the same time transcends consciousness.

As for personal immortality, Bradley admits that it is just possible. But he considers that a future life 'must be taken as decidedly improbable'.[70] And he evidently does not believe in it, though his main concern is with arguing that a belief in personal immortality is required neither for morality nor for religion. True, the finite self, as an appearance of the Absolute, must be included within it. But it is included only as somehow transformed. And it is clear that the transformation required is for Bradley of such a kind that an assertion of the personal immortality of the finite self would be quite inappropriate.

8. The Absolute, therefore, is all its appearances, every one of them; but 'it is not all equally, but one appearance is more real than another'.[71] That is to say, some appearances or phenomena are less far removed than others from all-inclusiveness and self-consistency. Hence the former require less alteration than the latter in order to fit into the harmonious, all-inclusive and self-consistent system which constitutes reality. 'And this is what we mean by degrees of truth and reality.'[72]

The criteria of truth are coherence and comprehensiveness. 'Truth is an ideal expression of the Universe, at once coherent and comprehensive. It must not conflict with itself, and there must be no suggestion which fails to fall inside it. Perfect truth in short must realize the idea of a systematic whole.'[73] Thought sunders, as Bradley puts it, the *what* from

the *that*. We try to reconstitute the unity of ideal content
and being by proceeding beyond singular judgments of perception to ever more comprehensive descriptions of the universe. Our goal is thus a complete apprehension of the universe in which every partial truth would be seen as internally,
systematically and harmoniously related to every other partial
truth in a self-coherent whole.

This goal is, however, unattainable. We cannot combine
comprehensiveness with an understanding of all particular
facts. For the wider and more comprehensive our relational
scheme becomes, the more abstract it becomes: the meshes
of the net become wider, and particular facts fall through.
Further, our relational thinking, as we have already seen, is
not in any case fitted to grasp reality as it is, as one fully
coherent and comprehensive whole. 'There is no possible
relational scheme which in my view in the end will be truth.
. . . I had long ago made it clear (so I thought) that for me
no truth in the end was quite true. . . .'[74]

Now, if we take it that for Bradley the standard in reference to which we have to measure degrees of truth is the
ideal truth which perpetually eludes our grasp, we seem to
be left without any standard or criterion which can be of
practical use. But Bradley's line of thought seems to be this.
'The criterion of truth, I should say, as of everything else, is
in the end the satisfaction of a want of our nature.'[75] We do
not know in advance what satisfies the intellect. But by using our intellect in the attempt to understand the world we
discover that what satisfies us is coherence and comprehensiveness, as far as we are able to find them. This, then, is
what we are aiming at, the ideal goal of perfect coherence
and comprehensiveness. But to be able to distinguish between different degrees of truth it is not necessary to have
attained this goal. For reflection on the degrees of satisfaction and dissatisfaction which we experience in our actual
attempt to understand the world will enable us to make corresponding distinctions between degrees of truth.

9. If the Absolute is its appearances, it must in some sense
be or contain error and evil. And though Bradley disclaims
the ability to explain precisely how they are transformed in
the Absolute, he at any rate feels that it is incumbent on

him to show that they are not positively incompatible with his theory of ultimate reality.

The line which Bradley takes in regard to error follows from his theory of degrees of truth. If undiluted truth, so to speak, is identified with the complete truth, every partial truth must be infected with some degree of error. In other words, any sharp distinction between truth and error disappears. An erroneous judgment does not constitute a peculiar kind of judgment. All human judgments are appearance; and all are transformed in the Absolute, though some need a more radical transformation than others. The transformation of what we call erroneous judgments, therefore, does not demand special treatment. It is all a question of degree.

As for evil in the sense of pain and suffering, Bradley suggests that it does not exist, as such, in the infinite act of experience which constitutes the Absolute. The possibility of this can be verified to some extent within the field of our own experience, by the way in which a small pain can be swallowed up, as it were, or neutralized by an intense pleasure. This suggestion is hardly a source of much consolation to the finite sufferer; but Bradley is understandably unwilling to envisage the Absolute as undergoing pain.

In treating of moral evil Bradley makes use of the interpretation to which reference has already been made. Moral evil is in a sense a condition of morality, inasmuch as the moral life consists in an overcoming of the lower self. But morality tends, as we have seen, to transcend itself. And in the Absolute it no longer exists as morality. Absolute experience transcends the moral order, and moral evil has no meaning in this context.

10. Can Bradley's Absolute be properly described as God? Bradley's answer is plain enough: 'for me the Absolute is not God'.[76] Obviously, if we meant by God simply ultimate reality, without any further specification, the Absolute would be God. But Bradley is thinking of the concept of God as a personal being; and he will not allow that personality can be predicated of the Absolute. True, to speak of the Absolute as impersonal would be misleading. For this would suggest that the Absolute is infra-personal. In point of fact personality must be contained within reality, so that the Absolute cannot

be less than personal. But, as so contained, personality is transformed to such an extent that we cannot speak of the Absolute as personal 'if the term "personal" is to bear anything like its ordinary sense'.[77] Reality 'is not personal, because it is personal and more. It is, in a word, suprapersonal.'[78]

Some theistic philosophers would obviously comment that they predicate personality of God in an analogical sense and not, as Bradley seems to suppose, in a univocal sense. As predicated of God, the term 'personal' does not imply finitude or limitation. This, however, is precisely the line of argument to which Bradley objects. In his view theistic philosophers begin by wishing to satisfy the demands of the religious consciousness.[79] That is to say, they desire to reach the conclusion that God is personal, a being to whom man can pray and who can hear man's prayers. But they then pursue a line of argument which progressively eliminates from the concept of personality all that gives it concrete content or meaning for us. And the proper conclusion of this line of argument is that God is not personal but superpersonal, above personality. The conclusion, however, which these philosophers actually assert is the one which they wish to arrive at, not the one which follows from the line of argument which they actually employ. It is not that they are deliberately dishonest. It is rather that they take a word which has a definite range of meaning when applied to human beings, evacuate it of its content and then imagine that it can be meaningfully applied to God. In point of fact, if we once admit that terms such as 'personal' cannot be applied to God in the sense which they ordinarily bear in our language, we create a chasm between personality and God. 'Nor will you bridge the chasm by the sliding extension of a word. You will only make a fog, where you can cry out that you are on both sides at once. And towards increasing this fog I decline to contribute.'[80]

The question, however, is not simply whether God should be called personal or super-personal. It must be remembered that Bradley's Absolute *is* its appearances. It is the universe as transformed. If therefore we understand by God a being who transcends the world in such a way that he cannot be identified with it, it is obvious that God and the Absolute cannot be equated. We *could* call the Absolute 'God'. But Bradley's contention is that the term already has in ordinary speech a meaning which is different from that of the term 'Absolute'. Hence confusion results if the two are identified. And in the interest of clarity, and of intellectual honesty, it is preferable to say that the Absolute is not 'God'.

This point of view affects what Bradley has to say of religion. If we assume that for the religious consciousness God is a being distinct from the external world and the finite self, we can only conclude that this consciousness is involved in a self-contradiction. On the one hand it looks on God as the one true reality. And in this case God must be infinite. On the other hand it conceives God as distinct from the multiplicity of creatures and so as one being, even if the greatest, among many. And in this case God must be limited, finite. If, therefore, when we speak of religion, we are thinking of its concept of ultimate reality, we are compelled to conclude that it belongs to the sphere of appearance, and that, just as morality passes into religion, so does religion pass into the metaphysics of the Absolute. 'If you identify the Absolute with God, that is not the God of religion. . . . Short of the Absolute God cannot rest, and having reached that goal, he is lost and religion with him.'[81]

There is, however, another point of view to which Bradley gives expression. The essence of religion he maintains is not knowledge. Nor is it feeling. 'Religion is rather the attempt to express the complete reality of goodness through every aspect of our being. And, so far as this goes, it is at once something more, and something higher, than philosophy.'[82] The precise meaning of this definition of religion may not be immediately evident; but it is at any rate clear that there is no question of religion, as so defined, passing into metaphysics. Religion may still be appearance; but so is philosophy. And 'the completion of each is not to be found except in the Absolute'.[83] It is obvious from what has been said that Bradley by no means has the desire of some of the earlier British idealists to use metaphysics to support the Christian religion. But it is equally obvious that he does not share Hegel's sublime confidence in the power of speculative philosophy.

In conclusion we can mention Bradley's passing suggestion of the need for a new religion and religious creed. He obviously does not think that metaphysics can justify Christianity, as Hegel thought that it could. Indeed, Bradley would doubtless think it misleading to apply the name of Christianity to 'absolute religion' as interpreted by Hegel. At the same time it might be possible to have 'a religious belief founded otherwise than on metaphysics, and a metaphysics able in some sense to justify that creed. . . . Though this fulfilment is a thing which I cannot myself expect to see, and though the obstacles in the way are certainly great, on the other hand I cannot regard it as impossible.'[84]

11. In the preface to *Appearance and Reality* Bradley quotes from his note-book the celebrated aphorism, 'metaphysics is the finding of bad reasons for what we believe upon instinct, but to find these reasons is no less an instinct'.[85] This remark is clearly not intended as a flat denial of the view expressed in the same preface that 'the metaphysician cannot perhaps be too much in earnest with metaphysics',[86] provided at any rate that he recognizes the limitations of metaphysics and does not exaggerate its importance. Bradley himself takes seriously his own contention that 'the chief need of English philosophy is, I think, a sceptical study of first principles . . . an attempt to become aware of and to doubt all preconceptions'.[87] This element of scepticism, 'the result of labour and education',[88] is represented by the dialectic of appearance, the critique of our ordinary ways of thought. At the same time the element of belief 'upon instinct' is represented by Bradley's explicit statement, to which reference has already been made, that metaphysics rests on a basic presupposition or assumption or initial act of faith,[89] and by the whole doctrine of the Absolute as a completely self-coherent and comprehensive totality.

This element of belief 'upon instinct' occupies a prominent position in the development of Bradley's metaphysics. Consider, for example, the theory of the transformation of appearances in the Absolute. The theory is not, of course, eschatological in character. That is to say, Bradley is not suggesting that at some future apocalyptic date the phenomena which give rise to contradictions or antinomies will undergo a transformation. He maintains that they exist here and now in the Absolute otherwise than they appear to us to exist. The completely harmonious and all-inclusive experience which constitutes the Absolute is a present reality, not simply something which will come into being in the future. But Bradley does not profess to be able to tell us precisely in what this transformation consists. What he does is to argue from possibility to actuality. We can show, for instance, that the transformation of error is not impossible. And if it is not impossible, it is possible. And if it is possible, it is an actual reality. 'For what is *possible*, and what a general principle compels us to say *must be*, that certainly *is*.'[90]

The same holds good of the transformation of pain. 'That which is both possible and necessary we are bound to think real.'[91] Similarly, of the transformation of moral evil Bradley remarks that 'if possible, then, as before, it is indubitably real'.[92] Again, 'the "this" and "mine" are now absorbed as elements within our Absolute. For their resolution must be, and it may be, and so certainly is *is*.'[93] And as a final example we can mention the transformation of finite centres of consciousness, which 'evidently is real, because on our principle it is necessary, and because again we have no reason to doubt that it is possible'.[94]

An obvious objection to this line of argument is that we can hardly be said to know that the required transformation is possible, unless we are able to show how it can take place. How, for example, can we legitimately claim to know that finite centres of consciousness can exist as elements within one infinite absolute experience without any disharmony or 'contradiction', unless we are able to show how they can so exist? It is really not enough to say that nobody can prove the impossibility of our thesis. After all, there is very considerable difficulty, *prima facie* at least, in seeing how finite centres of consciousness can be said to exist as elements within one unified and harmonious experience. And the burden of proof lies on the shoulders of those who claim that it is possible rather than of those who say that it is not possible.

It may be said in reply that as Bradley believes both that

reality is one infinite self-coherent and all-inclusive experience and that appearances are real, and not simply illusory, appearances, he must also believe that the required transformation of appearances is not only possible but also actual. This is quite true. The point is, however, that Bradley is forced to draw this conclusion only because of an initial assumption or presupposition or hypothesis about reality. The assumption is not proved by the dialectic of appearance. True, the elimination of substance, of the substantial, is skilfully used to suggest that all finite things are adjectival to one reality. But Bradley's criticism of substance is itself open to criticism. And in any case the fact, if it is a fact, that our ordinary ways of conceiving reality give rise to contradictions and antinomies does not of itself prove that reality is a self-coherent whole. For reality might be precisely what the dialectic reveals it as being, namely incoherent. If we go on to assert that reality, as contrasted with appearance, is a self-coherent totality, this is because we have already decided that reality *must* be of this nature. References to a primitive sentient experience of a 'felt totality' will not help us much. The idea of such an experience may indeed serve as an analogue for conceiving the Absolute, if we have already decided that there must be an Absolute. But it can hardly be said to prove that it is necessary to postulate the Absolute, as Bradley conceives it.

It is true that Bradley's line of thought can be presented in a plausible way. If we are going to try to understand reality at all, we must assume that reality is intelligible. Hence we must take it that the real is that which satisfies the demands of the intellect. An account of reality which is riddled with self-contradictions does not satisfy the intellect. We must therefore conclude that in reality, as contrasted with appearance, all contradictions are overcome. And in the end this means that we must accept the doctrine of a completely harmonious and all-inclusive totality, the Absolute.

Though, however, it is reasonable to claim that no account of reality which is riddled with contradictions can be accepted as true, it obviously does not follow that we have to accept Bradley's contention that all our ordinary and scientific ways of conceiving reality are in fact riddled with contradictions. True, concepts such as those of space, time and the self have for centuries provided philosophers with problems or puzzles. But we would probably not be inclined to acquiesce in the conclusion that the problems are insoluble on the ground that the concepts are inherently self-contradictory, unless we already believed that reality is different from what it appears to be.

Further, when Bradley makes statements about the Absolute, they are apt to cause no less difficulty than, say, the concept of an enduring self. For example, we are told that 'the Absolute has no history of its own, though it contains histories without number. . . . The Absolute has no seasons, but all at once it bears its leaves, fruit and blossoms.'[95] Now if Bradley's Absolute were transcendent, we could understand the statement that it has no history of its own. But, in his view, the appearances of the Absolute are internal to it: it is nothing apart from them. Hence history, change, development are internal to it. Yet at the same time it 'has no seasons'. The thesis is, of course, that change is 'transformed' in the Absolute. But if it is so transformed that it is no longer what we call change, it is difficult to see how the Absolute can be said to contain histories without number. And if change is not so transformed as to be no longer change, it is difficult to see how the Absolute can be said to have no history. For, to repeat, it *is* its appearances.

The obvious answer to this line of criticism is that it is illegitimate to expect perfect self-coherence from metaphysics. For, given Bradley's interpretation of the shortcomings of human thought, it follows necessarily that any concept of the Absolute which we are capable of forming belongs itself to the sphere of appearance. Indeed, the whole of metaphysics is appearance. Nor does Bradley hesitate to admit this. As we have seen, he declares that philosophy, no less than religion, reaches its completion in the Absolute. That is to say, philosophy is an appearance which, as transformed, is included in the infinite experience which constitutes the Absolute but which transcends our grasp. It is no matter for surprise, therefore, if metaphysical statements themselves fail to attain an ideal standard of self-coherence.

This is true enough. But it simply adds point to the contention that in the long run Bradley's assertion of the Absolute rests on an initial act of faith. In the long run it is the *'must* be' which is decisive. For Bradley's sceptical mind all constructions of human thought, including the metaphysics of the Absolute, must be relegated to the sphere of appearance. He allows indeed for degrees of truth. And he is convinced that the metaphysics of the Absolute in truer than, say, a concept of reality as consisting of many separate things linked by relations. But this does not alter the fact that speculative philosophy is appearance, and not identical with absolute experience. As has been already noted, Bradley does not share Hegel's confident 'rationalism'. Hence we can say that his scepticism extends even to metaphysics, as is indeed suggested by the aphorism quoted at the beginning of this section. This scepticism is combined, however, with a firm belief that reality in itself, transcending our powers of comprehension, is a comprehensive, completely harmonious totality, an all-embracing perfectly self-coherent eternal experience.

It is not altogether surprising if contemporary British philosophers, when writing on Bradley, have tended to concentrate on the puzzles which he raises in regard to our ordinary ways of thought and to pass over his doctrine of the Absolute in a rather cursory manner. One reason for this is that the logical puzzles raised by Bradley can often be treated on their own, without reference to any act of faith in the One, and that they are in principle capable of being definitely solved. For example, in order to decide whether it is true to say that space cannot be and at the same time must be a relation or set of relations, it is not necessary to discuss the transformation of space in the Absolute. What we need in the first place is to clarify the meaning or meanings of 'space'. Again, if we take Bradley's thesis that the concept of relation is self-contradictory, as on the one hand all relations make a difference to their terms and so must be internal to them, while on the other hand they must in some sense fall between and connect their terms and so be external to them, we have a problem which we can hope to solve, provided that we are prepared for the requisite clarificatory analysis. We can understand what is meant by Bradley's thesis and what questions have to be answered in order to decide whether or not it is true.

At the same time we obviously miss what one might call the essential Bradley, if we use *Appearance and Reality* simply as a quarry for detached logical puzzles. For the philosopher is clearly a man who is possessed by the idea of the Absolute, of a completely self-consistent and all-inclusive whole. And it is easy to understand how his philosophy has been able to arouse the interest of Indian thinkers who have not abandoned the native traditions of Hindu speculation, and of some Western philosophers who have an initial sympathy with this line of speculation. For there is at any rate some affinity between Bradley's theory of speculation and the Indian doctrine of Maya, the phenomenal world which veils the one true reality. Obviously, both Bradley and the Indian philosophers in question are faced with the same difficulty, namely that every concept which we can form of ultimate reality must itself belong to the sphere of appearance. But their initial 'visions' are similar, and it is a vision which can exercise a powerful attraction on some minds. Perhaps what we need is a serious inquiry into the bases of this vision or initial inspiration, an inquiry which is not dominated by the *a priori* assumption that what Bradley speaks of as a presupposition or act of faith must be devoid of objective value. It is an inquiry which possesses considerable importance in regard to the foundations of speculative metaphysics.

Chapter Nine

ABSOLUTE IDEALISM: BOSANQUET

Life and writings – Logic; judgment and reality – The meta-physics of individuality – Bosanquet's philosophy of the State – Hobhouse's criticism of Bosanquet – R. B. Haldane; Hegelianism and relativity – H. H. Joachim and the coherence theory of truth.

1. Bradley was a recluse. The other leading absolute idealist in Great Britain, Bernard Bosanquet (1848–1923), was not. After studying at Balliol College, Oxford, where he came under the influence of T. H. Green and R. L. Nettleship, he was elected a Fellow of University College, Oxford, in 1871. But in 1881 he took up residence in London with a view to devoting himself not only to writing but also to lecturing for the adult education movement, which was just beginning, and to social work. From 1903 until 1908 he occupied the chair of moral philosophy in the University of St. Andrews.

Bosanquet was a prolific writer. In 1883 his essay on *Logic as the Science of Knowledge* appeared in *Essays in Philosophical Criticism*, edited by A. Seth and R. B. Haldane. *Knowledge and Reality* was published in 1885 and the two-volume *Logic or the Morphology of Knowledge* in 1888.[1] There followed in quick succession *Essays and Addresses* (1889), *A History of Aesthetic* (1892, 2nd edition 1904), *The Civilization of Christendom and Other Studies* (1893), *Companion to Plato's Republic* (1895), *Essentials of Logic* (1895), and *The Psychology of the Moral Self* (1897). In 1899 Bosanquet published what is probably his best known work, *The Philosophical Theory of the State*.[2] Two sets of Gifford lectures, *The Principle of Individuality and Value* and *The Value and Destiny of the Individual*, appeared respectively in 1912 and 1913. Among other publications we may mention *The Distinction between Mind and Its Objects*

(1913), *Three Lectures on Aesthetic* (1915), *Social and International Ideals* (1917), *Some Suggestions in Ethics* (1918), *Implication and Linear Inference* (1920), *What Religion Is* (1920), *The Meeting of Extremes in Contemporary Philosophy* (1921) and *Three chapters on the Nature of Mind* (1923).

In spite of this extensive literary activity Bosanquet has tended to pass into oblivion and, in comparison with Bradley, is rarely mentioned nowadays, except perhaps in connection with a certain brand of political theory.[3] One reason is probably that Bosanquet is a duller and less paradoxical thinker than Bradley. A more important factor, however, seems to be the belief that, political and aesthetic theory apart, he has little to offer that is not to be found in the writings of his more famous contemporary. Indeed, in 1920 Bosanquet himself wrote to an Italian philosopher that from the publication of *Ethical Studies* in 1876 he had recognized Bradley as his master. But this modest remark hardly does justice to the facts. For example, Bosanquet strongly criticized Bradley's work *The Principles of Logic* on the ground that it created a gulf between thought and reality. And Bradley recognized his indebtedness to Bosanquet's ideas in connection with the material added to the second edition of *The Principles of Logic*. As for *Appearance and Reality*, Bosanquet was deeply influenced by it; but, though he was, like Bradley, a monist, he developed his own metaphysics which in some respects stood closer to Hegelianism. He was convinced of the truth of Hegel's principle that the rational is the real and the real the rational, and he did not share Bradley's marked sceptical tendencies.

2. In a certain sense, Bosanquet maintains, it is true to say that the world is for every individual *his* world, the course of his consciousness, built up out of his perceptions. 'The real world for every individual is emphatically *his* world; an extension and determination of his present perception, which perception is to him not indeed reality as such, but his point of contact with reality as such.'[4] That is to say, we must distinguish between the course of consciousness considered as a series of psychical phenomena and consciousness considered as 'intentional', as presenting a system of interrelated ob-

jects.[5] 'Consciousness is consciousness of a world only in so far as it *presents* a system, a whole of objects, acting on one another, and therefore independent of the presence or absence of the consciousness which presents them.'[6] We must also allow for a distinction between my objective world and the creations of my imagination. Hence we can say that 'the whole world, for each of us, *is* our course of consciousness, in so far as this is regarded as a system of objects which we are obliged to think'.[7]

Reflection on this factor of constraint shows us that the worlds of different individuals are constructed by definite processes common to intelligence as such. In a sense each of us begins with his or her private world. But the more the constructive process of building up a systematic world of objects is developed, so much the more do these several worlds correspond with one another and tend to merge into a common world.

This process of constructing a world is the same as knowledge, in the sense of coming to know. Thus knowledge is the mental construction of reality, the medium in which the world exists for us as a system of interrelated objects. And logic is the analysis of this constructive process. 'The work of intellectually constituting that totality which we call the real world is the work of knowledge. The work of analyzing the process of this constitution or determination is the work of logic, which might be described as the self-consciousness of knowledge, or the reflection of knowledge upon itself.'[8]

Now, knowledge exists in the judgment. And it follows, therefore, if logic is the self-consciousness of knowledge, that the study of the judgment is fundamental in logic. True, we can say that the proposition, the expression of the judgment, has 'parts'. And the enunciation of a proposition is a temporal process. But the judgment in itself is an identity-in-difference: it is 'not a relation between ideas, nor a transition from one idea to another, nor does it contain a third idea which indicates a particular kind of connection between two other ideal contents'.[9]

The ultimate subject of the judgment is reality as a whole, and 'the essence of Judgment is the reference of an ideal content to Reality'.[10] Hence every judgment could be intro-

duced by some such phrase as 'Reality is such that . . .'
or 'The real world is characterized by. . . .'[11]

As for inference, we can indeed make a *prima facie* distinction between judgment and inference by saying that the
former is the immediate and the latter the mediate reference
of an ideal content to reality. But on closer examination the
distinction tends to break down. For, properly speaking, no
judgment can be said to express knowledge unless it possesses the characteristics of necessity and 'precision', precision
depending on the mediating conditions being made explicit.
And in this case no absolute distinction between judgment
and inference is possible. Instead we have the ideal of one
ultimate judgment which would predicate the whole of reality, as an ideal content, of itself. This ultimate judgment
would not, of course, be simple. For it would include within
itself all partial truths as organically interrelated, as coherent.
It would be the all-inclusive identity-in-difference in the form
of knowledge. 'The whole is the truth.'[12] And particular
truths are true in so far as they cohere with other truths in
this whole.

Obviously, Bosanquet is in agreement with Bradley on
many points: on the fundamental importance of the judgment in logic, on reality as the ultimate subject of every judgment, and on truth in the full sense as being the complete
system of truth. But in spite of the many points of agreement there are important differences of attitude. Thus for
Bosanquet reality or the universe is 'not only of such a nature
that it can be known by intelligence, but further of such a
nature that it can be known and handled by *our* intelligence'.[13] True, Bosanquet carefully refrains from claiming
that the finite mind can fully comprehend reality. At the
same time he is anxious to avoid what he regards as Bradley's
marked tendency to drive a wedge between human thought
on the one hand and reality on the other. Every finite mind
approaches reality from a particular point of view and builds
up its own conception of reality. But though there are degrees of truth, and so of error, no judgment is entirely out
of touch with reality; and intelligence as such forces us to
conceive the universe in certain ways, so that, despite private
points of view, a common objective world is presented in

consciousness. Further, human thought as a whole approximates more and more to a comprehension of reality, even though the ideal ultimate judgment is a goal which transcends the capacity of any given finite mind.[14]

3. With Bosanquet, as with Bradley, there is evidently a close connection between logic and metaphysics. For both hold that the ultimate subject of every judgment is reality as a whole. But it would be a mistake to think that because Bosanquet describes logic as the self-consciousness of knowledge, he intends to imply that logic can provide us with factual knowledge about the world. He does not maintain this any more than Bradley does. Logic is the morphology of knowledge: it does not provide us with the content of knowledge.

Indeed, it is a mistake to look to philosophy at all for a knowledge of hitherto unknown facts. 'Philosophy can tell you no new facts, and can make no discoveries. All that it can tell you is the significant connection of what you already know. And if you know little or nothing, philosophy has little or nothing to tell you.'[15] In other words, we acquire factual knowledge by ordinary experience and by the study of physics, chemistry, and so on. Philosophy neither deduces nor adds to this knowledge. What it does is to exhibit a pattern of connections between already known facts.

Obviously, the sciences do not present us with unrelated atomic facts; they exhibit relations, connections, bringing facts under what we call laws. Hence, if philosophy has any such function to perform, to exhibit the 'significant connection' of what we already know must mean showing how the facts which are known otherwise than through philosophy are members of an overall system in which each member contributes to the total unity in virtue of the very characteristics which distinguish it from other members. In other words, the philosopher is not primarily concerned with class-concepts formed by abstraction from differentiating characteristics but rather with the concrete universal, which is an identity-in-difference, the universal existing in and through its particulars.

The concrete universal is called by Bosanquet, following Hegel, the 'individual'. And it is clear that in the fullest sense of the term there can be only one individual, namely the Absolute. For this universal of universals is the all-embracing system which alone can fully satisfy the criteria proposed by Bosanquet, that is, non-contradiction and wholeness. These criteria are said to be really one. For it is only in the complete whole or totality that there is complete absence of contradiction.

Though, however, individuality belongs in a pre-eminent sense to the Absolute, it is also attributed to human beings, even if in a secondary sense. And when examining this use of the term Bosanquet insists that individuality should not be understood in a predominantly negative fashion, as though it consisted chiefly in not being someone else. After all, in the case of the supreme individual, the Absolute, there is no other individual from which it can be distinguished. Rather should individuality be conceived positively, as consisting 'in the richness and completeness of a self'.[16] And it is in social morality, art, religion and philosophy that 'the finite mind begins to experience something of what individuality must ultimately mean'.[17] In social morality, for example, the human person transcends what Bosanquet calls the repellent self-consciousness, for the private will is united with other wills without being annulled in the process. Again, in religion the human being transcends the level of the narrow and poverty-stricken self and feels that he attains a higher level of richness and completeness in union with the divine. At the same time morality is subsumed within religion.

Reflection on the development of the individual self can thus give us some idea of how various levels of experience can be comprehended and transformed in the one unified and all-inclusive experience which constitutes the Absolute. And here Bosanquet has recourse to the analogy of Dante's mind as expressed in the *Divine Comedy*. The external world and the world of selves are both present in the poet's mind and find expression in the poem. The human selves are indeed presented as thinking and acting beings, as real selves existing in an external sphere. At the same time all these selves live only through their participation in the thoughts, emotions and acts which make up the poet's mind as expressed in the poem.

This analogy should not be interpreted as meaning that for Bosanquet the Absolute is a mind behind the universe, a mind which composes a divine poem. The Absolute is the totality. Hence it cannot be a mind. For mind is a perfection which depends on physical preconditions and constitutes a certain level of reality. Nor can the Absolute be simply equated with the God of the religious consciousness, who is a being distinct from the world and who does not contain evil. 'The whole, considered as a perfection in which the antagonism of good and evil is unnoted, is not what religion means by God, and must rather be taken as the Absolute.'[18] Here Bosanquet is at one with Bradley.

Though, however, the Absolute cannot be a mind or a self, reflection on self-consciousness, the chief characteristic of mind, can furnish us with clues for deciphering the nature of reality. For example, the self attains satisfaction and richness of experience only by passing out of itself: it must die, as it were, to live. And this suggests that a perfect experience embodies the character of the self to this extent at least, that it passes out of itself to regain itself. In other words, Bosanquet, unlike Bradley, is attempting to offer some explanation of the existence of finite experience. 'Not of course that the infinite being can lose and regain its perfection, but that the burden of the finite is inherently a part or rather an instrument of the self-completion of the infinite. The view is familiar. I can only plead that it loses all point if it is not taken in bitter earnest.'[19] One objection against this Hegelian idea of a self-developing Absolute is that it seems to introduce temporal succession into the infinite being. But unless we are prepared to say that the concept of the Absolute is for us a vacuous concept, we cannot help ascribing to the Absolute a content which, from our point of view, is developed in time.

It may be objected that Bosanquet has done nothing to show that there is an Absolute. He simply assumes its existence and tells us what it must be. His reply, however, is that at all levels of experience and thought there is a movement from the contradictory and partial to the noncontradictory and complete, and that the movement can find no end save in the concept of the Absolute. 'I am aware of no point at which an arrest in the process can be justified.'[20] The idea of the Absolute, the totality, is in fact the motive-force, the final end, of all thought and reflection.

Now, individuality is the criterion of value, a concept on which much more emphasis is laid by Bosanquet than by Bradley. And as individuality is to be found in its complete form only in the Absolute, the Absolute must be the ultimate standard of value, as well as of truth and reality. It follows from this that we cannot attribute an ultimate or absolute value to the finite self. And as Bosanquet conceives self-perfection as involving an overcoming of self-enclosedness and a conscious entry into membership of a greater whole, we would hardly expect him to regard personal immortality as the destiny of the finite self. He claims indeed that the best in the finite self is preserved, in a transformed state, in the Absolute. But he also admits that that which persists of myself would not appear to my present consciousness to be a continuation of 'myself'. This, however, is not for Bosanquet any cause for regret. The self, as we know it, is a mixture, as it were, of the finite and the infinite; and it is only in shedding the restricting vesture of finite limited self-hood that it achieves its destiny.

As has already been noted, Bosanquet is much less concerned than Bradley with illustrating the defectiveness of human thought as an instrument for grasping reality, and much more concerned with understanding the universe as a whole and with determining degrees of perfection or value. Yet in the long run both maintain that the universe is something very different from what it appears to be. Bosanquet rather plays down this aspect of the matter. And for this reason his thought may appear less exciting than that of Bradley. But both men represent the universe as an infinite experience, as something, that is to say, which it certainly does not appear to be at first sight. Though, however, there is a fundamental affinity, Bosanquet is notable as making explicit the value-judgment which is basic in idealist monism, namely that the supreme value and the ultimate criterion of all value is the totality, the all-inclusive concrete universal in which all 'contradictions' are overcome.

4. Given Bosanquet's absolute idealism, one would not ex-

pect him to favour the type of political theory which regards the State as a device for enabling individuals (in the ordinary sense of the term) to pursue their private ends in peace and security. All such theories are condemned as superficial, as theories 'of the first look'. 'It is the first look of the man in the street or of the traveller, struggling at a railway station, to whom the compact self-containedness and self-direction of the swarming human beings before him seems an obvious fact, while the social logic and spiritual history which lie behind the scene fail to impress themselves on his perceptive imagination.'[21]

These theories assume that every man is a self-enclosed unit which undergoes the impact of other such units. And government tends to appear as the impact of others when systematized, regularized and reduced to a minimum. In other words, it appears as something alien to the individual, bearing upon him from without, and so as an evil, though admittedly a necessary evil.

A quite different point of view is represented by Rousseau's theory of the General Will. Here we have the idea of an 'identity between my particular will and the will of all my associates in the body politic which makes it possible to say that in all social co-operation, and in submitting even to forcible restraint, when imposed by society in the true common interest, I am obeying only myself, and am actually attaining my freedom'.[22] Yet in the process of expressing his enthusiasm for direct democracy and his hostility to representative government Rousseau really enthrones the Will of All in the place of the General Will, which becomes a nonentity.

We must therefore go beyond Rousseau and give a real content to the idea of the General Will, without reducing it in effect to the Will of All. And this means identifying it with the State when considered not merely as a governmental structure but rather as 'a working conception of life . . . the conception by the guidance of which every living member of the commonwealth is enabled to perform his function, as Plato has taught us'.[23] If the State or political society is understood in this way, we can see that the relation of the individual mind and will to the mind of society and the

General Will is comparable to the relation between the individual physical object and Nature as a whole. In both cases the self-enclosed individual is an abstraction. The individual man's real will, therefore, by which he wills his own nature as a rational being, is identical with the General Will. And in this identification 'we find the only true account of political obligation'.[24] In obeying the State the individual obeys his real will. And when he is constrained by the State to act in a certain manner, he is constrained to act in accordance with his real will, and so to act freely.

In other words, the alleged antithesis between the individual and the State is for Bosanquet a false antithesis. And it follows that the alleged problem of justifying interference by the State with private liberty is not a genuine problem. But this is not to say that no genuine problem can arise in regard to some particular concrete issue. For the ultimate end of the State, as of its members, is a moral end, the attainment of the best life, the life which most develops man's potentialities or capacities as a human being. Hence we can always ask, in regard to a proposed law for example, 'how far and in what way the use of force and the like by the State is a hindrance to the end for which the States exists',[25] and which is at the same time the end of each of its members. An appeal simply to private liberty against so-called State interference in general betrays a misunderstanding of the nature of the State and of its relations to its members. But it by no means follows that any and every use of compulsion contributes to the end for which the State exists.

Bosanquet's point of view can be clarified in this way. As the end of the State is a moral end, it cannot be attained unless the citizens act morally, which includes intention as well as external action. Morality in this full sense, however, cannot be enforced by law. Individuals can be compelled, for instance, to refrain from certain actions; but they cannot be compelled to refrain from them for high moral motives. It is indeed clearly conducive to the common good that people should refrain from murder, even if their motive is simply the avoidance of punishment. It remains true, however, that the employment of force, so far as it is the determining cause of an action, reduces the resultant actions to a lower level than they would occupy if they were the result of reason and free choice. Hence the employment of force and compulsion should be restricted as far as possible, not because it is thought to represent an interference by society with self-enclosed individuals (for this is a false antithesis), but because it interferes with the attainment of the end for which the State exists.

In other words, Bosanquet shares the view of T. H. Green that the primary function of legislation is to remove hindrances to the development of the good life. How far, for example, social legislation should extend is not a question which can be answered *a priori*. As far as general principles go, we can only say that to justify compulsion we ought to be able to show that 'a definite tendency to growth, or a definite reserve of capacity, . . . is frustrated by a known impediment, the removal of which is a small matter compared to the capacities to be set free'.[26] On this principle we can justify, for instance, compulsory education as the removal of a hindrance to the fuller and wider development of human capacities. Obviously, the legislation itself is positive. But the object of the law is primarily that of removing hindrances to the attainment of the end for which political society exists, an end which is 'really' willed by every member as a rational being.

If we assume that the moral end is the fullest possible development of man's capacities, and that it is attained or at any rate approached only in the context of society, it seems only natural to look beyond the national State to the ideal of a universal society, humanity in general. And Bosanquet does at least admit that the idea of humanity must have a place 'in any tolerably complete philosophical thinking'.[27] At the same time he claims that the ethical idea of humanity does not form an adequate basis for an effective community. For we cannot presuppose in mankind at large a sufficient unity of experience, such as exists in a national State, for the exercise of a General Will. Further, Bosanquet condemns proposals for a World-State with plans for substituting a universal language for national languages, a substitution which, in his opinion, would destroy literature and poetry and reduce intellectual life to a level of mediocrity. Like Hegel, therefore, Bosanquet is unable to transcend the idea of the national State, animated by a common spirit which expresses itself in objective institutions and submits these institutions to a critical evaluation in the light of experience and present needs.

Again, like Hegel, Bosanquet is prepared to admit that no actual State is immune from criticism. It is possible in principle for the State to act 'in contravention of its main duty to sustain the conditions of as much good life as possible'.[28] But though this admission would appear to most people to be obviously justified, it creates a special difficulty for anyone who holds with Bosanquet that the State is in some sense identical with the General Will. For by definition the General Will wills only what is right. Hence Bosanquet tends to make a distinction between the State as such and its agents. The latter may act immorally, but the former, the State as such, cannot be saddled with responsibility for the misdeeds of its agents 'except under circumstances which are barely conceivable'.[29]

It can hardly be claimed that this is a logically satisfactory position. If the State as such means the General Will, and if the General Will always wills what is right, it seems to follow that there are no conceivable circumstances in which the State as such could be said to act immorally. And in the long run we are left with a tautology, namely that a will which always wills what is right, always wills what is right. Indeed, Bosanquet himself seems to feel this, for he suggests that on a strict definition of State action we ought to say that the State does not really will an immoral action which we would ordinarily attribute to 'the State'. At the same time he understandably feels bound to admit that there may be circumstances in which we can legitimately speak of the State acting immorally. But by speaking of 'barely conceivable' circumstances he inevitably gives the impression that for practical purposes the State is immune from criticism. For those who maintain that statements about action by the State are always reducible in principle to statements about individuals, there is obviously no difficulty in speaking about the State as acting immorally. But if we assume that we can make meaningful statements about 'the State as such' which are not reducible in principle to a set of statements about assignable individuals, the question certainly arises whether we can legitimately apply the criteria of personal morality when judging the actions of this somewhat mysterious entity.

5. It is understandable that when some British writers undertook to show that ultimate responsibility for the First World War rested fairly and squarely on the shoulders of German philosophers such as Hegel, Bosanquet's political philosophy came in for its share of criticism. For example, in *The Metaphysical Theory of the State* (1918) by L. T. Hobhouse,[30] the author, though principally concerned with Hegel, devoted a good deal of criticism to Bosanquet, in whom he rightly saw the British political philosopher who stood nearest to Hegel.

Hobhouse sums up what he calls the metaphysical theory of the State in the three following propositions. 'The individual attains his true self and freedom in conformity to his real will'; 'this real will is the general will'; and 'the general will is embodied in the State'.[31] The State is thus identified to all intents and purposes with the entire social fabric, with society in general; and it is regarded as the guardian and expression of morality, as the highest moral entity. But if the State is identified with society, the result is the absorption of the individual by the State. And why should the national State be regarded as the highest product of social development? If we assume for the sake of argument that there is such a thing as the General Will and that it is the real or true will of man,[32] it should find a much more adequate expression in a universal world-society than in the national State. True, a world-society is not yet in existence. But the creation of such a society should be held up as an ideal towards which we ought to strive effectively, whereas in point of fact Bosanquet, following Hegel, shows an unwarranted prejudice in favour of the national State. In this sense idealist political theory is unduly conservative. Further, if the State is regarded as the guardian and expression of morality and as the highest moral entity, the logical consequence is a disastrous moral conformism. In any case, if the State is really, as Bosanquet supposes it to be, a moral entity of a higher order than the individual moral agent, it is very odd that these sublime moral entities, namely different States, have not succeeded in regularizing their mutual relations according to moral standards.[33] In brief, 'to confuse the State with society and political with moral obligation is the central fallacy of the metaphysical theory of the State'.[34]

Having summed up the metaphysical theory of the State in a number of theses, Hobhouse then finds himself driven to admit that Bosanquet sometimes speaks in ways which do not easily fit into this abstract scheme. But his way of coping with this difficulty is to argue that Bosanquet is guilty of inconsistency. He notes, for example, that in the introduction to the second edition of *The Philosophical Theory of the State* Bosanquet refers to a social co-operation which does not belong strictly either to the State or to private individuals simply as such. And he finds this inconsistent with the thesis that every man's true self finds its adequate embodiment in the State. Again, Hobhouse notes that in *Social and International Ideals* Bosanquet speaks of the State as an organ of the community, which has the function of maintaining the external conditions required for the development of the best life. And he finds this way of speaking inconsistent with the thesis that the State is identical with the whole social fabric. Hobhouse's conclusion, therefore, is that if such passages represent what Bosanquet really thinks about the State, he ought to undertake 'the reconstruction of his entire theory'.[35]

By and large, of course, Hobhouse is quite justified in finding in Bosanquet the so-called metaphysical theory of the State.[36] True, it is an exaggeration to say that according to Bosanquet a man's true self finds its adequate embodiment in the State, if we mean by this that man's potentialities are completely actualized in what would normally be regarded as his life as a citizen. Like Hegel, Bosanquet considers art, for instance, separately from the State, even if it presupposes society. At the same time it is undoubtedly true that he maintains an organic theory of the State, according to which statements about the State 'as such' are irreducible in principle to statements about assignable individuals. It is also true that Bosanquet ascribes to the national State a pre-eminent role as the embodiment of the General Will, and that he is comparatively insensitive to the ideal of a wider human society. As for the confusion of political with moral obligation, which Hobhouse mentions as a cardinal feature of the metaphysical theory of the State and to which he strongly objects, it seems to the present writer that a distinction must be made.

If we hold a teleological interpretation of morality, in which obligation is regarded as falling on us in regard to those actions which are required for the attainment of a certain end (for example, the actualization and harmonious integration of one's potentialities as a human being), and if at the same time we regard life in organized society as one of the normally requisite means for attaining this end, we can hardly avoid looking on political obligation as one of the expressions of moral obligation. But it by no means follows that we are committed to confusing moral with political obligation, if by this is meant reducing the former to the latter. This confusion can arise only if the State is regarded as being itself the basis and interpreter of the moral law. If we do look on the State in this way, a disastrous conformism is, as Hobhouse notes, the result. But though Bosanquet's theory of the General Will as finding its adequate embodiment in the State undoubtedly favours this exalted view of the latter's moral function, we have seen that he allows, even if with reluctance, for moral criticism of any actual State. Hobhouse's comment, however, is that Bosanquet is here guilty of inconsistency, and that if he really wishes to allow for moral criticism of the State, he should revise his theory of the General Will. The comment seems to the present writer to be just.

6. We have noted that Bosanquet stood closer than Bradley to Hegel. But if we are looking for a British philosopher who openly shared Stirling's enthusiastic veneration for Hegel as the great master of speculative thought, we must turn rather to Richard Burdon Haldane (1856–1928), the distinguished statesman who in 1911 was created Viscount Haldane of Cloan. In his two-volume work The Pathway to Reality (1903–4) Haldane declared that Hegel was the greatest master of speculative method since Aristotle, and that he himself was not only prepared but also desirous to be called an Hegelian.[37] Indeed, his undisguised admiration for German

thought and culture led to a rather shameful attack on him at the beginning of the First World War.[38]

Haldane made an attempt to show that the theory of relativity is not only compatible with Hegelianism but also demanded by it. In *The Pathway to Reality* he proposed a philosophical theory of relativity; and when Einstein published his papers on the subject, Haldane regarded them as providing confirmation of his own theory, which he developed in *The Reign of Relativity* (1921). In brief, reality as a whole is one, but knowledge of this unity is approached from various points of view, such as those of the physicist, the biologist and the philosopher. And each point of view, together with the categories which it employs, represents a partial and relative view of the truth and should not be absolutized. This idea not only fits in with but is also demanded by a philosophical outlook for which reality is ultimately Spirit and for which truth is the whole system of truth, reality's complete self-reflection or self-knowledge, a goal which is approached through dialectical stages.

It can hardly be claimed that this general philosophical theory of relativity was, in itself, a novelty. And in any case it was rather late in the day for an attempt to infuse fresh life into Hegelianism by emphasizing the relativistic aspects of the system and by invoking the name of Einstein as a patron. However, it is worth mentioning Haldane as one of those prominent figures in British public life who have had a lasting interest in philosophical problems.

7. We have already had occasion to mention the coherence theory of truth, namely that any particular truth is true in virtue of its place in a total system of truth. This theory was discussed and defended in *The Nature of Truth* (1906) by Harold Henry Joachim (1868–1938), who occupied the Wykeham chair of logic at Oxford from 1919 until 1935. And it is not altogether superfluous to say something about the book, because the author showed his awareness of the difficulties to which the theory gives rise and did not attempt to slur them over.

Joachim approaches the coherence theory of truth by way of a critical examination of other theories. Consider, for example, the correspondence theory, according to which a factual statement is true if it corresponds with extra-linguistic reality. If somebody asks us to tell him what the reality is with which, say, a true scientific statement corresponds, our reply will necessarily be expressed in a judgment or set of judgments. When therefore we say that the scientific statement is true because it corresponds with reality, what we are really saying is that a certain judgment is true because it coheres systematically with other judgments. Hence the correspondence of truth is seen to pass into the coherence theory.

Or take the doctrine that truth is a quality of certain entities called 'propositions', a quality which is simply perceived immediately or intuitively. According to Joachim the claim of an immediate experience to be an experience of truth can be recognized only in so far as the intuition is shown to be the outcome of rational mediation, that is, in so far as the truth in question is seen to cohere with other truths. A proposition considered as an independent entity which possesses the quality of truth or of falsity, is a mere abstraction. Hence once more we are driven on to the interpretation of truth as coherence.

Joachim is thus convinced that the coherence theory of truth is superior to all rival theories. 'That the truth itself is one, and whole, and complete, and that all thinking and all experience moves within its recognition and subject to its manifest authority; this I have never doubted.'[39] Similarly, Joachim does not doubt that different judgments and partial systems of judgments are 'more or less true, i.e. as approximating more or less closely to the one standard'.[40] But once we begin to make the coherence theory explicit, really to think out its meaning and implications, difficulties arise which cannot be ignored.

In the first place coherence does not mean simply formal consistency. It refers in the long run to one all-inclusive significant whole in which form and matter, knowledge and its object, are inseparably united. In other words, truth as coherence means absolute experience. And an adequate theory of truth as coherence would have to provide an intelligible account of absolute experience, the all-inclusive totality, and to show how the various levels of incomplete experience form constitutive moments in it. But it is impossible in principle that these demands should be met by any philosophical theory. For every such theory is the result of finite and partial experience and can be at best only a partial manifestation of the truth.

In the second place truth, as it is attained in human knowledge, involves two factors, thought and its object. And it is precisely this fact which gives rise to the correspondence theory of truth. An adequate theory of truth as coherence must therefore be able to explain how we are to conceive that self-diremption of the totality, absolute experience, which brings about the relative independence of subject and object, of ideal content and external reality, within human knowledge. But no such explanation, Joachim admits, has ever been given.

In the third place, as all human knowledge involves thought about an Other (that is, an other than itself), every theory of the nature of truth, including the coherence theory, must be a theory about truth as its Other, as something about which we think and pronounce judgment. And this is equivalent to saying that 'the coherence theory of truth *on its own admission* can never rise above the level of knowledge which at the best attains to the "truth" of correspondence'.[41]

With admirable candour Joachim is quite ready to speak of the 'shipwreck' of his endeavours to state an adequate theory of truth. In other words, he cannot meet the difficulties to which the coherence theory gives rise. At the same time he is still convinced that this theory carries us further than rival theories into the problem of truth, and that it can maintain itself against objections which are fatal to them, even if it itself gives rise to questions which cannot be answered. It is, however, clear enough that the ultimate reason why Joachim sticks to the coherence theory, in spite of the difficulties to which it admittedly gives rise, is a metaphysical reason, a belief about the nature of reality. Indeed, he explicitly says that he does not believe that 'the Metaphysician is entitled to acquiesce in logical theories, when their success demands that he should accept within the sphere of Logic assumptions which his own metaphysical theory condemns'.[42] In other words, absolute idealism in metaphysics demands the coherence theory of truth in logic. And in spite of the difficulties to which this theory gives rise we are justified in accepting it, if other theories of truth inevitably pass into the coherence theory when we try to state them precisely.

In judging whether other theories of truth do in fact pass into the coherence theory we have to bear in mind Joachim's own observation that coherence in this context does not mean simply formal consistency. An admission that two mutually incompatible propositions cannot both be true at the same time is not equivalent to embracing the coherence theory of truth. As Joachim presents the theory, when he is discussing the difficulties to which it gives rise, it is clearly a metaphysical theory, part and parcel of absolute idealism. Hence it is a question of whether all other theories of truth can be seen ultimately either to suffer complete collapse under critical examination or to imply the validity of absolute idealism. And nobody who is not already an absolute idealist is likely to admit that this is the case. It is not indeed the intention of the present writer to suggest that coherence has nothing to do with truth. In point of fact we often use coherence as a test, coherence with already established truths. And it is arguable that this implies a metaphysical belief about the nature of reality. But it does not necessarily follow that this is an implicit belief in absolute idealism. In any case, as Joachim himself frankly recognizes, if a true proposition is true only in so far as it is included as a moment in an absolute experience which transcends our grasp, it is very difficult to see how we can ever know that any proposition is true. And yet we are sure that we can have some knowledge. Perhaps an essential preliminary to any attempt to formulate 'the' theory of truth is a careful examination of the ways in which terms such as 'true' and 'truth' are used in ordinary discourse.

Chapter Ten

THE TURN TOWARDS PERSONAL IDEALISM

Pringle-Pattison and the value of the human person – The pluralistic idealism of McTaggart – The pluralistic spiritualism of J. Ward – General comments.

1. The attitude adopted by Bradley and Bosanquet to finite personality not unnaturally led to a reaction even within the idealist movement. One of the chief representatives of this reaction was Andrew Seth Pringle-Pattison (1856–1931).[1] In his first work, *The Development from Kant to Hegel* (1882), he described the transition from the critical philosophy of Kant to the metaphysical idealism of Hegel as an inevitable movement. And he always maintained that the mind cannot rest in a system which involves the doctrine of unknowable things-in-themselves. But in 1887 he published *Hegelianism and Personality* in which, somewhat to the surprise of his readers, he submitted absolute idealism to outspoken criticism.

At first sight, Pringle-Pattison admits, Hegelianism appears to magnify man. For, obscure though Hegel's utterances may be, his philosophy certainly suggests that God or the Absolute is identical with the whole historical process, considered as developing dialectically towards self-knowledge in and through the human mind. 'The philosopher's knowledge of God is God's knowledge of himself.'[2] The ground is thus prepared for the Left-wing Hegelian transformation of theology into anthropology.

Reflection, however, shows that in Hegelianism the individual person is of little account. For human beings become 'the foci in which the impersonal life of thought momentarily concentrates itself, in order to take stock of its own contents. These foci appear only to disappear in the perpetual process of this realization.'[3] The human person, in other words, is simply a means whereby impersonal Thought comes to a knowledge of itself. And from the point of view of anyone who attaches a real value to personality it is clear that 'Hegel's determination to have one process and one subject was the original fountain of error'.[4] The radical mistake both of Hegelianism itself and of its British derivatives is 'the identification of the human and the divine self-consciousness or, to put it more broadly, the unification of consciousness in a single self'.[5] This unification is ultimately destructive of the reality of both God and man.

Pringle-Pattison insists, therefore, on two points. First, we should recognize a real self-consciousness in God, even though we have to avoid ascribing to it the features of finite self-consciousness considered precisely as finite. Secondly, we must assert the value and relative independence of the human person. For each person has a centre of its own, a will, which is 'impervious' to any other person, 'a centre which I maintain even in my dealings with God Himself'.[6] 'The two positions—the divine personality and human dignity and immortality—are two complementary sides of the same view of existence.'[7]

This sounds like an abandonment of absolute idealism in favour of theism. But in his later writings Pringle-Pattison reaffirms absolute idealism or, more accurately, attempts to revise it in such a way that it permits more value being attached to finite personality than in the philosophies of Bradley and Bosanquet. The result is an unsatisfactory amalgam of absolute idealism and theism.

In the first place we cannot prove, by the sort of arguments employed by the earlier British idealists, that the world of Nature can exist only as object for a subject. Ferrier's line of argument, for example, is quite unsound. It is indeed obviously true that we cannot conceive material things without conceiving them; but 'this method of approach cannot possibly prove that they do not exist out of that relation'.[8] As for Green's argument that relations cannot exist except through the synthesizing activity of a universal consciousness, this presupposes a defunct psychology, according to which experience begins with unrelated sensations. In point of fact relations are just as much given realities as the things related.

It does not follow, however, that, as the 'lower naturalism' maintains, Nature exists apart from a total system which embodies value. On the contrary, we can see in Nature a continuity of process combined with the emergence of qualitatively distinct levels. Man appears as 'the organ through which the universe beholds and enjoys itself'.[9] And among the emergent qualities which characterize the universe we must recognize not only the so-called secondary qualities but also 'the aspects of beauty and sublimity which we recognize in nature and those finer insights which we owe to the poet and the artist'.[10] Moral values too must be taken as qualifying the universe. And the whole process of Nature, with the emergence of qualitatively different levels, is to be looked on as a progressive manifestation of the Absolute or God.

According to Pringle-Pattison, the idea of God as existing 'before' the world and as creating it out of nothing is philosophically untenable. 'The idea of creation tends to pass into that of manifestation';[11] and the infinite and the finite stand to one another in a relation of mutual implication. As for man, 'he exists as an organ of the universe or of the Absolute, the one Being',[12] which should be conceived in terms of its highest manifestation and so as one spiritual life or absolute experience.

Whatever *Hegelianism and Personality* may have seemed to imply, there is thus no radical rejection of absolute idealism in Pringle-Pattison's later work. On the contrary, there is a large measure of agreement with Bosanquet. At the same time Pringle-Pattison is not prepared to accept Bosanquet's view of the destiny of the human individual. In his view differentiation constitutes the very essence of absolute life, and 'every individual is a unique nature . . . an expression or focalization of the universe which is nowhere else repeated'.[13] The higher we ascend in the scale of life, the clearer becomes the uniqueness of the individual. And if value increases in proportion to unique individuality, we cannot suppose that distinct selves achieve their destiny by being merged without distinction in the One. Each must be preserved in its uniqueness.

Pringle-Pattison is thus not prepared to say with Bradley that the temporal world is appearance. And as he retains the doctrine of the Absolute, he seems to be committed to saying that the Absolute is subject to temporal succession. But he also wishes to maintain that there is a real sense in which the Absolute or God transcends time. Hence he has recourse to the analogies of the drama and the symphony. Where, for example, a symphony is played, the notes succeed one another; yet in a real sense the whole is there from the beginning, giving meaning to and unifying the successive units. 'Somewhat in this fashion we may perhaps conceive that the time-process is retained in the Absolute and yet transcended.'[14]

If such analogies were pressed, the natural conclusion would be that the Absolute is simply the Idea, or perhaps more properly the Value, of the entire cosmic and historical process. But Pringle-Pattison clearly wishes to maintain that God is an absolute personal experience, which could hardly be described as simply the meaning and value of the world. In other words, he tries to combine absolute idealism with elements of theism. And the ambiguous result suggests that he would have done better either to retain the Absolute and identify it with the historical process considered as moving towards the emergence of new values or to make a clear break with absolute idealism and embrace theism. However, it is at any rate clear that within the general framework of absolute idealism he tried to preserve and assert the value of the finite personality.

2. We can now turn to a Cambridge philosopher, John McTaggart Ellis McTaggart (1866–1925), for whom the problem of the relation between finite selves and the Absolute did not and could not arise, inasmuch for him there was no Absolute apart from the society or system of selves. In his philosophy the Absolute as understood by Bradley and Bosanquet simply disappeared from the scene.

McTaggart was elected a Fellow of Trinity College, Cambridge, in 1891. In his view Hegel had penetrated further than any other philosopher into the nature of reality. And he devoted himself to a prolonged study of Hegelianism, which bore fruit in *Studies in the Hegelian Dialectic* (1896; second edition, 1922), *Studies in the Hegelian Cosmology* (1901; second edition, 1918), and A *Commentary on Hegel's Logic* (1910). But McTaggart was by no means only a student of and commentator on Hegel: he was an original thinker. This fact shows itself indeed in the commentaries but much more in the two volumes of *The Nature of Existence*,[15] which together contain his system of philosophy.

In the first part of his system McTaggart is concerned with determining the characteristics which belong to all that exists or, as he puts it, to existence as a whole.[16] More accurately, he is concerned with determining the characteristics which the existent *must* have. Hence the method to be employed will be that of *a priori* deduction. McTaggart is thus very far from being what is often described as an inductive metaphysician.

Even in the first part of the system, however, McTaggart admits two empirical premisses, namely that something exists and that what exists is differentiation. The truth of the first premiss is known by immediate experience. For everyone is aware that he at any rate exists. And he cannot deny this without implicitly affirming it. As for the second premiss, 'it would indeed be possible to reach this result *a priori*. For I shall argue later that it is certain *a priori* that no substance can be simple.'[17] But an appeal to perception 'seems more likely to command assent'.[18] What McTaggart really wishes to show is that existence as a whole is differentiated, that there is a plurality of substances. And this is shown by the very fact of perception. If, for example, perception is interpreted as a relation, there must be more than one term.

We can take it, therefore, that something exists. This cannot be existence itself.[19] For if we say that what exists is existence, we are left with an absolute blank. That which exists must possess some quality besides existence. And the compound quality, composed of all the qualities of a thing, can be called its nature. But we cannot resolve a thing without residue into its qualities. 'At the head of the series there will be something existent which has qualities without being itself a quality. The ordinary name for this, and I think the best name, is substance.'[20] It may be objected that substance apart from its qualities is an inconceivable nothing; but it does not follow that substance is 'not anything in conjunction with its qualities'.[21]

If therefore there is anything existing, and we know from experience that there is, there must be at least one substance. But we have already accepted the empirical premiss of pluralism, of the differentiation of existence as a whole. It follows therefore that there must be relations.[22] For if there is a plurality of substances, they must be similar and dissimilar, similar in being substances, dissimilar in being distinct.[23] And similarity and dissimilarity are relations.

Now, according to McTaggart every relation generates a derivative quality in each of its terms, namely the quality of being a term in this relationship. Further, a derivative relationship is generated between every relation and each of its terms. We therefore get infinite series. But 'these infinite series are not vicious, because it is not necessary to complete them to determine the meaning of the earlier terms'.[24] Hence Bradley's argument to show that qualities and relations cannot be truly real loses its force.

Substances, we have seen, must be dissimilar in some way. But there are similarities which permit their arrangement in collections and collections of collections. A collection is called a 'group', and the substances which compose it are its 'members'.[25] Taken by itself, this is a straightforward idea. But there are several points to notice. First, a group is for McTaggart a substance. Thus the group of all French citizens is a substance which possesses qualities of its own, such as being a nation. Secondly, as no substance is ever absolutely simple, a compound substance cannot have simple substances as its members. Thirdly, we cannot assume without more ado that two groups are necessarily two substances. If the contents are the same, the groups are one substance. For example, the counties of England and the parishes of England form two groups but only one substance.

Now, there must be one compound substance which contains all existent content and of which every other substance is a part. 'This substance is to be called the Universe.'[26] It is an organic unity in which 'all that exists, both substances and characteristics, are bound together in one system of extrinsic determination'.[27] At the same time there seems to be a major objection against admitting this idea of an all-inclusive substance. On the one hand McTaggart takes it that a sufficient description of any substance must be possible in principle. On the other hand no sufficient description of the universe seems to be possible. For a sufficient description would have, it appears, to indicate the parts and also their relations to one another and to the whole. But how can this be possible if no substance is simple and is consequently infinitely divisible?[28]

The details of McTaggart's solution of this difficulty are too complicated for discussion here. His general principle, as stated in his summary of his system, is that to avoid a contradiction between the thesis that a sufficient description of any substance is possible and the thesis that no substance is simple 'there must be some description of any substance, A, which implies sufficient descriptions of the members of all its sets of parts which are sequent to some given sets of parts'.[29] Taken by itself, this statement does not indeed convey very much. But McTaggart's line of thought is this. A sufficient description of a substance is possible in principle, if certain conditions are fulfilled. Consider the all-inclusive substance, the universe. This consists of one or more primary wholes, which in turn consist of primary parts. These parts can be differentiated by, for example, distinct qualities. And a sufficient description of the universe is possible in principle, provided that descriptions of the primary parts *imply* sufficient descriptions of the secondary parts, the series of which is indefinitely prolonged. For this implication to be a reality, however, the secondary parts must be related to one another by what McTaggart calls the relation of determining correspondence. For example, let us suppose that A and B are primary parts of a given substance, and that A and B are sufficiently described in terms of the qualities of x and y respectively. The relation of determining correspondence demands that a secondary part of A should be sufficiently describable in terms of y and that a secondary part of B should be sufficiently describable in terms of x. Given such interlocking determining correspondences throughout the whole hierarchy of consequent sets of parts, sufficient descriptions of the primary parts will imply sufficient descriptions of the secondary parts. And a sufficient description of the substance is thus possible in principle, notwithstanding the fact that it is indefinitely divisible.

As McTaggart maintains that a sufficient description of every substance must be possible, it follows that the relation of determining correspondence must hold between the parts of a substance. And if we look on determining correspondence as a label for types of causal relations, we can then say that McTaggart attempts to prove *a priori* the necessity of a certain pattern of causal relations within the universe. That is to say, if, as he assumes, the universe is an intelligible organic unity, there must exist in the hierarchy of its parts a certain pattern of determining correspondence.

Now, we have referred, for instance, to the counties of England, and we have been speaking of the universe. But though in the first part of the system some empirical illustrations are given to facilitate understanding, the conclusions reached are intended to be purely abstract. For example, though it is argued *a priori* that, if anything exists, there must be an all-inclusive substance which we can call the universe, it is a mistake to suppose that this term necessarily refers to the whole complex of entities which we are ordinarily accustomed to think of as the universe. The first part of the system established simply that there must be a universe. It does not tell us which, if any, empirical entities are members of the all-inclusive group which is called the universe. It is only in the second part of the system that McTaggart applies the conclusions of the first part, asking, for instance, whether the characteristics of substance which have been determined *a priori* can belong to those kinds of things which at first sight appear to be substances, or, rather, whether the characteristics which are encountered in or suggested by experience really belong to the existent.

In this field of inquiry, however, McTaggart insists, we cannot obtain absolute certainty. We may indeed be able to show that certain characteristics presented in or suggested by experience cannot belong to the existent, and that they must therefore be assigned to the sphere of appearance. But we cannot show with absolute certainty that characteristics suggested by experience *must* belong to the existent. For there might be characteristics never experienced or imagined by us which would equally well or better satisfy the *a priori* requirements of the first part of the system. However, if it can be shown that characteristics suggested by experience do in fact satisfy these *a priori* demands, and that no others which we know of or can imagine will do so, we have reasonable, though not absolute, certainty. In other words, McTaggart ascribes absolute certainty only to the results of *a priori* demonstration.

'The universe appears, *prima facie*, to contain substances of two very different kinds—Matter and Spirit.'[30] But McTaggart refuses to admit the reality of matter, mainly on the ground that nothing which has the quality of being material can have between its parts that relation of determining correspondence which must exist between the secondary parts of a substance. Let us suppose, for the sake of argument, that a given material thing has two primary parts, one of which can be sufficiently described as blue, while the other can be sufficiently described as red. According to the requirements of the principle of determining correspondence there would have to be a secondary part of the primary part described as blue which would correspond with the primary part described as red. That is to say, this secondary part would be red. But this is not logically possible. For a primary part could not be sufficiently described as blue, if one of its secondary parts were red. And analogous conclusions can be drawn if we consider qualities such as size and shape. Hence matter cannot belong to the existent: it cannot qualify the universe.[31]

We are left therefore with spirit. There is indeed no demonstrative proof that nothing exists save spirit. For there might possibly be a form of substance, which we had never experienced or imagined, which would satisfy the requirements for being a substance and yet not be spiritual. But we have no positive ground for claiming that there is such a substance. Hence it is reasonable to conclude that all substance is spiritual.

As for the nature of spirit, 'I propose to define the quality of spirituality by saying that it is the quality of having content, all of which is the content of one or more selves'.[32]

Thus selves are spiritual, and so are parts of selves and groups of selves, though in deference to common usage the term 'a spirit' can be reserved for a self.[33]

If spirit, therefore, is the only form of substance, the universe or Absolute will be the all-inclusive society or system of selves, selves being its primary parts. The secondary parts, of all grades, are perceptions, which form the contents of selves. In this case there must be relations of determining correspondence between these parts. True, this demands the fulfilment of certain conditions; that 'a self can perceive another self, and a part of another self',[34] that a perception is part of a percipient self, and that a perception of a part of a whole can be part of a perception of this whole. But the fulfilment of these conditions cannot be shown to be impossible; and there are reasons for thinking that they are in fact fulfilled. So we can take it that the Absolute is the system or society of selves.

Are selves immortal? The answer to this question depends on the point of view which we adopt. On the one hand McTaggart denies the reality of time, on the ground that an assertion of the reality of the temporal series of past, present and future compels us to attribute to any given event mutually incompatible determinations.[35] Hence if we adopt this point of view, we should describe selves as timeless or eternal rather than as immortal, a term which implies unending temporal duration. On the other hand time certainly belongs to the sphere of appearance. And the self will appear to persist through all future time. 'In consequence of this, I think we may properly say that the self is immortal',[36] though immortality must then be understood as including pre-existence, before, that is, its union with the body.

Professor C. D. Broad has remarked[37] that he does not suppose that McTaggart made a single disciple, though he exercised a considerable influence on his pupils by his logical subtlety, his intellectual honesty and his striving after clarity. It is not indeed surprising if McTaggart failed to make disciples. For, apart from the fact that he does not explain, any more than Bradley did, how the sphere of appearance arises in the first place, his system provides a much clearer example than the philosophies of either Bradley or Bosanquet of the account of metaphysics which has sometimes been given by anti-metaphysicians, namely as an alleged science which professes to deduce the nature of reality in a purely *a priori* manner. For having worked out in the first part of his system what characteristics the existent must possess, McTaggart blithely proceeds in the second part to reject the reality of matter and time on the ground that they do not fulfil the requirements established in the first part. And though his conclusions certainly make his philosophy more interesting and exciting, their strangeness is apt to make most readers conclude without more ado that there must be something wrong with his arguments. Most people at any rate find it difficult to believe that reality consists of a system of selves, the contents of which are perceptions. 'Ingenious but unconvincing', is likely to be their verdict about McTaggart's arguments.

It may be objected that this is a very philistinian point of view. If McTaggart's arguments are good ones, the strangeness of his conclusions does not alter the fact. And this is true enough. But it is also a fact that few philosophers have been convinced by the arguments adduced to show that reality must be what McTaggart says it is.

3. McTaggart combined the doctrine that existing reality consists of spiritual selves with atheism.[38] But the personal idealists generally adopted some form of theism. We can take as an example James Ward (1843–1925), naturalist, psychologist and philosopher, who studied for a while in Germany, where he came under the influence of Lotze, and eventually occupied the chair of logic and mental philosophy at Cambridge (1897–1925).

In 1886 Ward contributed to the *Encyclopaedia Britannica* a famous article on psychology, which later provided the basis for his *Psychological Principles* (1918), a work which clearly shows the influence of German philosophers such as Lotze, Wundt and Brentano. Ward was strongly opposed to the associationist psychology. In his view the content of consciousness consists of 'presentations'; but these form a continuum. They are not discrete isolated events or impressions, into which the presentational continuum can be broken up. Obviously, a new presentation introduces fresh material; but it does not constitute simply an additional item in a series, for it modifies or partially changes the pre-existing field of consciousness. Further, every presentation is a presentation for a subject, being an experience of the subject. The idea of the 'soul' is not for Ward a concept of psychology; but we cannot dispense with the idea of the subject. For consciousness involves selective attention to this or that feature or aspect of the presentational continuum; and this is an activity of the subject under the influence of feelings of pleasure and pain. It is, however, a mistake to regard the subject of consciousness as merely a spectator, a purely cognitive subject. For the conative aspect of experience is fundamental, and the selective activity in question is teleological in character, the active subject selecting and attending to presentational data in view of an end or purpose.[39]

In the first series of his Gifford Lectures, published in 1899 as *Naturalism and Agnosticism*, Ward attacked what he called the naturalistic view of the world. We must distinguish between natural science on the one hand and philosophical naturalism on the other. For example, mechanics which deals simply 'with the quantitative aspects of physical phenomena'[40] should not be confused with the mechanical theory of Nature, 'which aspires to resolve the actual world into an actual mechanism'.[41] The philosopher who accepts this theory believes that the formulas and laws of mechanics are not simply abstract and selective devices for dealing with an environment under certain aspects, devices which possess a limited validity, but that they reveal to us the nature of concrete reality in an adequate manner. And in this belief he is mistaken. Spencer, for instance, attempts to deduce the movement of evolution from mechanical principles and is blind to the fact that in the process of evolution different levels emerge which require their own appropriate categories and concepts.[42]

Dualism, however, as a possible alternative to naturalism, is untenable. It is true that the fundamental structure of experience is the subject-object relationship. But this distinction is not equivalent to a dualism between mind and matter. For even when the object is what we call a material thing, the fact that it is comprised together with the subject within the unity of the subject-object relationship shows that it cannot be entirely heterogeneous to the subject. No ultimate dualism between mind and matter can stand up to criticism.

Having rejected, therefore, materialism, in the form of the mechanical theory of Nature, and dualism, Ward has recourse to what he calls spiritualistic monism. This term does not, however, express a belief that there is only one substance or being. Ward's view is that all entities are in some sense spiritual. That is to say, they all possess a psychical aspect. His theory is thus pluralistic; and in his second set of Gifford Lectures, which appeared in 1911 under the title *The Realm of Ends or Pluralism and Theism* he speaks of pluralistic spiritualism rather than of spiritualistic monism, though, if the latter term is properly understood, both names have the same meaning.

To some readers it may appear extraordinary that a Cambridge professor of comparatively recent date should embrace a theory of panpsychism. But Ward does not intend to imply, any more than Leibniz did,[43] that every entity or monad enjoys what we call consciousness. The idea is rather that there is no such thing as 'brute' matter, but that every centre of activity possesses some degree, often a very low degree, of 'mentality'. Moreover, Ward claims that pluralistic spiritualism is not a doctrine which has been deduced *a priori* but is based on experience.[44] 'The world is taken simply as we find it, as a plurality of active individuals unified only in and through their mutual interactions. These interactions again are interpreted throughout on the analogy of social transactions, as a mutuum commercium; that is to say, as based on cognition and conation.'[45]

Now, Ward admits that it is possible to stop at this idea of a plurality of finite active centres of experience. For Kant has exposed the fallacies in the alleged demonstrative proofs of God's existence. At the same time theism supplies a unity which is missing in pluralism without God. Further, the concepts of creation and conservation throw light on the existence of the Many, though creation should be understood in terms of ground and consequent rather than of cause and effect. 'God is the ground of the world's being, its *ratio essendi.*'[46] In addition, Ward argues in a pragmatist-like way that acceptance of the idea of God has the benefit of increasing the pluralist's confidence in the significance of finite existence and in the eventual realization of the ideal of the kingdom of ends. Without God as both transcendent and immanently active in the universe, 'the world may well for ever remain that *rerum concordia discors*, which at present we find it'.[47]

4. We can safely venture the generalization that one of the basic factors in personal idealism is a judgment of value, namely that personality represents the highest value within the field of our experience. This statement may indeed appear inapplicable to the philosophy of McTaggart, who professes to demonstrate by *a priori* reasoning what characteristics must belong to the existent and then inquires which of the kinds of things that are *prima facie* substances actually possess these characteristics. But it does not necessarily follow, of course, that a judgment of value does not constitute an effective implicit factor even in his philosophy. In any case it is clear that Pringle-Pattison's revision of absolute idealism was prompted by a conviction of the ultimate value of personality, and that James Ward's pluralistic spiritualism was connected with a similar conviction.

Obviously, personal idealism does not consist simply of this judgment of value. It involves also the conviction that personality should be taken as the key to the nature of reality, and a sustained attempt to interpret reality in the light of this conviction. This means that personal idealism tends to pluralism rather than to monism. In the philosophies of McTaggart and Ward a pluralistic conception of the universe is clearly dominant. With Pringle-Pattison it is held in check by his retention of the idea of the Absolute as a single all-inclusive experience. At the same time the value which he attaches to finite personality drives him to endeavour to interpret the doctrine of the One in such a way as not to involve the submerging or obliteration of the Many in the One.

The natural result in metaphysics of the turning from monism to pluralism in the light of a conviction of the value of personality is the assertion of some form of theism. In the exceptional case of McTaggart the Absolute is indeed interpreted as the society or system of finite spiritual selves. And with Pringle-Pattison the change to unequivocal theism is checked by the influence which the tradition of absolute idealism still exercises on his mind. But the inner dynamic, so to speak, of personal idealism is towards the interpretation of ultimate reality as being itself personal in character and of such a kind as to allow for the dependent reality of finite persons. According to the absolute idealists, as we have seen, the concept of God must be transformed into the concept of the Absolute. In personal idealism the concept of the Absolute tends to be re-transformed into the concept of God. True, McTaggart looks on his idea of the society or system of spiritual selves as the proper interpretation of the Hegelian Absolute. But with James Ward we find a clear transition to theism. And it is no matter for surprise that he explicitly asserts his affinity with Kant rather than with Hegel.

How far we extend the application of the term 'personal idealism' is, within limits, a matter of choice. Consider, for example, William Ritchie Sorley (1855–1935), who occupied the chair of moral philosophy at Cambridge from 1900 until 1932. He was mainly concerned with problems connected with the nature of values and the judgment of value, and it may be preferable to label him a philosopher of value. But he also inquired into the sort of general philosophical theory which we must embrace when we take values seriously into account as factors in reality. Thus he insisted that persons are 'the bearers of value',[48] and that metaphysics culminates in the idea of God, conceived not only as creator but also as 'the essence and source of all values, and as willing that these values should be shared by the free minds who owe their being to him'.[49] And the total result of his reflections is such that he can reasonably be labelled as a personal idealist.

We cannot, however, be expected to outline the ideas of all those British philosophers who can reasonably be described as personal idealists. Instead we can draw attention to the differences in attitude towards the sciences between the absolute idealists and the personal idealists. Bradley does not, of course, deny the validity of science at its own level. But inasmuch as he relegates all discursive thought to the sphere of appearance, he is involved in holding that the sciences are incapable of revealing to us the nature of reality as distinct from appearance. True we find much the same attitude in McTaggart, for whom the spatio-temporal world is appearance. And even James Ward, in his polemic against naturalism and the mechanical theory of the world, plays down the ability of science to disclose to us the nature of reality and emphasizes the man-made character of abstract scientific concepts, which have to be judged by their utility rather than by any claim to absolute truth. At the same time he is convinced that the concrete sciences, such as biology and psychology, suggest and confirm his pluralistic philosophy. And, in general, the personal idealists are concerned not so much with sitting in judgment on science and relegating it to the sphere of appearance as with challenging the claim of materialist and mechanist philosophies to be the logical outcome of the sciences. The general tendency at any rate of personal idealism is to appeal to the fact that different sciences require different categories to cope with different levels of experience or aspects of reality, and to regard metaphysics as a legitimate and indeed necessary enlargement of the field of interpretation rather than as the unique path to a knowledge of reality from which the empirical sciences, confined to the sphere of appearance, are necessarily debarred. This observation may not apply to McTaggart. But he is really *sui generis*. The general attitude of the personal idealists is to argue that experience and an empirical approach to philosophy support pluralism rather than the type of monism characteristic of absolute idealism, and that if we bear in mind the different types of science,[50] we can see that metaphysical philosophy is not a counterblast to science but a natural crown to that interpretation of reality in which the sciences have their own parts to play.

A final point. If we except the system of McTaggart, personal idealism was calculated by its very nature to appeal to religiously minded philosophers, to the sort of philosophers who would be considered suitable persons to receive invitations to give series of Gifford Lectures. And what the personal idealists wrote was generally religiously edifying. Their style of philosophy was obviously much less destructive of Christian faith than the absolute idealism of Bradley.[51] But though the various philosophies which can reasonably be regarded as representative of personal idealism are edifying enough from the moral and religious points of view, they tend to give the impression, at least in their more metaphysical aspects, of being a series of personal statements of belief which owe less to rigorous argument than to a selective emphasis on certain aspects of reality.[52] And it is understandable that during the lifetime of Ward and Sorley other Cambridge philosophers were suggesting that instead of rushing to produce large-scale interpretations of reality we should do better to make our questions as clear and precise as possible and treat them one by one. However, though this sounds a very reasonable and practical suggestion, the trouble is that philosophical problems are apt to interlock. And the idea of breaking up philosophy into clearly defined questions which can be answered separately has not in practice proved to be as fruitful as some people hoped. Still, it is undeniable that the idealist systems appear, in the present climate of British philosophy, to belong to a past phase of thought. This makes them indeed apt material for the historian. But it also means that the historian cannot help wondering whether there is really much justification for devoting space to minor systems which do not strike the imagination in the way that the system of Hegel makes an impression. There is, however, this to be said, that personal idealism represents the recurrent protest of the finite personality to absorption in a One, however it is conceived. It is easy to say that personality is 'appearance'; but no monistic system has ever explained how the sphere of appearance arises in the first place.

APPENDIX

A SHORT BIBLIOGRAPHY

General Works

For the sake of brevity titles of general histories of philosophy mentioned in the first section of the Bibliography in Volume VII of this *History* have not been repeated here. Nor have I attempted to supply bibliographies for all the philosophers mentioned in the text of the present volume. In the case of a considerable number of philosophers works are mentioned in the text or in footnotes, which have not been listed here.

Adams, G. P. and Montague, W. P. (editors). *Contemporary American Philosophy*. 2 vols. New York, 1930. (Personal Statements.)

Anderson, P. R. and Fisch, M. H. *Philosophy in America*. New York, 1939.

Blau, J. L. *Men and Movements in American Philosophy*. New York, 1939.

Bochenski, I. M. *Contemporary European Philosophy*, translated by D. Nicholl and K. Aschenbrenner. London and Berkeley, 1956.

Brinton, Crane. *English Political Thought in the Nineteenth Century*. Cambridge (Mass.), 1949.

Deledalle, G. *Histoire de la philosophie américaine de la guerre de sécession à la seconde guerre mondiale*. Paris, 1955.

Lamanna, A. P. *La filosofia del novecento*. Florence, 1964.

Merz, J. T. *History of European Thought in the Nineteenth Century*. 4 vols. London, 1896–1914.

Metz, R. *A Hundred Years of British Philosophy*, translated by J. W. Harvey, T. E. Jessop and H. Sturt. London, 1938. (An account of British philosophy from about the middle of the nineteenth century onwards.)

Muelder, W. E. and Sears, L. *The Development of American Philosophy*. Boston, 1940.

Muirhead, J. H. (editor). *Contemporary British Philosophy: Personal Statements*. 2 vols. London, 1924–5. (The first volume includes statements by, for example, Bosanquet, McTaggart, Bertrand Russell and Schiller, the second by James Ward and G. E. Moore.)

Passmore, J. *A Hundred Years of Philosophy*. London, 1957. (A useful account of philosophy, mainly but not exclusively British, from J. S. Mill, with a concluding chapter on existentialism.)

Riley, I. W. *American Thought from Puritanism to Pragmatism and Beyond*. New York, 1923 (2nd edition).

Schneider, H. W. *A History of American Philosophy*. New York, 1946.

Seth (Pringle-Pattison), A. *English Philosophers and Schools of Philosophy*. London, 1912. (From Francis Bacon to F. H. Bradley.)

Warnock, G. J. *English Philosophy Since 1900*. London, 1958. (A clear and succinct account of the development of the modern analytic movement.)

Warnock, M. *Ethics Since 1900*. London, 1960.

Werkmeister, W. H. *A History of Philosophical Ideas in America*. New York, 1949.

Part I: Chapters I–V

1. GENERAL WORKS RELATING TO THE UTILITARIAN MOVEMENT

Albee, E. *A History of English Utilitarianism*. London, 1902.

Davidson, W. L. *Political Thought in England: Bentham to J. S. Mill*. London, 1950.

Guyau, J. M. *La morale anglaise contemporaine*. Paris, 1904 (5th ed.).

Halévy, E. *The Growth of Philosophic Radicalism*, translated by M. Morris, with a preface by A. D. Lindsay. London, 1928.

Laski, H. J. *The Rise of European Liberalism*. London, 1936.

Leslie, S. W. *Political Thought in England. The Utilitarians from Bentham to Mill.* London and New York, 1947.

Mondolfo, R. *Saggi per la storia della morale utilitaria.* 2 vols. Verona and Padua, 1903–4.

Plamentaz, J. *The English Utilitarians.* Oxford, 1949.

Stephen, L. *The English Utilitarians.* 3 vols. London, 1900. (The volumes are devoted respectively to Bentham, James Mill and J. S. Mill.)

2. BENTHAM

Texts

The Works of Jeremy Bentham, edited by John Bowring. 11 vols. Edinburgh, 1838–43.

Benthamiana, Select Extracts from the Works of Jeremy Bentham, edited by J. H. Burton. Edinburgh, 1843.

Oeuvres de Jérémie Bentham, translated by E. Dumont. 3 vols. Brussels, 1829–30.

Colección de obras del célebre Jeremias Bentham, compiled by E. Dumont with commentaries by B. Anduaga y Espinosa. 14 vols. Madrid, 1841–3.

An Introduction to the Principles of Morals and Legislation, edited by L. Lafleur. New York, 1948. (The 1876 Oxford edition is a reprint of the 1823 edition.)

Theory of Legislation, translated from the French of E. Dumont by R. Hildreth. London, 1896.

Bentham's Theory of Legislation, edited by C. K. Ogden. London, 1950.

A Fragment on Government, edited by F. C. Montague. London, 1891.

Bentham's Theory of Fictions, edited by C. K. Ogden. London, 1932.

Bentham's Handbook of Political Fallacies, edited by H. A. Larrabee. Baltimore, 1952.

Deontology, or the Science of Morality, edited by J. Bowring. 2 vols. London, 1834.

The Limits of Jurisprudence Defined, edited by C. W. Everett. New York, 1945.

Jeremy Bentham's Economic Writings, Critical Edition based on his Printed Works and Unprinted Manuscripts, edited by W. Stark. 3 vols. London, 1952–4. (Each volume contains an introductory essay. The second appendix, contained in the third volume, is a systematic survey of the surviving Bentham manuscripts.)

Catalogue of the Manuscripts of Jeremy Bentham in the Library of University College, London, edited by A. T. Milne. London, 1937.

Studies

Atkinson, C. M. *Jeremy Bentham, His Life and Work*. London, 1905.

Baumgardt, D. *Bentham and the Ethics of Today*. Princeton (U.S.A.) and London, 1952.

Busch, J. *Die moralische und soziale Ethik Benthams*. Neisse, 1938.

Everett, C. W. *The Education of Jeremy Bentham*. New York, 1931.

Jones, W. T. *Masters of Political Thought: From Machiavelli to Bentham*. London, 1947.

Keeton, G. W. and Schwarzenberger, G. (editors). *Jeremy Bentham and the Law*. London, 1948.

Laski, H. J. *Political Thought in England: Locke to Bentham*. London, 1950.

Mack, M. P. *Jeremy Bentham: An Odyssey of Ideas, 1748–1792*. London, 1962.

Mill, J. S. *Mill on Bentham and Coleridge*, edited by F. R. Leavis. London, 1950.

Quintodamo, N. *La morale utilitaristica del Bentham e sua evoluzione nel diritto penale*. Naples, 1936.

Stephen, L. *The English Utilitarians: Vol. I, Jeremy Bentham*. London, 1900.

3. JAMES MILL

Texts

History of India. 3 vols. London, 1817. (4th edition, 9 vols., 1848; 5th edition, with continuation by M. H. Wilson, 10 vols., 1858.)

Elements of Political Economy. London, 1821 (3rd and revised edition, 1826).

Analysis of the Phenomena of the Human Mind, edited by

J. S. Mill, with notes by A. Bain, A. Findlater and G. Grote. 2 vols. London, 1869.

A *Fragment on Mackintosh*. London, 1835.

Studies

Bain, A. *James Mill, A Biography*. London 1882.

Bower, G. S. *Hartley and James Mill*. London, 1881.

Hamburger, J. *James Mill and the Art of Revolution*. Yale, 1964.

Ressler, A. *Die Beiden Mill*. Cologne, 1929.

Stephen, L. *The English Utilitarians: Vol. II, James Mill*. London, 1900.

4. J. S. MILL

Texts

Collected Works of John Stuart Mill, general editor F. E. L. Priestley. Toronto and London. Vols. XII–XIII, *The Earlier Letters, 1812–1848*, edited by F. E. Mineka, 1963; vols. II–III, *The Principles of Political Economy*, with an introduction by V. W. Bladen, edited by J. M. Robson, 1965.

Autobiography, edited by H. J. Laski. London, 1952. (Among other editions there is the one edited by J. J. Cross, New York, 1924.)

The Early Draft of J. S. Mill's Autobiography, edited by J. Stillinger. Urbana (Ill.), 1961.

Mill's Utilitarianism reprinted with a Study of the English Utilitarians, by J. Plamentaz. Oxford, 1949.

On Liberty, Considerations on Representative Government, edited with an introduction by R. B. McCallum. Oxford, 1946.

Considerations on Representative Government, edited with an introduction by C. V. Shields. New York, 1958.

A System of Logic. London, 1949 (reprint).

Examination of Sir William Hamilton's Philosophy. London, 1865.

John Stuart Mill's Philosophy of Scientific Method, edited by E. Nagel. New York, 1950. (Selections, with introductory material, from the *Logic* and the *Examination*.)

Dissertations and Discussions. 5 vols. Boston (U.S.A.), 1865–75.

Mill on Bentham and Coleridge, edited by F. R. Leavis. London, 1950.

Auguste Comte and Positivism. London, 1865.

Inaugural Address at St. Andrews. London, 1867.

Three Essays on Religion. London, 1874. (*Theism,* edited by R. Taylor. New York, 1957.)

John Stuart Mill and Harriet Taylor: Their Freindship and Subsequent Marriage, edited by F. A. Hayek. Chicago, 1951. (Contains the Mill–Taylor correspondence.)

Lettres inédites de John Stuart Mill à Auguste Comte, publiées avec les résponses de Comte, edited by L. Lévy-Bruhl. Paris, 1899.

Bibliography of the Published Works of John Stuart Mill, edited by N. MacMinn, J. R. Hinds and J. M. McCrimmon. London, 1945.

Studies

Anschutz, R. P. *The Philosophy of J. S. Mill.* Oxford, 1953. (Illustrates very well the different tendencies in Mill's thought.)

Bain, A. *John Stuart Mill: A Criticism with Personal Recollections.* London, 1882.

Borchard, R. *John Stuart Mill, the Man.* London, 1957.

Britton, K. *John Stuart Mill.* Penguin Books, 1953.

Casellato, S. *Giovanni St. Mill e l'utilitarismo inglese.* Padua, 1951.

Castell, A. *Mill's Logic of the Moral Sciences: A Study of the Impact of Newtonism on Early Nineteenth-Century Social Thought.* Chicago, 1936.

Courtney, W. L. *The Metaphysics of John Stuart Mill.* London, 1879.

Cowling, M. *Mill and Liberalism.* Cambridge, 1963.

Douglas, C. *J. S. Mill: A Study of His Philosophy.* London, 1895.

Ethics of John Stuart Mill. Edinburgh, 1897.

Grude-Oettli, N. *John Stuart Mill zwischen Liberalismus und Sozialismus.* Zürich, 1936.

Hippler, F. *Staat und Gesellschaft bei Mill, Marx, Lagarde.* Berlin, 1934.

Jackson, R. *An Examination of the Deductive Logic of John Stuart Mill.* London, 1941.

Kantzer, E. M. *La religion de John Stuart Mill.* Caen, 1914.

Kennedy, G. *The Psychological Empiricism of John Stuart Mill.* Amsterdam, 1928.

Kubitz, O. A. *The Development of John Stuart Mill's System of Logic.* Urbana (Ill.), 1932.

McCosh, J. *An Examination of Mr. J. S. Mill's Philosophy.* New York, 1890 (2nd edition).

Mueller, I. W. *John Stuart Mill and French Thought.* Urbana (Ill.), 1956.

Packe, M. St. John. *The Life of John Stuart Mill.* New York, 1954.

Pradines, M. *Les postulats métaphysiques de l'utilitarisme de Stuart Mill et Spencer.* Paris, 1909.

Ray, J. *La méthode de l'économie politique d'après John Stuart Mill.* Paris, 1914.

Roerig, F. *Die Wandlungen in der geistigen Grundhaltung John Stuart Mills.* Cologne, 1930.

Russell, Bertrand. *John Stuart Mill.* London, 1956. (Bristol Academy Lecture.)

Saenger, S. *John Stuart Mill, Sein Leben und Lebenswerk.* Stuttgart, 1901.

Schauchet, P. *Individualistische und sozialistische Gedanken im Leben John Stuart Mills.* Giessen, 1926.

Stephen, L. *The English Utilitarians:* vol. III, *John Stuart Mill.* London, 1900.

Towney, G. A. *John Stuart Mill's Theory of Inductive Logic.* Cincinnati, 1909.

Watson, J. *Comte, Mill and Spencer.* Glasgow, 1895.

Zuccante, G. *La morale utilitaristica dello Stuart Mill.* Milan, 1899.

  Giovanni S. Mill e l'utilitarismo. Florence, 1922.

5. HERBERT SPENCER

Texts

A System of Synthetic Philosophy. 10 vols. London, 1862–93.
(For some detailed information about the various editions of the books comprising the *System* see pp. 240–1.)

Epitome of the Synthetic Philosophy, by F. H. Collins. London, 1889 (5th edition, 1901).

Essays, Scientific, Political and Speculative. 3 vols. London, 1891. (Two volumes of *Essays, Scientific, Political and Speculative* appeared at London in 1857 and 1863 respectively and one volume of *Essays, Moral, Political and Aesthetic* at New York in 1865.)

Education, Intellectual, Moral, Physical. London, 1861.

The Man versus The State. London, 1884.

The Nature and Reality of Religion. London, 1885.

Various Fragments. London, 1897.

Facts and Comments. London, 1902.

Autobiography. 2 vols. New York, 1904.

Studies

Allievo, G. *La psicologia di Herbert Spencer.* Turin, 1914 (2nd edition).

Ardigò, R. *L'Inconoscibile di Spencer e il noumeno di Kant.* Padua, 1901.

Asirvatham, E. *Spencer's Theory of Social Justice.* New York, 1936.

Carus, P. *Kant and Spencer.* Chicago, 1889.

Diaconide, E. *Étude critique sur la sociologie de Herbert Spencer.* Paris, 1938.

Duncan, D. *The Life and Letters of Herbert Spencer.* London, 1912.

Elliott, H. *Herbert Spencer.* London, 1917.

Ensor, R. C. *Some Reflections on Spencer's Doctrine that Progress is Differentiation.* Oxford, 1947.

Fiske, J. *Outlines of Cosmic Philosophy.* 2 vols. London, 1874. (These lectures are critical as well as expository of Spencer's thought.)

Gaupp, O. *Herbert Spencer.* Stuttgart, 1897.

Guthmann, J. *Entwicklung und Selbstentfaltung bei Spencer.*
   Ochsenfurt, 1931.

Häberlin, P. *Herbert Spencers Grundlagen der Philosophie.*
   Leipzig, 1908.

Hudson, W. H. *Introduction to the Philosophy of Herbert
   Spencer.* London, 1909.

Jarger, M. *Herbert Spencers Prinzipien der Ethik.* Hamburg,
   1922.

Macpherson, H. *Herbert Spencer, The Man and His Work.*
   London, 1900.

Parisot, E. *Herbert Spencer.* Paris, 1911.

Parker-Bowne, B. *Kant and Spencer.* New York, 1922.

Ramlow, L. A. *Riehl und Spencer.* Berlin, 1933.

Royce, J. *Herbert Spencer: An Estimate and Review with a
   chapter of Personal Reminiscences by J. Collier.* New
   York, 1904.

Rumney, J. *Herbert Spencer's Sociology: A Study in the History of Social Theory.* London, 1934.

Sergi, G. *La sociologia di Herbert Spencer.* Rome, 1903.

Sidgwick, H. *Lectures on the Ethics of T. H. Green, Mr.
   Herbert Spencer, and J. Martineau.* London, 1902.

Solari, G. *L'opera filosofica di Herbert Spencer.* Bergamo,
   1904.

Stadler, A. *Herbert Spencers Ethik.* Leipzig, 1913.

Thompson, J. A. *Herbert Spencer.* London, 1906.

Tillett, A. W. *Spencer's Synthetic Philosophy: What It is All
   About. An Introduction to Justice, 'The Most Important
   Part'.* London, 1914.

Part II: Chapters VI–X

1. GENERAL WORKS RELATING TO BRITISH IDEALISM

Abbagnano, N. *L'idealismo inglese e americano.* Naples,
   1926.

Cunningham, G. W. *The Idealistic Argument in Recent British and American Philosophy.* New York, 1933.

Dockhorn, K. *Die Staatsphilosophie des englischen Idealis-
   mus, ihre Lehre und Wirkung.* Pöppinghaus, 1937.

Haldar, H. *Neo-Hegelianism*. London, 1927.

Milne, A. J. M. *The Social Philosophy of English Idealism*. London, 1962.

Muirhead, J. M. *The Platonic Tradition in Anglo-Saxon Philosophy*. London, 1931.

Pucelle, J. *L'idéalisme en Angleterre de Coleridge à Bradley*. Neuchatel and Paris, 1955. (Can be highly recommended.)

2. COLERIDGE

Texts

Works, edited by W. G. T. Shedd. 7 vols. New York, 1884.

The Friend. 3 vols. London, 1812. (2 vols, 1837).

Biographia Literaria. London, 1817. (Everyman Library, 1906 and reprints.)

Aids to Reflection. 2 vols. London, 1824–5 (with addition of the *Essay on Faith*, 1890).

On the Constitution of Church and State, edited by H. N. Coleridge. London, 1839.

Confessions of an Inquiring Spirit, edited by H. N. Coleridge. London, 1840.

Treatise on Method. London, 1849 (3rd edition).

Essays on His Own Times. 3 vols. London, 1850.

Anima Poetae, edited by E. H. Coleridge. London, 1895.

Letters, edited by E. H. Coleridge. London, 1895.

Unpublished Letters. London, 1932.

The Political Thought of Coleridge, selected by R. J. White. London, 1938.

The Philosophical Lectures of S. T. Coleridge, Hitherto Unpublished, edited by K. Coburn. London, 1949.

The Notebooks of S. T. Coleridge, edited by K. Coburn. 2 vols. London, 1957–62.

Studies

Blunden, E. and Griggs, E. L. (editors). *Coleridge Studies*. London, 1934.

Campbell J. D. *Life of S. T. Coleridge*. London, 1894.

Chambers, E. K. *S. T. Coleridge: A Biographical Study*. Oxford, 1938.

Chinol, E. *Il pensiero di S. T. Coleridge*. Venice, 1953.

Coburn, K. *Inquiring Spirit. A New Presentation of Coleridge* (from published and unpublished writings). London, 1931.

Ferrando, G. *Coleridge*. Florence, 1925.

Green, J. H. *Spiritual Philosophy, Founded on the Teaching of the late S. T. Coleridge*. 2 vols. London, 1865.

Hanson, L. *Life of S. T. Coleridge: Early Years*. London, 1938.

Kagey, R. *Coleridge: Studies in the History of Ideas*. New York, 1935.

Lowes, J. L. *The Road to Xanadu: A Study in Ways of the Imagination*. London, 1927 (revised edition 1930).

Muirhead, J. H. *Coleridge as Philosopher*. London, 1930.

Richards, I. A. *Coleridge on Imagination*. London, 1934.

Snyder, A. D. *Coleridge on Logic and Learning*. New Haven, 1929.

Wellek, R. *Immanuel Kant in England*. Princeton, 1931. (Only partly on Coleridge.)

Winkelmann, E. *Coleridge und die kantische Philosophie*. Leipzig, 1933.

Wunsche, W. *Die Staatsauffassung S. T. Coleridge's*. Leipzig, 1934.

3. CARLYLE

Texts

Works, edited by H. D. Traill. 31 vols. London, 1897–1901.

Sartor Resartus. London, 1841, and subsequent editions.

On Heroes, Hero-Worship and the Heroic in History. London, 1841.

Correspondence of Carlyle and R. W. Emerson. 2 vols. London, 1883.

Letters of Carlyle to J. S. Mill, J. Stirling and R. Browning, edited by A. Carlyle. London, 1923.

Studies

Baumgarten, O. *Carlyle und Goethe*. Tübingen, 1906.

Fermi, L. *Carlyle*. Messina, 1939.

Garnett, R. *Life of Carlyle*. London, 1887.

Harrold, C. F. *Carlyle and German Thought, 1819–34*. New Haven, 1934.

Hensel, P. *Thomas Carlyle*. Stuttgart, 1901.

Lammond, D. *Carlyle*. London, 1934.

Lea, F. *Carlyle, Prophet of Today*. London, 1944.

Lehman, B. H. *Carlyle's Theory of the Hero*. Duke, 1939.

Neff, E. *Carlyle and Mill: Mystic and Utilitarian*. New York, 1924.

  Carlyle. New York, 1932.

Seillière, E. *L'actualité de Carlyle*. Paris, 1929.

Storrs, M. *The Relation of Carlyle to Kant and Fichte*. Bryn Mawr, 1929.

Taylor, A. C. *Carlyle et la pensée latine*. Paris, 1937.

Wilson, D. A. *Carlyle*. 6 vols. London, 1923–34.

4. T. H. GREEN

Texts

Works, edited by R. L. Nettleship, 3 vols. London, 1885–8. (Contains Green's *Introductions to Hume's Treatise*, lectures on Kant, on Logic and on *The Principles of Political Obligation*, together with a memoir of the philosopher by Nettleship.)

Introductions to Hume's Treatise in vols. 1 and 2 of the *Philosophical Works of David Hume* edited by T. H. Green and T. M. Grose. London, 1874.

Prolegomena to Ethics, edited by A. C. Bradley. London, 1883.

Principles of Political Obligation. London, 1895.

Studies

Günther, O. *Das Verhältnis der Ethik Greens zu der Kants*. Leipzig, 1915.

Fairbrother, W. H. *The Philosophy of T. H. Green*. London, 1896.

Fusai, M. *Il pensiero morale di T. H. Green*. Florence, 1943.

Lamont, W. D. *Introduction to Green's Moral Philosophy*. New York, 1934.

Muirhead, J. H. *The Service of the State: Four lectures on the Political Teaching of Green*. London, 1908.

Pucelle, J. *La nature et l'esprit dans la philosophie de T. H. Green. I, Métaphysique–Morale.* Louvain, 1961. (A thorough and sympathetic study.)

5. E. CAIRD

Texts

A Critical Account of the Philosophy of Kant. Glasgow, 1877. (Revised edition in 2 vols. with the title *The Critical Philosophy of Kant,* Glasgow, 1889.)

Hegel. Edinburgh, 1883.

The Social Philosophy and Religion of Comte. Glasgow, 1885.

Essays on Literature and Philosophy. 2 vols. Glasgow, 1892.

The Evolution of Religion. 2 vols. Glasgow, 1893.

The Evolution of Theology in the Greek Philosophers, 2 vols. Glasgow, 1904.

Studies

Jones, H. and Muirhead, J. H. *The Life and Philosophy of Edward Caird.* London, 1921.

6. BRADLEY

Texts

The Presuppositions of Critical History. London, 1874.

Ethical Studies. London, 1876 (2nd edition, 1927).

Mr. Sidgwick's Hedonism. London, 1877.

The Principles of Logic. London, 1883 (2nd edition with Terminal Essays in 2 vols, 1922.)

Appearance and Reality. London, 1893 (2nd edition with Appendix, 1897).

Essays on Truth and Reality. London, 1914.

Aphorisms. Oxford, 1930.

Collected Essays. 2 vols. Oxford, 1935. (This work includes *The Presuppositions of Critical History.*)

Studies

Antonelli, M. A. *La metafisica di F. H. Bradley.* Milan, 1952.

Campbell, C. A. *Scepticism and Construction. Bradley's Scep-*

tical Principle as the Basis of Constructive Philosophy. London, 1931.

Chappuis, A. *Der theoretische Weg Bradleys*. Paris, 1934.

Church, R. W. *Bradley's Dialectic*. London, 1942.

De Marneffe, J. *La preuve de l'Absolu chez Bradley. Analyse et critique de la méthode*. Paris, 1961.

Kagey, R. *The Growth of Bradley's Logic*. London, 1931.

Keeling, S. V. *La nature de l'expérience chez Kant et chez Bradley*. Montpellier, 1925.

Lomba, R. M. *Bradley and Bergson*. Lucknow, 1937.

Lofthouse, W. F. *F. H. Bradley*. London, 1949.

Mack, R. D. *The Appeal to Immediate Experience. Philosophic Method in Bradley, Whitehead and Dewey*. New York, 1945.

Ross, G. R. *Scepticism and Dogma: A Study in the Philosophy of F. H. Bradley*. New York, 1940.

Schüring, H.-J. *Studie zur Philosophie von F. H. Bradley*. Meisenheim am Glan, 1963.

Segerstedt, T. T. *Value and Reality in Bradley's Philosophy*. Lund, 1934.

Taylor, A. E. *F. H. Bradley*. London, 1924. (British Academy lecture.)

Wollheim, R. *F. H. Bradley*. Penguin Books, 1959.

In *Mind* for 1925 there are articles on Bradley by G. D. Hicks, J. H. Muirhead, G. F. Stout, F. C. S. Schiller, A. E. Taylor and J. Ward.

7. BOSANQUET

Texts

Knowledge and Reality. London, 1885.

Logic, or the Morphology of Knowledge. 2 vols. London, 1888.

Essays and Addresses. London, 1889.

A History of Aesthetic. London, 1892.

The Civilization of Christendom and Other Studies. London, 1893.

Aspects of the Social Problem. London, 1895.

The Essentials of Logic. London, 1895.

Companion to Plato's Republic. London, 1895.

Rousseau's Social Contract. London, 1895.

Psychology of the Moral Self. London, 1897.

The Philosophical Theory of the State. London, 1899.

The Principle of Individuality and Value. London, 1912.

The Value and Destiny of the Individual. London, 1913.

The Distinction between Mind and Its Objects. London, 1913.

Three Lectures on Aesthetics. London, 1915.

Social and International Ideals. London, 1917.

Some Suggestions in Ethics. London, 1918.

Implication and Linear Inference. London, 1920.

What Religion Is. London, 1920.

The Meeting of Extremes in Contemporary Philosophy. London, 1921.

Three Chapters on the Nature of Mind. London, 1923.

Science and Philosophy and Other Essays, edited by J. H. Muirhead and R. C. Bosanquet. London, 1927.

Studies

Bosanquet, H. *Bernard Bosanquet.* London, 1924.

Houang, F. *La néo-hégelianisme en Angleterre: la philosophie de Bernard Bosanquet.* Paris, 1954.

  De l'humanisme à l'absolutisme. L'évolution de la pensée religieuse du néo-hégelien anglais Bernard Bosanquet. Paris, 1954.

Muirhead, J. H. (editor). *Bosanquet and His Friends: Letters Illustrating Sources and Development of His Philosophical Opinions.* London, 1935.

Pfannenstil, B. *Bernard Bosanquet's Philosophy of the State.* Lund, 1936.

8. MC TAGGART

Texts

Studies in the Hegelian Dialectic. Cambridge, 1896 (2nd edition 1922).

Studies in the Hegelian Cosmology. Cambridge, 1901 (2nd edition, 1918).

Some Dogmas of Religion. London, 1906 (2nd edition, with biographical introduction by C. D. Broad, 1930).

A Commentary on Hegel's Logic. Cambridge, 1910 (new edition, 1931).

The Nature of Existence. 2 vols. Cambridge, 1921–7. (The second vol. is edited by C. D. Broad.)

Philosophical Studies, edited, with an introduction by S. V. Keeling, London, 1934. (Mainly a collection of published articles, including that on the unreality of time.)

Studies

Broad, C. D. *Examination of McTaggart's Philosophy.* 2 vols. Cambridge, 1933–8.

Dickinson, G. Lowes. *McTaggart, a Memoir.* Cambridge, 1931.

NOTES

CHAPTER ONE

¹ See Vol. V, Pt. II, of this *History*, pp. 167–96.

² See Vol. V, Pt. I, of this *History*, pp. 202–4.

³ See Vol. VI, Pt. I, of this *History*, pp. 49–52.

⁴ Cf. Vol. V, Pt. II, of this *History*, pp. 65–8, 122–3 and 145–6.

⁵ See Vol. V, Pt. I, of this *History*, p. 193.

⁶ *An Enquiry concerning the Principles of Morals*, 3, 1, 145.

⁷ Allusion to the influence of Helvétius's writings on Bentham's mind has already been made. We may add that he corresponded with d'Alembert.

⁸ This work had been printed in 1788.

⁹ A partial English text appeared in 1791.

¹⁰ Obviously, the prisoners whom Bentham had in mind were not at all of the type of those who later became victims of the Jacobin Terror. He turned to the new French Assembly in the hope that now at last the reign of unclouded reason was beginning, that philosophy was coming into its own.

¹¹ The work had been written at a considerably earlier period.

¹² In the *Works* Bowring included a number of fragments, some of which are of philosophical interest. Thus in the fragment entitled *Ontology* Bentham distinguishes between real entities and fictitious entities. The latter, which are not to be compared with fabulous entities, the products of the free play of the imagination, are creations of the exigencies of language. For example, we require to be able to speak of relations, using the noun 'relation'. But though things can be related, there are no separate entities called 'relations'. If such entities are postulated through the influence of language, they are 'fictitious'.

¹³ For Tucker see Vol. V, Pt. I, of this *History*, pp. 204–6.

¹⁴ *An Introduction to the Principles of Morals and Legislation*, ch. 1, sect. 1. This work will be referred to in future as *Introduction*.

¹⁵ *Theory of Legislation*, translated from the French of Étienne Dumont by R. Hildreth, p. 3 (London, 1896).

¹⁶ *Introduction*, ch. 1, sect. 1.

¹⁷ For example, under the attraction of an immediate pleasure a man might neglect the fact that the course of action which causes this pleasure leads to a sum total of pain which outweighs the pleasure.

¹⁸ Strictly speaking, an action which tends to add to the sum total of pleasure is for Bentham a 'right' action, in the sense of an action which we ought to perform, or at any rate not an action which we are

obliged not to perform, that is, a 'wrong' action. It may not always be the case that an addition to the sum of pleasure cannot exist otherwise than through my action here and now. Hence I may not be obliged to act, though, if I do, the action will certainly not be wrong.

19 *Introduction*, ch. 1, sect. 1, note 1.

20 Bentham insists that the rightness or wrongness of actions depends on an objective criterion and not simply on the motive with which they are performed. 'Motive' and 'intention' are often confused, though they ought, Bentham maintains, to be carefully distinguished. If 'motive' is understood as a tendency to action when a pleasure, or the cause of a pleasure, is contemplated as the consequent of one's action, it makes no sense to speak of a bad motive. But in any case the criterion of right and wrong is primarily an objective criterion, not a subjective one.

21 See Vol. V, Pt. I, of this *History*, pp. 133–7.

22 *Essay*, Bk. 2, ch. 20, sect. 2.

23 *Introduction*, ch. 1, sect. 3.

24 *Ibid.*, ch. 4.

25 *Ibid.*, ch. 1, sect. 7.

26 *Ibid.*, ch. 1, sect. 4. For Bentham's use of the word 'fictitious' see Note 1 on p. 15.

27 *Ibid.*

28 Bentham and his followers were indeed convinced that in the sphere of the economic market the removal of legal restrictions and the introduction of free trade and competition would, in the long run at any rate, inevitably make for the greater happiness of the community. But further reference to Benthamite economics will be made in the last section of this chapter.

29 *Introduction*, ch. 5, sect. 10. 'Sensitive beings' includes animals.

30 This theme will be treated in connection with James Mill.

31 In Bentham's time the British monarch was able to exercise considerably more effective influence in political life than is possible today.

32 *Introduction*, ch. 13, sect. 2.

33 It was certainly not unknown at the time for juries to refuse to convict even when they were well aware that the accused was guilty. Further, the death sentence, when passed for what would now be considered comparatively minor offences and even on children, was frequently commuted. In other words, there was a growing discrepancy between the actual state of the law and educated opinion as to what it should be.

34 *Dissertations and Discussions*, 1, pp. 339–40 (2nd edition, 1867).

35 *Ibid.*, 1, p. 353.

36 *Ibid.*, 1, p. 339.

37 See Vol. V, Pt. II, of this *History*, pp. 179–85.

38 This circle comprised, among others, the economists David Ricardo and J. R. McCulloch, T. R. Malthus, the famous writer on population, and John Austin, who applied utilitarian principles to jurisprudence in his work *The Province of Jurisprudence Determined* (1832).

39 Mill was indeed quite right in thinking that the House of Commons of his time was effec-

tively representative of only a small part of the population. He seems, however, to have thought that a legislature which represented the prosperous middle classes would represent the interests of the country as a whole. At the same time he saw no logical stopping-point in the process of extending the suffrage, though he assumed, rather surprisingly, that the lower classes would be governed by the wisdom of the middle class.

40 *Analysis of the Phenomena of the Human Mind*, II, p. 217 (1869, edited by J. S. Mill). Commenting on his father's statement, J. S. Mill draws attention to its ambiguity. To say that if I take pleasure in another man's pleasure, the pleasure which I feel is my own and not the other man's, is one thing. And it is obviously true. To imply that if I seek another man's pleasure I do so as a means to my own, is something different.

41 Similarly, the sentiments which we feel in contemplating the undesirable qualities of a bad man need not involve any reference to their lack of utility.

42 This determination also shows itself in Mill's attack on Mackintosh for making the morality of actions depend on motive, when Bentham had shown that it does not.

43 See Vol. VI, Pt. I, of this *History*, pp. 41–9.

44 *Analysis*, I, p. 52.

45 *Ibid.*, I, p. 110.

46 *Ibid.*, II, p. 177.

47 *Ibid.*, II, p. 179, note 34.

48 See Vol. V, Pt. II, of this *History*, pp. 157–8.

49 See Vol. VII, Pt. II, of this *History*, p. 81.

CHAPTER TWO

1 *Autobiography*, p. 38 (2nd edition, 1873). Though James Mill was an agnostic rather than a dogmatic atheist, he refused to admit that the world could possibly have been created by a God who combined infinite power with infinite wisdom and goodness. Moreover, he thought that this belief had a detrimental effect upon morality.

2 Mill started to read Wordsworth in 1828.

3 Comte Claude Henri de Rouvroy de Saint-Simon (1760–1825) was a French socialist, whose ideas gave rise to a group or School.

4 *Autobiography*, p. 167. Mill is referring to the aim or ideal of organizing labour and capital for the general good of the community.

5 The fifth essay was partially rewritten in 1833.

6 Auguste Comte (1798–1857) published the first volume of this work in 1830.

7 Subsequent editions appeared in 1849 and 1852.

8 This short work had previously appeared in instalments in *Fraser's Magazine*.

9 *Autobiography*, p. 294.

10 *Utilitarianism*, pp. 9–10 (2nd edition, 1864).

11 *Ibid.*, p. 16.

12 *Ibid.*, p. 32. Mill recognizes that the expedient may mean that which is expedient or useful for securing some temporary advantage when the securing of this advantage involves violation

of a rule 'whose observance is expedient in a much higher degree' (*ibid.*). And it is clear that not only the individual but also the community, as represented by public authority, might succumb to the temptation to seek its immediate temporary advantage in this way. But Mill argues that the expedient in this sense is not really 'useful' at all. It is harmful. Hence there can be no question of choice of the expedient being justified by the principle of utility.

13 Mill agrees with Bentham that the principle of utility cannot be proved by deduction from any more ultimate principle or principles. For the point at issue is the ultimate end of human action. And 'questions of ultimate ends do not admit of proof, in the ordinary acceptation of the term' (*Utilitarianism*, p. 52). It can, however, be shown that all men seek happiness, and only happiness, as the end of action. And this is sufficient proof of the statement that happiness is the one ultimate end of action.

14 *Utilitarianism*, p. 53.

15 *Ibid.*, pp. 56-7.

16 *Ibid.*, p. 11.

17 *Ibid.*, pp. 11-12.

18 *Dissertations and Discussions*, I, pp. 358-9.

19 *Ibid.*

20 *On Liberty*, p. 9 (edited by R. B. McCallum, Oxford, 1946).

21 *Utilitarianism*, pp. 13 and 16.

22 *On Liberty*, p. 50.

23 *Ibid.*, p. 56.

24 *Utilitarianism*, p. 56.

25 *Ibid.*, p. 53.

26 *Ibid.*

27 *Ibid.*, p. 46.

28 *Ibid.*, p. 46.

29 *Ibid.*, p. 50.

30 This line of objection is not confined, of course, to utilitarianism. It can be brought against any form of teleological ethics which interprets the moral imperative as what Kant would call an assertoric hypothetical imperative. (See Vol. VI, Pt. II, of this *History*, pp. 114-16.)

31 *On Liberty*, p. 9. All page references to this essay and to that *On Representative Government* are to the edition of the two essays in one volume by R. B. McCallum (Oxford, 1946).

32 *Ibid.*, p. 50.

33 *Ibid.*, p. 49.

34 *Ibid.*, p. 9.

35 *Ibid.*

36 *Ibid.*

37 *Ibid.*, p. 8.

38 *Ibid.*, p. 50.

39 *Ibid.*, p. 73.

40 Mill makes a distinction between violating specific duties to society and causing perceptible hurt to assignable individuals on the one hand and merely 'constructive injury' on the other (cf. *On Liberty*, p. 73). But though most people would make a clear distinction between, say, driving a car to the danger of the public when the driver is drunk and getting drunk in the privacy of one's own home, there are bound to be many cases in which the application of general categories is a matter for dispute.

41 *On Representative Government*, p. 115.

42 *Ibid.*, p. 141.

43 *Ibid.*, p. 151.

44 Mill envisages the possibility of a majority of unskilled

workers obtaining legislation to protect what it conceives to be its own interest, to the detriment of the interests of skilled workers and of other classes. Cf. *On Representative Government*, p. 183.

45 *Ibid.*, p. 179.

46 *Ibid.*, p. 102.

47 *On Liberty*, p. 94.

48 *Ibid.*, p. 95.

49 *Ibid.*

50 Mill insists, for example, that some education is a prerequisite for exercise of the suffrage, and so for democracy.

51 *A System of Logic*, II, p. 421 (10th edition, 1879). All further page-references to this work will be to this edition, denoted by the title *Logic*.

52 *Logic*, II, p. 423.

53 *Ibid.*, II, p. 422.

54 *Ibid.*, II, p. 426.

55 *An Examination of Sir William Hamilton's Philosophy*, p. 505 (2nd edition, 1865). This work will be referred to in future page-references as *Examination*.

56 *Ibid.*, p. 511.

CHAPTER THREE

1 *Logic*, I, p. 2 (I, *Introduction*, 2). Whately's *Elements of Logic* appeared in 1826.

2 Whately regarded the description of logic as the art of reasoning as inadequate. Logic is also the science of reasoning. As far as this emendation is concerned, Mill agrees with him.

3 *Logic*, I, p. 4 (I, *Introduction*, 4).

4 *Ibid.*, I, p. vii (in the Preface to the first edition).

5 See Vol. V, Pt. II, of this *History*, pp. 65–7.

6 *Logic*, II, p. 368 (II, 5, 5, 5).

7 *Ibid.*, II, p. 363 (II, 5, 5, 4).

8 *Ibid.*, II, p. 368 (II, 5, 5, 4).

9 *Auguste Comte and Positivism*, p. 121 (2nd edition, 1866).

10 *Logic*, I, p. 5 (I, *Introduction*, 4).

11 *Ibid.*, I, footnote (I, *Introduction*, 4).

12 *Autobiography*, p. 225.

13 *Ibid.*, pp. 225–6.

14 *Logic*, I, p. 17 (I, 1, 1, 1).

15 The phrase 'the wife of Socrates' would be for Mill a name, but not a proper name. For it is a connotative name, whereas proper names, such as John, are not connotative but solely denotative.

16 *Logic*, I, p. 151 (I, 1, 8, 1). As proper names do not possess meaning, they cannot be defined.

17 This is, for Mill, a real proposition, and not an 'essential' or purely verbal proposition.

18 *Logic*, I, p. 13 (I, 1, 6, 5).

19 *Ibid.*, I, p. 129, footnote (I, 1, 6, 4, footnote). Mill tends to use the term 'metaphysics' in the sense of theory of knowledge.

20 It is not denied, of course, that there can be true propositions which state matters of linguistic fact, propositions about the English language, for example.

21 *Logic*, I, p. 373 (I, 3, 5, 1).

22 *Ibid.*, II, p. 147 (II, 3, 24, 3).

23 *Examination*, p. 526.

24 *Logic*, I, p. 165 (I, 1, 8, 5).

25 *Ibid.*, I, p. 171 (I, 1, 8, 6).

26 *Ibid.*

27 *Ibid.*, II, pp. 148–9 (II, 3, 24, 4).

28 *Ibid.*, I, p. 265 (I, 2, 5, 3).

29 *Ibid.*, I, p. 262 (I, 2, 5, 1).

30 *Logic*, I, p. 261 (I, 2, 5, 1).

31 *Ibid.*, I, p. 263 (I, 2, 5, 2).

32 *Ibid.*, I, p. 261, note (I, 2, 5, 1, note).

33 *Ibid.*, I, p. 262 (I, 2, 5, 1).

34 *Autobiography*, p. 226.

35 *Examination*, p. 533.

36 *Logic*, II, p. 150 (II, 3, 24, 5).

37 *Ibid.*, II, p. 149 (II, 3, 24, 4).

38 *Ibid.*

39 Notably R. P. Anschutz in *The Philosophy of J. S. Mill*, ch. 9.

40 *Logic*, I, p. 187 (I, 2, 1, 3).

41 *Ibid.*, I, p. 209 (I, 2, 3, 1).

42 *Ibid.*, I, p. 130 (I, 1, 6, 5).

43 *Ibid.*, I, p. 221 (I, 2, 3, 4). The notion of a formula 'according to which' was suggested to Mill by Dugald Stewart's doctrine that the axioms of geometry are principles according to which, not from which, we reason.

44 *Ibid.*, I, p. 225 (I, 2, 3, 5).

45 *Ibid.*, I, p. 221 (I, 2, 3, 4).

46 *Ibid.*, I, p. 223 (I, 2, 3, 4).

47 *Ibid.*, I, p. 328 (I, 3, 1, 2).

48 *Ibid.*

49 *Ibid.*, I, p. 333 (I, 3, 2, 1). The use of the word 'will' should not be taken to mean that inductive inference is exclusively a process of inferring the future from the past. The general proposition refers also, of course, to unobserved contemporary members of a class, and indeed to unobserved past members.

50 If, for instance, I first discover that each Apostle is a Jew and then say, 'all the Apostles are Jews', this general proposition does not represent any real advance in knowledge.

51 *Logic*, I, p. 355 (I, 3, 3, 1).

52 *Ibid.*

53 *Logic*, I, p. 364 (I, 3, 4, 1).

54 *Ibid.*, I, p. 357 (I, 3, 3, 1).

55 *Ibid.*, I, p. 366 (I, 3, 4, 1).

56 *Ibid.*

57 *Ibid.*, I, p. 376 (I, 3, 5, 1).

58 *Ibid.*, I, p. 377 (I, 3, 5, 2).

59 Adopting a distinction made by Reid, Mill says that he is concerned only with 'physical' causes, and not with 'efficient' causes.

60 *Logic*, I, p. 377 (I, 3, 5, 2).

61 *Ibid.*, I, p. 392 (I, 3, 5, 6).

62 *Ibid.*, I, p. 392 (I, 3, 5, 6).

63 *Ibid.*, I, p. 378 (I, 3, 5, 2).

64 Mill recognizes in the universe 'permanent causes', natural agents which precede all human experience and of whose origin we are ignorant.

65 *Logic*, I, p. 400 (I, 3, 5, 8).

66 *Ibid.*, II, p. 102 (II, 3, 21, 3).

67 *Ibid.*, II, p. 103 (II, 3, 21, 3).

68 *Ibid.*, II, p. 104 (II, 3, 21, 3).

69 *Ibid.*, II, p. 106 (II, 3, 21, 4).

70 *Ibid.*, II, p. 108 (II, 3, 21, 4).

71 *Ibid.*, I, p. 437 (I, 3, 7, 1).

72 *Ibid.*, II, pp. 16–17 (II, 3, 14, 5).

73 *Ibid.*, I, p. 538 (I, 3, 11, 3).

74 *Ibid.*, II, p. 15 (II, 3, 14, 4).

75 *Ibid.*, I, p. 437 (I, 3, 7, 1).

76 *Ibid.*

77 *Ibid.*, I, p. 451 (I, 3, 8, 1).

78 *Ibid.*, I, p. 458 (I, 3, 8, 4).

79 *Ibid.*, I, p. 460 (I, 3, 8, 5).

80 *Ibid.*, I, p. 470 (I, 3, 8, 7).

81 *Ibid.*, I, p. 502 (I, 3, 9, 6).

82 *Ibid.*, I, p. 443 (I, 3, 7, 3).

83 *Ibid.*, I, p. 446 (I, 3, 7, 4).

84 *Ibid.*, II, p. 546 (II, 6, 12, 1).

85 The study of the formation of national character had been suggested, for example, by Montesquieu.

86 *Logic*, II, p. 439 (II, 6, 4, 3).

87 *Ibid.*, II, p. 458 (II, 6, 5, 5).

88 *Ibid.*

89 *Ibid.*, II, p. 464 (II, 6, 6, 1).

90 *Ibid.*, II, p. 490 (II, 6, 9, 1). That is to say, the empirical generalizations are verified by ascertaining whether they follow from known general principles relating to human nature.

91 *Autobiography*, p. 211.

92 *Logic*, II, p. 496 (II, 6, 9, 3).

93 Mill can, of course, evade fatalism, if fatalism is understood as omitting the human will from the chain of operative causes. At the same time if, given the antecedent conditions, a human volition cannot be otherwise than it is, it is difficult to see how he can evade fatalism if this is understood as synonymous with rejection of liberty of indifference.

94 For instance, statistically-based generalizations may enable us to predict the approximate number of people in a given county who will post letters incorrectly addressed. But the statistician is not in a position to say which individual citizens will be guilty of this oversight.

95 *Examination*, p. 192.

96 Obviously, in the illustration which has just been given of someone sitting at a table, a belief in the existence of an external world is already present. But it can serve to show the general line of Mill's psychological reconstruction of the belief.

97 *Examination*, p. 196.

98 *Ibid.*, p. 198.

99 *Ibid.* Needless to say, Mill does not accept the theological conclusions which Berkeley drew from his theory of material things as 'ideas'. But he regards his own analysis of what it means to say that there are material things which continue to exist even when unperceived, as being substantially the same as that given by the good bishop.

100 *Three Essays on Religion*, p. 86 (1904 edition).

101 *Ibid.*, p. 85.

102 It is widely recognized that the only sufficient proof of the possibility of such a translation would be to perform it, and that no adequate translation has in fact been made.

103 *Examination*, p. 205. According to Mill's use of the term, metaphysics is 'that portion of mental philosophy which attempts to determine what part of the furniture of the mind belongs to it originally, and what part is constructed out of materials furnished to it from without'. *Logic*, I, p. 7 (I, Introduction, 4). For the use of the term 'feeling' see reference on p. 21 to James Mill's use of the word.

104 *Examination*, p. 212.

105 *Ibid.*, p. 213.

106 *Ibid.*, p. 207.

107 *Three Essays on Religion*, p. 70. This work will be referred to as *Three Essays*.

108 *Ibid.*, p. 67.

109 *Ibid.*, p. 72.

110 Mill does not think that an account of the matter simply in terms of the survival of the fittest is at all conclusive.

111 *Three Essays*, p. 75.

112 *Ibid.*

113 *Autobiography*, p. 40.

114 *Three Essays*, p. 48.

115 *Ibid.*, p. 50.

116 *Ibid.*, p. 54. Mill maintains that while science does not provide any cogent evidence against immortality, there is no positive evidence in favour of it.

117 *Ibid.*, p. 108.

118 *Ibid.*, p. 102.

CHAPTER FOUR

1 See J. S. Mill's *Autobiography*, p. 245, note.

2 Though certainly not blind to the relevance of physiological investigations, J. S. Mill, like his father, was chiefly interested in the psychology of consciousness and in its philosophical relevance.

3 Bain introduced, however, a good many modifications into the associationist psychology as received from his predecessors.

4 Mind is thus described from the start. 'It has Feeling, in which term I include what is commonly called Sensation and Emotion. It can Act according to Feeling. It can Think.' *The Senses and the Intellect*, p. 1 (1st edition).

5 *Ibid.*, p. 371.

6 *Ibid.*

7 *Ibid.*, p. 372.

8 *Ibid.*

9 *Ibid.*, p. 371.

10 *Ibid.*, p. 372.

11 According to Bain, we cannot even discuss the existence of a material world entirely apart from consciousness.

12 *The Emotions and the Will*, p. 524 (2nd edition).

13 *Ibid.*, p. 525.

14 *Ibid.*, p. 538.

15 *Ibid.*, p. 548.

16 *Ibid.*, p. 585.

17 *Ibid.*

18 *Ibid.*, p. 272.

19 *Ibid.*, p. 258. Bain also notes that we can have disinterested antipathies and aversions.

20 *Ibid.*, p. 274.

21 *Ibid.*, p. 277.

22 *Ibid.*, p. 283.

23 *Ibid.*

24 *Ibid.*, p. 281.

25 *The Methods of Ethics*, p. XV (6th edition.)

26 *Ibid.*, p. XX.

27 This does not mean that we ought to prefer a future uncertain good to a lesser but certain present one. As self-evident, the principle simply states that priority in time, considered simply by itself, is not a reasonable ground for preferring one good to another. Cf. *The Methods of Ethics*, p. 381.

28 *The Methods of Ethics*, p. 380. The difference might be one of circumstances or between the persons considered. We would not necessarily think it right to treat a child in the way that we consider we ought to be treated.

29 *Ibid.*, p. 382.

30 *Ibid.*, pp. 406–7.

31 For Samuel Clarke see Vol. V, Pt. I, of this *History*, pp. 171–2.

32 *Lectures and Essays* (The People's Library edition), pp. 178–9. Huxley was commenting on an essay by a certain Professor Kolliker of Würzburg who had interpreted Darwin as a teleologist and had criticized him on this score.

33 *Lay Sermons, Addresses and Reviews*, p. 294 (6th edition).

The quotation is taken from an 1860 article on *The Origin of Species*.

[34] *Ibid.*, p. 295.

[35] In regard to Lamarck's theory that environmental changes produce new needs in animals, that new needs produce new desires, and that new desires result in organic modifications which are transmitted by heredity, Huxley remarks that it does not seem to have occurred to Lamarck to inquire 'whether there is any reason to believe that there are any limits to the amount of modifications producible, or to ask how long an animal is likely to endeavour to gratify an impossible desire;' *Lectures and Essays*, p. 124. The quotation is taken from an 1859 essay on 'The Darwinian Hypothesis'.

[36] *Evolution and Ethics and Other Essays*, p. 80. The discourse on *Evolution and Ethics* was originally given at Oxford as the second Romanes lecture.

[37] *Ibid.*, p. 81.

[38] *Ibid.*, p. 83.

[39] *Ibid.*, p. 83.

[40] *Ibid.*, p. 135.

[41] The Marxist, for example, does not deny the reality of mind. Nor does he identify psychical with physical processes. But he looks on himself none the less as a materialist. And so he is in a metaphysical sense.

[42] *Evolution and Ethics, and Other Essays*, p. 130. *Kraft und Stoff* is the title of a well-known book by the German materialist, Ludwig Büchner. See Vol. VII, Pt. II, of this *History*, pp. 125–6.

[43] *Ibid.*, p. 133.

[44] *Lay Sermons, Addresses and Reviews*, p. 18.

[45] On Faraday's death in 1867 Tyndall succeeded him as Superintendent of the Institution.

[46] *Fragments of Science for Unscientific People*, pp. 121–2 (2nd edition).

[47] *Ibid.*, p. 122.

[48] *Lectures and Essays*, p. 40 (Rationalist Press Association edition, 1903).

[49] *Fragments of Science*, p. 166.

[50] *Ibid.*, p. 163.

[51] *Lectures and Essays*, p. 40.

[52] *Fragments of Science*, p. 93.

[53] *Lectures and Essays*, p. 47.

[54] *Ibid.*

[55] 'No atheistic reasoning can, I hold, dislodge religion from the human heart. Logic cannot deprive us of life, and religion is life to the religious. As an experience of consciousness it is beyond the assaults of logic', *ibid.*, p. 45.

[56] *An Agnostic's Apology and Other Essays*, p. 52 (Rationalist Press Association edition, 1904). The quotation is taken from an 1886 essay. *What is Materialism?*

[57] *Ibid.*, p. 66.

[58] *Ibid.*, p. 57.

[59] *Ibid.*

[60] *Ibid.*, p. 20.

[61] *Thoughts on Religion*, p. 87.

[62] *Ibid.*, p. 124.

[63] *Ibid.*, p. 140.

[64] *Ibid.*, p. 132.

[65] *Ibid.*, p. 168.

[66] *Ibid.*, p. 131.

[67] In 1864 Spencer wrote his *Reasons for Dissenting from the Philosophy of Comte*.

68 In 1893 the London Positivist Committee founded *The Positivist Review*. But the periodical ceased publication in 1925, after having been called *Humanity* during the last two years of its life.

69 As Clifford presupposed something like the phenomenalism of Hume, he had to maintain that impressions or sensations, composed of mind-stuff, can exist antecedently to consciousness. When consciousness arises, they become, or can become, its objects; but to be objects of consciousness is not essential for their existence.

70 Sir Francis Galton (1822–1911), a cousin of Darwin, was the founder of the science of eugenics and envisaged the deliberate application in human society of the principle of selection which works automatically in Nature.

71 *The Grammar of Science*, p. 6 (2nd edition, revised and enlarged, 1900).

72 *Ibid.*, p. 17.

73 *Ibid.*, p. 64.

74 Science, Pearson insists, is purely descriptive, and not explanatory. Scientific laws 'simply *describe*, they never explain the routine of our perceptions, the sense-impressions we project into an "outside world"', *ibid.*, p. 99.

75 *Ibid.*, p. 91. No argument from 'design' to the existence of God, therefore, could ever be valid.

76 *Ibid.*, p. 95.

77 *Ibid.*, p. 9.

78 See Vol. VII, Pt. II, of this *History*, p. 132.

79 As we have seen, T. H. Huxley was an exception, inasmuch as he believed that moral progress runs counter to the process of evolution in Nature.

CHAPTER FIVE

1 Spencer's attitude to the Boer War prompted an attack on him by *The Times*.

2 We shall return later to Spencer's doctrine of the 'unknowable'.

3 *First Principles*, p. 119 (6th edition).

4 *Ibid.*, p. 120.

5 *Ibid.*

6 *Ibid.*, p. 123.

7 *Ibid.*

8 *Ibid.*, p. 122.

9 *Ibid.*, p. 123.

10 *Ibid.*

11 *Ibid.*

12 *Ibid.*

13 *Ibid.*, p. 125.

14 Some of these may have their remoter origin in animal experience.

15 *Ibid.*, p. 125.

16 *Ibid.*, p. 127.

17 *Ibid.*, p. 145.

18 In Spencer's opinion the idea of co-existence is derived from that of sequence, inasmuch as we find that the terms of certain relations of sequence can be presented with equal facility in reverse order. Co-existence cannot be an original datum of a consciousness which consists in serial states.

19 *First Principles*, p. 146.

20 *Ibid.*, p. 149.

21 *Ibid.*, p. 151.

22 *Ibid.*

23 *Ibid.*, p. 167.

24 *Ibid.*, p. 175.

25 *Ibid.*, p. 249.

26 *Ibid.*, p. 175.

27 *Ibid.*, p. 176.

28 *First Principles*, p. 367. In a note Spencer remarks that the word 'relatively', omitted in the original text, needs to be inserted in two places as above.

29 *Ibid.*, p. 506.

30 *The Principles of Sociology*, I, p. 3.

31 The study of what Spencer calls super-organic evolution, which presupposes organic or biological evolution, would include, if understood in the widest sense, the study of, for example, the societies of bees and ants.

32 *The Study of Sociology*, p. 44 (26th thousand, 1907).

33 *Ibid.*, p. 70.

34 *Ibid.*, I, pp. 9–10.

35 *Ibid.*, I, p. 479.

36 *Ibid.*

37 *Ibid.*, II, p. 288.

38 *Ibid.*, I, p. 577.

39 *Ibid.*, II, p. 607.

40 The militant type of society also tends to manifest itself in characteristic forms of law and judicial procedure.

41 *Ibid.*, II, p. 610.

42 *Ibid.*

43 *Ibid.*, II, p. 607.

44 This is the title of one of his essays.

45 *The Man Versus the State*, p. 78 (19th thousand, 1910).

46 *Ibid.*, p. 107.

47 *The Data of Ethics*, p. V (1907 edition). This preface is reprinted in the first volume of *The Principles of Ethics*, the reference being to p. VII (1892 edition).

48 Purposeless actions are excluded from 'conduct'.

49 *The Data of Ethics*, p. 238.

50 *The Principles of Ethics*, I, p. 318.

51 *The Data of Ethics*, p. 241.

52 Obviously, the idea of moral precepts must be understood in such a way as to admit the distinction between principles of conduct in an imperfectly evolved society and the ideal principles which would obtain in a perfectly evolved society.

53 *The Data of Ethics*, p. 140.

54 *Ibid.*, p. 148.

55 *Ibid.*

56 *Justice* (*The Principles of Ethics*, Part IV), p. 17.

57 *First Principles*, p. 9.

58 It may occur to the reader that religion and the offering of explanations are not precisely the same thing. But in ordinary language 'religion' is generally understood as involving an element or elements of belief. And Spencer obviously understands the term in this way.

59 *First Principles*, p. 29.

60 Henry L. Mansel (1820–71), who became Dean of St. Paul's, developed Sir William Hamilton's doctrine about the unknowable unconditioned and gave the Bampton lectures on *The Limits of Religious Thought* (1858) from which Spencer quotes (*First Principles*, pp. 33–6) in support of his own agnosticism.

61 *First Principles*, p. 55.

62 *Ibid.*, p. 57.

63 *Ibid.*, pp. 82–3.

64 *Ibid.*, p. 92.

65 Spencer actually employs the Kantian terms.

66 *First Principles*, p. 74.

67 *Ibid.*, p. 80.

68 *Ibid.*, p. 143.

69 *Ibid.*, pp. 143–4.

70 *The Data of Ethics*, p. 106.

71 *Ibid.*

CHAPTER SIX

1 The foregoing remarks constitute a generalization which is open to criticism on a number of counts. But in such introductory observations one has to prescind from the differences between the various idealist systems.

2 Empiricism, it is true, had its own implicit metaphysics. And the empiricists not infrequently used the term 'metaphysics' in regard to some of their tenets. But in so far as metaphysics involves an attempt to disclose the nature of ultimate reality, idealism can legitimately be said to represent a revival of metaphysics.

3 In Catholic countries idealism, with its tendency to subordinate theology to speculative philosophy, was commonly regarded as a disintegrating influence, so far as the Christian religion was concerned. In England the situation was somewhat different. A good many of the British idealists were themselves religious men, who found in their philosophy both an expression of and a support for their religious view of the world and of human life.

4 In *The Platonic Tradition in Anglo-Saxon Philosophy* (1931).

5 Fichte and Schelling exercised little influence, though the former had some stimulative effect on Carlyle, and the latter on Coleridge. There is one obvious reason for this. The classical German idealist movement was already over when the British began; and it was regarded as having culminated in Hegel, considered as the true successor of Kant.

6 That is to say, it is from one point of view somewhat surprising to find that the romantic poet was ever an enthusiast for Hartley of all people. But the associationist psychology was then regarded as 'advanced', and this doubtless helped to commend it to the intellectually alive undergraduate.

7 For the matter of that, Hartley himself had been a religious believer.

8 See Coleridge's *Biographia Literaria*, ch. 6.

9 See Mill's *Dissertations and Discussions*, I, p. 405.

10 'The writings of the illustrious sage of Koenigsberg, the founder of the Critical Philosophy, more than any other works, at once invigorated and disciplined my understanding', *Biographia Literaria*, p. 76 (Everyman's Library edition).

11 See Vol. VI, Pt. I, of this *History*, pp. 169–72.

12 *Philosophical Lectures*, edited by K. Coburn, p. 186.

13 *Biographia Literaria*, p. 78.

14 *Ibid.*, p. 79.

15 *Ibid.*, p. 136.

16 *Ibid.*, p. 145.

17 *Ibid.*

18 *Ibid.*, p. 144.

19 Fichte did not, of course, make the finite ego or self his ultimate principle. And Coleridge tends to caricature his thought.

20 *Biographia Literaria*, p. 144.

21 *Exodus*, 3, 14.

22 *Dissertations and Discussions*, I, p. 436.

23 As no publisher would accept this work, it first appeared in instalments in *Fraser's Magazine*, 1833–4. An American edition of the book appeared in

1836, and an English edition in 1838.

24 *Sartor Resartus*, I, 10, p. 57 (Scott Library edition). The 'Garment' is, of course, the body.

25 *Ibid.*, I, 8, p. 48.

26 *On Heroes*, lecture I, p. 193 (London, Chapman and Hall).

27 *Ibid.*, p. 185.

28 Hegel, however, regarded his 'word-historical individuals' as instruments of the World-Spirit.

29 *Ibid.*, lecture V, p. 323.

30 *Ibid.*

31 According to Ferrier, if we wish to find the solution to a metaphysical problem, we might well inquire what the psychologists have said about the matter and then assert the exact opposite.

32 This did not prevent Ferrier from writing articles on Schelling and Hegel for the *Imperial Dictionary of Universal Biography*.

33 We can hardly exclude all influence of German thought on Ferrier's mind. But he was doubtless right in claiming that his system was his own creation, and not the result of borrowing.

34 *Institutes of Metaphysics*, I, prop. 1, p. 79 (Works, I, 3rd edition). This work will henceforth be referred to simply as *Institutes*.

35 *Ibid.*, I, prop. 13, observation 3, p. 312.

36 *Ibid.*, observation 2, p. 311.

37 *Institutes*, III, prop. 11, p. 522. It will be noted that for Ferrier the Absolute is not God alone but the synthesis of God and the world, of the infinite subject and its object in relation to one another.

38 According to Grote, in its construction of an articulated world the self discovers or recognizes categories in Nature, which are the expression of the divine mind.

39 In Grote's view, things-in-themselves are known intuitively, even if not distinctly, through knowledge by acquaintance, as contrasted with knowledge about.

40 While he explicitly acknowledged the stimulus which he had received from Hegel, Jowett gradually moved further away from rather than nearer to Hegelianism.

41 A one-volume edition appeared in 1898. Stirling never held an academic post; but he gave the Gifford Lectures at Edinburgh in 1889–90. These were published in 1890 with the title *Philosophy and Theology*.

42 Stirling published a *Text-Book to Kant* in 1881.

CHAPTER SEVEN

1 This work will be referred to as *Introductions*.

2 *Ibid.*, I, 2–3. Green and Grose edition of Hume's *Treatises*, I, p. 2.

3 *Ibid.*, 3.

4 Green is clearly thinking of philosophers such as the two Mills.

5 *Introductions*, I, 3. Green and Grose, I, pp. 2–3.

6 *Ibid.* Green and Grose, I, p. 3.

7 *Prolegomena to Ethics*, p. 9 (first edition). This work will be

referred to henceforth as *Prolegomena*.

8 *Prolegomena*, p. 14. The phrase 'cosmos of experience' is taken from G. H. Lewes, one of Green's targets of attack.

9 *Ibid.*, p. 22. Clearly, Kant's transcendental ego is given an ontological status.

10 *Ibid.*, p. 28.

11 *Ibid.*, p. 38.

12 *Ibid.*, pp. 72–3.

13 *Ibid.*, p. 72.

14 *Ibid.*, p. 198.

15 *Ibid.*, pp. 103–4.

16 Obviously, metaphysical idealists are by no means the only philosophers whose criticism of their opponents has been more telling than their own positive contributions to philosophy. Indeed, the frequency with which this situation occurs raises general problems about philosophy. But they cannot be discussed here.

17 *Ibid.*, p. 169.

18 *Ibid.*, p. 109.

19 Obviously, if Green had lived at a later date, he would have had to cope with theories of the infra-conscious springs of human action.

20 *Ibid.*, p. 102.

21 *Lectures on the Principles of Political Obligation*, p. 146 (1901 edition). This work will be referred to as *Political Obligation*.

22 *Prolegomena*, p. 193.

23 *Ibid.*, p. 193. Hegel could, of course, say the same. For the universal, in his view, exists only in and through particulars. At the same time, in speaking of the State, Green does not employ the exalted epithets used by the German philosopher.

24 Society in this context does not necessarily mean the State. The members of a family, for example, enjoy rights. The point is that 'right' is, so to speak, a social term.

25 *Political Obligation*, p. 144. The State, of course, presupposes the family, a form of society in which the claims of individuals are already recognized. The State maintains these rights.

26 *Ibid.*, p. 41.

27 *Ibid.*, p. 125.

28 *Ibid.*, p. 147.

29 *Ibid.*, p. 149.

30 *Ibid.*, p. 195.

31 *Ibid.*

32 *Hegel*, published in Blackwood's Philosophical Classics series.

33 On this subject see Caird's Preface to *Essays in Philosophical Criticism*, edited by A. Seth and R. B. Haldane (1883).

34 *The Evolution of Religion*, I, p. 65.

35 This is obviously true in regard to the *terms* 'subject' and 'object'.

36 *Ibid.*, I, p. 67.

37 *Ibid.*, I, p. 68.

38 Caird's three stages correspond more or less to Hegel's stages; natural religion, the religion of spiritual individuality and absolute religion.

39 *Ibid.*, I, p. 189.

40 *Ibid.*, I, p. 195.

41 *Ibid.*, I, p. 140.

42 *Evolution of Religion*, I, p. 65.

43 This idea appears, for example, though in a rather different setting, in the philosophy of Karl Jaspers, under the form of The Comprehensive.

44 In the organism, John Caird argues, we find immanent

teleology which shows itself in the way that an internal spontaneity or energy differentiates members and functions and at the same time reintegrates them into a common unity, realizing the immanent end of the whole organism. As for the life of reflective consciousness, the idea of mechanical causality loses all relevance in this sphere.

45 *An Introduction to the Philosophy of Religion*, p. 112.

46 *Ibid.*, p. 125.

47 In more recent times, it has sometimes been said that the traditional proofs of God's existence, while logically invalid, possess value as 'pointers' to God. But unless we know what is meant by saying this, it is difficult to discuss the thesis. We need to be told something more than that the traditional proofs are 'pointers to God' or, as by Caird, that they possess great value as phenomenological analyses. This is the point that I have been trying to make.

48 This is, of course, the so-called shorter or lesser *Logic*, of Hegel.

49 *Prolegomena to the Study of Hegel, and especially of his Logic.*

50 Cf. for example, *Darwin and Hegel, with Other Philosophical Studies* (1893).

CHAPTER EIGHT

1 The second edition appeared in two volumes in 1922.

2 A second edition, with an added Appendix, appeared in 1897.

3 *The Presuppositions of Crit-*

ical History is reprinted in the first volume.

4 See Vol. VII, Pt. II, of this *History*, p. 14.

5 See *Contemporary British Philosophy, Second Series*, p. 271, edited by J. H. Muirhead (1925).

6 *Collected Essays*, I, p. 24.

7 *Ibid.*, I, p. 20.

8 *Ibid.*, I, p. 21.

9 *Ibid.*, I, pp. 69–70.

10 *Ethical Studies*, p. 36 (2nd edition). It is in this context that Bradley makes his famous comment: 'Mr Bain collects that the mind is a collection. Has he ever thought who collects Mr Bain?' (p. 39, note 1).

11 *Ibid.*, p. 12.

12 The book includes indeed some metaphysical excursions; but Bradley does not explicitly introduce his metaphysics of the Absolute.

13 *Ethical Studies*, p. 125.

14 *Ibid.*, pp. 125–6.

15 *Ibid.*, p. 159.

16 *Ibid.*, p. 148, note 1.

17 *Ibid.*, p. 180.

18 *Ibid.*, p. 166.

19 *Ibid.*, pp. 199–200.

20 *Ibid.*, p. 192.

21 *Ibid.*

22 *Ibid.*, p. 223.

23 *Ibid.*

24 *Ibid.*

25 *Ibid.*, p. 201.

26 *Ibid.*, p. 313.

27 *Ibid.*, p. 316.

28 *Ibid.*, p. 322.

29 *Ibid.*, p. 74.

30 *The Principles of Logic*, I, p. 2 (2nd edition).

31 *Ibid.*, I, pp. 2–3.

32 *Ibid.*, I, p. ix.

33 It is presupposed that the judgment is not what Bradley calls a 'collective' judgment, a

mere summation of observed cases, but a genuine abstract universal judgment.

34 Hegel had already drawn attention to this point. See Vol. VII, Pt. I, of this *History*, p. 220.

35 *The Principles of Logic*, I, p. 49.

36 *Ibid.*, I, p. 56.

37 *Ibid.*, II, p. 623 (terminal essays, 2).

38 As Bradley turned his back on Hume, so have modern logical atomists turned their back on Bradley. Thus for Bertrand Russell analysis is the path to truth, to a knowledge of reality, rather than a distortion or mutilation of reality. In actual fact, however, we need both analysis and synthesis.

39 *The Principles of Logic*, I, p. 95.

40 *Ibid.*

41 *Ibid.*, II, p. 591.

42 In Bradley's developed metaphysics movement, becoming, belongs to the sphere of appearance.

43 *Appearance and Reality*, p. 1 (2nd edition, 1897).

44 *Ibid.*, p. 4.

45 *Essays on Truth and Reality*, p. 15.

46 *Appearance and Reality*, pp. 553–4.

47 *Essays on Truth and Reality*, p. 200.

48 *Ibid.*, p. 159.

49 *Ibid.*, p. 200.

50 *Ibid.*

51 *Ibid.*, p. 174. Bradley argued against James Ward that there is in fact such an experience.

52 *Appearance and Reality*, p. 31.

53 Obviously, if we wish to avoid Bradley's conclusion, we must refuse to be compelled to choose between these bald theses. For example, we can distinguish two possible meanings of the statement 'a relation is nothing'.

54 *Appearance and Reality*, p. 33.

55 *Essays on Truth and Reality*, p. 238.

56 *Appearance and Reality*, p. 34.

57 *Ibid.*, p. 37.

58 *Ibid.*, p. 80.

59 *Ibid.*, p. 87.

60 *Ibid.*, p. 119.

61 *Ibid.*, p. 132.

62 *Ibid.*

63 *Ibid.*, p. 146.

64 *Ibid.*, pp. 146–7.

65 *Ibid.*, p. 552.

66 *Ibid.*, p. 530.

67 *Ibid.*, p. 498.

68 *Ibid.*, p. 499.

69 *Ibid.*, p. 159.

70 *Ibid.*, p. 506.

71 *Ibid.*, p. 487.

72 *Ibid.*, p. 365.

73 *Essays on Truth and Reality*, p. 223.

74 *Ibid.*, p. 239.

75 *Ibid.*, p. 219.

76 *Ibid.*, p. 335.

77 *Appearance and Reality*, p. 531.

78 *Ibid.*

79 When speaking of the religious consciousness, it is primarily Christianity which Bradley has in mind. It can hardly be claimed that in all forms of religion the divine, or ultimate reality, is conceived as personal.

80 *Ibid.*, p. 533.

81 *Ibid.*, p. 447.

82 *Ibid.*, p. 453.

[83] *Appearance and Reality*, p. 454.

[84] *Essays on Truth and Reality*, pp. 446–7.

[85] *Appearance and Reality*, p. XIV.

[86] *Ibid.*, p. XIV.

[87] *Ibid.*, p. XII.

[88] *Ibid.*

[89] As we have seen, this is also described by Bradley as a dim virtual knowledge.

[90] *Ibid.*, p. 196.

[91] *Ibid.*, p. 201.

[92] *Ibid.*, p. 203.

[93] *Ibid.*, p. 240.

[94] *Ibid.*, p. 227.

[95] *Ibid.*, pp. 499–500.

CHAPTER NINE

[1] A second edition appeared in 1911.

[2] A fourth edition appeared in 1923, the year of Bosanquet's death.

[3] Bosanquet's history of aesthetic theory remains, however, a valuable contribution to the subject.

[4] *Logic*, I, p. 3.

[5] Bosanquet is concerned with phenomenology rather than with psychology. The individual's world is not built up out of his perceptions considered as psychological entities, but rather out of his perceptions considered as presenting objects.

[6] *Essentials of Logic*, p. 15.

[7] *Ibid.*, pp. 14–15.

[8] *Ibid.*, I, p. 3.

[9] *Ibid.*, I, pp. 83–4. By 'a third idea' Bosanquet means the copula considered as a distinct element in the judgment.

[10] *Ibid.*, II, p. 1.

[11] *Ibid.*, I, p. 78.

[12] *The Principle of Individuality and Value*, p. 43.

[13] *Essentials of Logic*, p. 166.

[14] To a certain extent Bradley would be prepared to speak in much the same way. But it is true that he so emphasizes the deficiencies of human thought that Bosanquet is justified in seeing in Bradley's philosophy the creation of a gap between thought and reality.

[15] *Essentials of Logic*, p. 166.

[16] *The Principle of Individuality and Value*, p. 69.

[17] *Ibid.*, p. 80.

[18] *The Value and Destiny of the Individual*, p. 251.

[19] *The Principle of Individuality and Value*, pp. 243–4.

[20] *Ibid.*, pp. 267–8.

[21] *The Philosophical Theory of the State*, p. 80 (1st edition).

[22] *Ibid.*, p. 107.

[23] *Ibid.*, p. 151.

[24] *Ibid.*, p. 154.

[25] *Ibid.*, p. 183.

[26] *Ibid.*, p. 192.

[27] *Ibid.*, p. 328.

[28] *Ibid.*, p. 327.

[29] *Ibid.*, p. 322.

[30] Leonard Trelawny Hobhouse (1864–1929), professor of sociology in the University of London from 1907 until the year of his death, was a philosopher of wide interests and the author of a number of books on philosophical and sociological topics. The work mentioned in the text represents a course of lectures given at the London School of Economics in 1917.

[31] *The Metaphysical Theory of the State*, pp. 117–18.

[32] As a matter of fact, Hobhouse denies all three propositions mentioned above.

33 According to Bosanquet, 'moral relations presuppose an organized life; but such a life is only within the State, not in relations between the States and other communities'. *The Philosophical Theory of the State*, p. 325.

34 *The Metaphysical Theory of the State*, p. 77.

35 *Ibid.*, p. 121, note 1.

36 If one sums up a trend of thought common to several philosophers in a number of theses, it is not surprising if the resultant scheme is not fully applicable to all of them, or perhaps to any of them. And one can then find examples of 'inconsistency'. Still, the inconsistency may be with the main operative ideas of a given philosopher's thought.

37 In the biographical note which prefaces his contribution to the first volume of *Contemporary British Philosophy*, edited by J. H. Muirhead, Haldane remarks that he was influenced more by Hegel's method than by his detailed theory of the Absolute. But he adds that in his opinion Hegel came nearer to the ultimately true view than anyone since the ancient Greeks.

38 Though he had become Lord Chancellor in 1912, after having done excellent work as Secretary of State for War, Haldane was omitted from the reconstituted ministry of 1915, not indeed because his colleagues had any doubt of his patriotism but rather as a measure of expediency in view of popular prejudice.

39 *The Nature of Truth*, p. 178.

40 *Ibid.*, pp. 178-9.

41 *Ibid.*, p. 175.

42 *Ibid.*, p. 179.

CHAPTER TEN

1 Originally called Andrew Seth, he adopted the name Pringle-Pattison in 1898 in fulfilment of a condition for succeeding to an estate. He successively occupied chairs of philosophy at Cardiff (1883-7), St. Andrews (1887-91) and Edinburgh (1891-1919).

2 *Hegelianism and Personality*, p. 196 (2nd edition).

3 *Ibid.*, p. 199.

4 *Ibid.*, p. 203.

5 *Ibid.*, p. 226. Strictly speaking, neither Bradley nor Bosanquet regarded the Absolute as a 'self'. But they did, of course, merge all finite experiences in the unity of a single absolute experience.

6 *Ibid.*, p. 217.

7 *Ibid.*, p. 238.

8 *The Idea of God in the Light of Recent Philosophy* (1917), p. 192. This work will be referred to as *The Idea of God*.

9 *Ibid.*, p. 211.

10 *Ibid.*, p. 212.

11 *Ibid.*, p. 308.

12 *Ibid.*, p. 259.

13 *Ibid.*, p. 267.

14 *Ibid.*, p. 363.

15 The first volume appeared in 1921. The second, edited by Professor C. D. Broad, was published posthumously in 1927. A summary of the system is presented by McTaggart himself in his contribution to the first volume of *Contemporary British Philosophy*, edited by J. H. Muirhead.

16 Existence is said to be an

indefinable quality which is such that everything which exists is real, though not everything which is real is necessarily existent. In other words, reality or being is for McTaggart a wider concept than that of existence.

[17] *The Nature of Existence*, 45. The work is divided into sections numbered successively from the beginning of the first to the end of the second volume. And references are given here according to these numbered sections.

[18] *Ibid*.

[19] Obviously, McTaggart, interpreting existence as an indefinable quality, could not accept the Thomist thesis that ultimate reality is precisely *ipsum esse subsistens*.

[20] *The Nature of Existence*, 65.

[21] *Ibid*., 68.

[22] The term 'relation' is for McTaggart indefinable, though we can clarify the difference in meaning between words such as 'relation' and 'quality'. For instance, qualities are not said to exist 'between' terms, whereas relations are.

[23] According to McTaggart, following Leibniz, if two substances had precisely the same nature, they would be indistinguishable, and therefore one and the same substance.

[24] *The Nature of Existence*, 88.

[25] We must distinguish between members and parts. 'If we take the group of all the counties in Great Britain, neither England nor Whitechapel are members of the group, but they are parts, of which the group is the whole.' *Ibid*., 123.

[26] *Ibid*., 135.

[27] *Ibid*., 137. If, for instance, a substance X possesses qualities *a*, *b* and *c*, an alteration in one quality produces an alteration in the nature (composed of the qualities) and so in the substance which is manifested in the nature. The qualities are then said to stand to one another in a relation of extrinsic determination.

[28] As no substance is absolutely simple, the difficulty occurs in regard to every substance.

[29] *Contemporary British Philosophy*, First Series, p. 256.

[30] *The Nature of Existence*, 352.

[31] According to McTaggart, it is no good saying that the existence of matter can be proved inferentially from sense-data. For what we call sense-data might be caused by spiritual causes. And if we claim that sense-data are themselves material substances, we shall have to meet the arguments which show, in general, that substance cannot be material.

[32] *The Nature of Existence*, 381.

[33] For McTaggart the self is indefinable and is known by acquaintance.

[34] *Ibid*., 408.

[35] Cf. *Ibid*., 332, and McTaggart's article on *The Unreality of Time* in *Mind*, 1908.

[36] *The Nature of Existence*, 503.

[37] In *British Philosophy in the Mid-Century*, edited by C. A. Mace, p. 45.

[38] McTaggart admitted the bare possibility of there being within the society of selves a self which from the standpoint of ex-

perience might appear to exercise some controlling, though not creative, function. But he added that we have no reason to suppose that there is in fact such a self. And even if there were, it would not be equivalent to God as customarily represented in theistic thought.

39 In the opinion of the present writer this approach to psychology was much superior to that of the associationists.

40 *Naturalism and Agnosticism*, 1, p. viii.

41 *Ibid.*

42 Ward is not always careful to observe his own distinction between natural science and philosophical naturalism. And he tends to speak as though the science of mechanics does not treat of 'the actual'.

43 Ward's pluralism resembles the monadology of Leibniz, except that Ward's monads are not 'windowless' but act on one another.

44 According to Ward, the only *a priori* statements which are beyond challenge are 'purely formal statements' (*The Realm of Ends*, p. 227), those of logic and mathematics. These do not give factual information about the world. If, however, a philosopher professes to deduce the nature of reality from a table of categories and these are found to apply to the world, it will also be found that they were taken from experience in the first place.

45 *The Realm of Ends*, p. 225. Obviously, the less fantastic panpsychism is made to appear, the more does it lie open to the comment that no new information is being given, but that it consists simply in interpreting the empirically observable behaviour of things according to certain selected analogies. The question whether it is true or not then appears as a question whether a certain description is appropriate, not whether certain behaviour takes place or not.

46 *Ibid.*, p. 234.

47 *Ibid.*, p. 421.

48 *Contemporary British Philosophy*, Second Series, p. 254.

49 *Ibid.*, p. 265.

50 When Ward writes as though science does not provide us with knowledge of the concretely real, he is thinking primarily of mechanics which he regards as a branch of mathematics. As already noted, he was himself a psychologist.

51 I do not mean to imply that Bradley can properly be described as an irreligious thinker. At the same time the concept of 'God' belongs for him to the sphere of appearance, and it would be absurd to claim him as a Christian thinker. He was not.

52 McTaggart certainly professed to reach his conclusion by rigorous argument. But then his conclusions were not particularly edifying from the religious point of view, unless one is prepared to maintain that the existence or non-existence of God is a matter of indifference to religion.

IMAGE BOOKS

Image Books constitute a quality library of Catholic writings, broad in human interest and deep in Christian insight. They will include classical Christian writings, devotion, philosophy, education and history; biographies, novels and poetry; and books on contemporary social problems. They represent a planned program of making available to the widest possible audience the finest Catholic literature in attractive, paper-bound, inexpensive editions. They have been selected with these criteria in mind: that they must in every instance be well written, inspiring to the spirit, and of lasting value to the general audience who will purchase them.

The majority of Image Books will consist of reprints made possible through the cooperation of the publishers of the original editions. Occasionally certain much-needed volumes which are not available will also be initiated for this series.

A descriptive catalogue of the Image Books already published may be obtained by writing directly to the publisher. Comments and suggestions from those interested in the series are welcomed by the publisher.